PEARSON   ALWAYS LEARNING

Rhetorical Choices
Analyzing and Writing Arguments

English 101
The University of Tennessee, Knoxville

Assembled by:

Emily Murphy Cope, Jeffrey M. Ringer, and Kirsten F. Benson

Taken from:

Scenes of Writing: Strategies for Composing with Genres
by Amy Devitt, Mary Jo Reiff, and Anis Bawarshi

Reading Rhetorically, Fourth Edition
by John C. Bean, Virginia A. Chappell, and Alice M. Gillam

The Brief Penguin Handbook, Fifth Edition
by Lester Faigley

Writing Arguments: A Rhetoric with Readings, Ninth Edition
by John D. Ramage, John C. Bean, and June Johnson

Compose, Design, Advocate: A Rhetoric for Integrating Written, Oral, and
Visual Communication
by Anne Frances Wysocki and Dennis A. Lynch

Ancient Rhetorics for Contemporary Students, Fifth Edition
by Sharon Crowley and Debra Hawhee

The DK Handbook, Third Edition
by Anne Frances Wysocki and Dennis A. Lynch

Cover Photographs: "Knoxville Suffragettes" and "Torchbearer at Dawn" by Teresa Hooper. "Alex Haley in Hodges Library" by David Hooper.

Excerpts taken from:

Scenes of Writing: Strategies for Composing with Genres
by Amy Devitt, Mary Jo Reiff, and Anis Bawarshi
Copyright © 2004 by Pearson Education, Inc.
Published by Pearson Longman
New York, New York 10036

Reading Rhetorically, Fourth Edition
by John C. Bean, Virginia A. Chappell, and Alice M. Gillam
Copyright © 2014, 2011, 2007 by Pearson Education, Inc.
Upper Saddle River, New Jersey 07458

The Brief Penguin Handbook, Fifth Edition
by Lester Faigley
Copyright © 2015, 2012, 2009, 2006, 2003 by Pearson Education, Inc.

Writing Arguments: A Rhetoric with Readings,
Ninth Edition
by John D. Ramage, John C. Bean, and June Johnson
Copyright © 2012, 2010, 2007, 2004 by Pearson Education, Inc.

Compose, Design, Advocate: A Rhetoric for Integrating Written, Oral, and Visual Communication
by Anne Frances Wysocki and Dennis A. Lynch
Copyright © 2013, 2007 by Pearson Education, Inc.

Ancient Rhetorics for Contemporary Students, Fifth Edition
by Sharon Crowley and Debra Hawhee
Copyright © 2012, 2009, 2004, 1999 by Pearson Education, Inc.

The DK Handbook, Third Edition
by Anne Frances Wysocki and Dennis A. Lynch
Copyright © 2014, 2011, 2009 by Pearson Education, Inc.

Pearson Learning Solutions, 501 Boylston Street, Suite 900, Boston, MA 02116
A Pearson Education Company
www.pearsoned.com

Printed in the United States of America

8   16

000200010271884907

EEB

ISBN 10: 1-269-88580-4
ISBN 13: 978-1-269-88580-5

Brief Contents

1   Introduction to English 101 at The University of Tennessee, Knoxville   1

Units 1 and 2   **Understanding Persuasion and Analyzing Rhetorical Situations**

2   Reading Rhetorically   7

3   Analyzing Rhetorical Situations: Purpose, Genre, and Context   21

4   Writing Rhetorical Analyses   41

5   Understanding and Summarizing Others' Arguments   57

6   Mapping an Ongoing Debate   71

Units 3 and 4   **Composing Arguments for Academic and Public Audiences**

7   Understanding Genres and Writing for Academic Audiences   87

8   Planning your Argument: Composing a Rhetorical Purpose Statement   111

9   Convincing Your Audience: *Logos*   131

10   Using Evidence Effectively   143

11   Moving Your Audience: *Ethos, Pathos,* and *Kairos*   161

12   Writing for Public Audiences   175

13   Additional Guides to Writing for Public Audiences   207

Detailed Contents

1   **Introduction to English 101 at The University of Tennessee, Knoxville**   1

Units 1 and 2   **Understanding Persuasion and Analyzing Rhetorical Situations**

2   **Reading Rhetorically**   7

What Do We Mean by "Reading Rhetorically"?   8

The Demands and Pleasures of Academic Reading   9

Reading and Writing as Conversation   10

Reading and Writing as Acts of Composing   13

Reading Rhetorically as a Strategy for Academic Writing   14

Questions Rhetorical Readers Ask   15

3   **Analyzing Rhetorical Situations: Purpose, Genre, and Context**   21

Rhetorical Context: Purpose, Audience, and Genre   21

Analyzing Your Own Rhetorical Context as Reader/Writer   30

How Expert Readers Use Rhetorical Knowledge to Read Efficiently   32

Typical Reading-Based Writing Assignments Across the Curriculum   35

4   **Writing Rhetorical Analyses**   41

Examining a Writer's Credibility and Appeals to *Ethos*   42

Examining a Writer's Appeals to Reason or *Logos*   43

Examining a Writer's Strategies for Engaging Readers, or *Pathos*   46

Writing About What Texts Say and Do   47

Writing a Rhetorical Analysis Paper: Guidelines   49

ATUL GAWANDE: "A Lifesaving Checklist"   53

5   **Understanding and Summarizing Others' Arguments**   57

Writing as You Read   57

Listening as You Read Initially   58

Listening as You Reread   60

Writing About How Texts Work: Guidelines and Two Examples   62

KIRK SAVAGE: The Conscience of the Nation   66

6   Mapping an Ongoing Debate   71

On Inventing: How to Proceed   72

The Importance of Achieving Stasis   73

Theoretical versus Practical Questions   75

The Four Questions   78

Expanding the Questions   80

Using the Stases   86

Units 3 and 4   Composing Arguments for Academic and Public Audiences

7   Understanding Genres and Writing for Academic Audiences   87

Genres as Social Scripts   87

Analyzing Genres   89

The Values of Academic Genres   97

Writing an Academic Position Paper   98

Two Sample Academic Position Papers   103

**8   Planning Your Argument:
Composing a Rhetorical Purpose Statement   111**

Working Toward a Statement of Purpose   111

Purpose   112

Audience   116

Context   122

Statment of Purpose   125

9   Convincing Your Audience: *Logos*   131

Classical Appeals and the Rhetorical Triangle   133

Issue Questions as the Origins of Argument   134

Frame of an Argument: A Claim Supported by Reasons   138

10   Using Evidence Effectively   143

Rhetorical Understanding of Evidence   144

Examining Visual Arguments: Angle of Vision   149

Gathering Evidence   155

11 Moving Your Audience: *Ethos, Pathos,* and *Kairos* 161

How to Create an Effective *Ethos:* The Appeal to Credibility 163

How to Create *Pathos*: The Appeal to Beliefs and Emotions 163

Using Images for Emotional Appeal 167

Kairos: The Timeliness and Fitness of Arguments 168

How Audience-Based Reasons Enhance *Logos, Ethos,* and *Pathos* 170

12 Writing for Public Audiences 175

The Public and Its Genres 176

Civic Genres and Public Participation 182

Examples of Civic Genres 186

Analyzing Letters to the Editor 187

Analyzing Editorials 197

Writing for Specific Publics 204

13 Additional Guides to Writing for Public Audiences 207

How to Plan and Deliver Presentations 207

How to Compose in Online Genres 212

Sample of a Newsletter 221

Sample of a Letter to an Authority 225

Sample of a Web Site 227

Rhetorical Choices

Analyzing and Writing Arguments

Introduction to English 101 at The University of Tennessee, Knoxville

Welcome to First-Year Composition at The University of Tennessee, Knoxville, and to English 101 in particular. We are proud of our composition program and the national recognition it has received. In 2012, our program won the "Writing Program Certificate of Excellence" from the Conference on College Composition and Communication (CCCC), an affiliate of the National Council of Teachers of English (NCTE).[1] We believe that our first-year composition courses offer a great start to your college experience here at UTK, and we're glad you're here.

Undergraduate Success Depends upon Strong Writing Abilities

We see our first-year composition (FYC) courses as part of a larger effort, one that begins in your first year and continues throughout your undergraduate career. The FYC sequence, English 101 and 102, is designed to help you become a knowledgeable and skillful writer. Strong writing, research, and communication abilities are the cornerstones of successful academic performance, crucial to ensuring that you succeed in your academic coursework and in your eventual professional and civic life. The FYC sequence immerses you in a culture of writing and helps you acquire composing and research skills that will transfer across multiple disciplines and writing situations. In general, we aim to support your ability to produce good writing in any situation. UTK seeks to graduate a diverse body of well-educated undergraduate students who possess the essential writing and communication skills they need to succeed, and the first-year composition courses help you begin that journey.

Overview of the First-Year Composition Sequence

Our FYC sequence moves students from analyzing to producing arguments—from studying and practicing persuasive techniques to conducting extended research inquiries using a variety of disciplinary approaches. English 101 focuses primarily on rhetorical analysis of how texts work, how and why writers make the choices they do, and how writers use their understandings

---

[1]A video about UTK's writing program is available at http://english.utk.edu/first-year-composition/.

of audience, purpose, genre, context, and style to formulate their own rhetorically effective arguments. In English 102, students define productive questions for academic inquiry, learn how to conduct research using various methods and types of source material, and produce and revise original research projects.

Both English 101 and 102 share the following requirements and features:

- 5000 words of writing, both formal (essays) and informal (drafts and revisions, journals, reading responses, in-class writing);
- Two individual conferences between instructor and student to discuss drafts-in-progress and to address particular writing concerns;
- Emphasis on the writing process, including invention, drafting, feedback, and revision. Most teachers require that students maintain a folder of all written drafts;
- Activities to become familiar with the University Libraries; and
- Instruction in methods of locating, integrating, and documenting external source material.

English 101

In English 101 you will learn about *rhetoric*—about what makes a text persuasive and how writers appeal to their intended audiences. You will learn about and practice strategies for researching and understanding ongoing debates, planning your own contribution to debates, clarifying your rhetorical purpose, and researching and composing arguments that use good reasons and persuasive appeals to change your audience's moods, minds, and actions. You will learn how all acts of communication take place in *rhetorical situations*—situations when individuals or groups have a sense that a change is needed and are motivated to communicate with others in order bring about change. In rhetorical situations, writers construct their arguments to influence their readers.

English 101 has a set of core outcomes that all instructors aim to meet as well as a set of core assignments. Individual teachers have flexibility in designing their course schedule and the particulars of assignments, but the overall structure of the course and paper assignments of each section follow a plan shared by all sections of the course.

Outcomes for English 101

By the end of English 101, students should be able to:

- read texts critically and analyze the varied situations that motivate writers, the choices that writers make, and the effects of those choices on readers;
- analyze how writers employ content, structure, style, tone, and conventions appropriate to the demands of a particular audience, purpose, context, or culture;
- write persuasive arguments that articulate a clear, thoughtful position; deploy support and evidence appropriate to audience and purpose; and consider counterclaims and multiple points of view, including international and intercultural perspectives;
- respond constructively to drafts-in-progress, applying rhetorical concepts to revisions of their own and peers' writing;

■ analyze multiple modes of communication and the ways in which a wide range of rhetorical elements (both written and visual) and cultural elements operate in the act of persuasion; and

■ evaluate sources and integrate the ideas of others into their own writing (through paraphrase, direct quotation, summary, analysis, and evaluation).

Sequence of Units and Assignments in English 101

In English 101, the overall arc of assignments over the semester moves students from analyzing others' persuasive texts towards producing their own. There are four units, each with a required paper. The units are taught in the following sequence.

Unit 1: Understanding Rhetorical Situation and Persuasion   The overall goal of this unit is for you to understand how writers respond to situations or ongoing debates and how writers persuade others to accept new information or insights, change their minds about something, or prompt them to take some action. We want you to understand rhetorical situations, how and why writers try to persuade others, and to recognize why some rhetorical choices are more effective than others. You will write rhetorical situation analysis reports in order to better understand the contexts in which particular texts were created.

Paper #1: Comparative Rhetorical Analysis

The formal paper assignment for this unit asks you to compare two texts that have similar rhetorical purposes and evaluate which writer you think is *more effective* in accomplishing his or her persuasive purpose.

Unit 2: Entering a Rhetorical Situation—Analyzing the Issues in an Ongoing Argument   In the second unit, you will begin to identify the issues at stake within a particular ongoing debate, an actual rhetorical situation. (You will develop your own position about this debate in a later paper.)

To help you enter an ongoing debate, your instructor will provide a selection of readings that involve multiple perspectives and positions. The goal is to identify the important questions at issue within that debate—the nature of the unresolved issues that keep people talking about it actively. Instruction includes information on stasis analysis (four types of arguments and disagreements) and on helping you to "map" the nature of an ongoing argument. Most instructors assign an annotated bibliography of the readings within the selected debate.

Paper #2: Informative Analysis of a Debate

For the formal paper in this unit, you will write an informative analysis of an ongoing debate, drawing upon your understanding of the sources you've read in order describe the current state of this debate. Your paper will engage with these questions: What are the main questions at issue in this debate? Where do participants have common ground and where do they disagree? Why does this debate remain unresolved? In terms of academic genres, your paper will be similar to a "literature review."

Unit 3: Creating an Argument for an Academic Audience   Once you have analyzed the common ground and the questions at issue in the ongoing debate the class analyzed in Unit 2, you will get your turn to stake out a position within that debate and to use rhetorical appeals effectively to persuade others.

In Unit 2 you will have identified a part of an ongoing debate that offers productive ground for further argument, and that will be the starting point for your reading and writing in Unit 3. Instruction includes an introduction to academic genres; approaches to argument; finding, evaluating, and integrating sources; and methods for proper citation and documentation—how to avoid plagiarism. In most classes, an introduction to using the University Libraries is included at this point in the semester. As you work toward the formal paper, you may be asked to write a short proposal requesting approval to write your position paper on a particular part of the debate.

Paper #3: Position Paper for an Academic Audience

In this unit, your formal writing assignment will be a position paper written for an academic audience that seeks to intervene in the debate you analyzed in Unit 2. For example, you might have found in your Unit 2 analysis that a particular debate is stalled because of a lack of agreement over certain facts or key definitions, so your position paper would then aim to *inform* people whose arguments represent a lack of consideration for some factual matter or an unclear understanding of a key definition. Or, again depending on what you discovered in your Unit 2 analysis, you may need to try to *change some people's position* by getting them to better understand the negative effects of the position they hold. Another possibility is that your Unit 2 analysis leads you to realize that it's necessary to advocate that certain people *take a particular course of action.* There are many productive directions for successful position arguments.

Your teacher will also ask you to write a short reflective essay about your academic position paper, identifying your persuasive purpose, explaining why you chose to make the particular argument you did and describing your rationale for the rhetorical strategies you chose: how you think your ethos, *logos*, and *pathos* appeals might affect academic readers and accomplish your rhetorical purpose. These reflections help you develop "big-picture" understandings of your own writing and its effectiveness.

Unit 4: Entering the Conversation: Argument for a Public Audience   In the last unit of the course, you will use the rhetorical skills you've developed over the semester to persuade a *public* audience. You will stake out a position within a debate and use the rhetorical strategies you learned during the semester to convince a public audience to accept new information or insights, change their minds about something, or prompt them to take some kind of action.

Paper #4: Position Paper for a Public Audience

Like the third unit paper, the final formal assignment for this course requires you to produce your own rhetorically effective argument within a real debate. Some instructors will ask you to intervene in a local debate, perhaps one that is related to the general issue the course has been focusing on during the semester. Your goal is to rhetorically affect a group of targeted *public* readers to get them to accept new information or insights, change their minds about something, or prompt them to take some kind of action. You will choose to use ethos, logos, and pathos appeals in ways you think will be effective with your specific audience. Most assignments require you to find some relevant outside sources through your own research. Also, most students are asked to follow the conventions and formatting of an actual public genre, such as an op-ed column that would be appropriate for publication in a newspaper, or a website, magazine article, or another type of "real-world" writing.

For this unit, you also may be asked to write another short, reflective essay identifying your persuasive purpose, explaining why you chose to make the particular argument you did and describing your rhetorical strategies and evaluating their effectiveness: How do you think your *ethos*, *logos*, and *pathos* appeals might affect the real world audience you chose? Did you accomplish your rhetorical purpose?

About This Text

Rhetorical Choices: Analyzing and Writing Arguments is a custom text created for UTK's English 101 course. We revised our English 101 curriculum in 2013–14, and in doing so we discovered there were no existing textbooks that matched our curriculum as closely as we hoped for. So, we created our own, using a selection of chapters from various existing textbooks. The benefit for students and teachers is that each part of this text is presented in the order that matches the units of our 101. Additionally, it includes materials that present the content knowledge you will need to understand the assignments of the course—the principles of rhetoric and argument and how to practice and apply those principles within your academic and "real-world" writing. We're aware, though, that one downside to this type of text is that it may include a few repetitions or some overlap of material. At times, you may notice that the style or tone changes from one chapter to the next. This is due to the fact that we've included excerpts from different books by different authors. Also, the transitions from one chapter to the next are not as smooth as they would be if everything came from the same source. We hope you will overlook these minor issues and focus on the content of the chapters themselves and how they support your understanding of the English 101 course. This is our first edition of this particular custom-created text, and we will refine it over the next several years to iron out some of the minor issues. In the meantime, we hope you find that the materials themselves will contribute to developing your understanding of rhetoric and effective argument—which is, after all, the main goal of English 101.

We wish you the best as you get started with your English 101 course!

FOR INFORMAL WRITING

1. Write a one- to one and a half-page description of your understanding of and previous experiences with *rhetoric, analysis,* and *argument*—for example from your high school courses or from other settings.

2. See the section on "Outcomes for English 101." An "outcome" is a measure that all students should be able to meet upon successfully completing the course. Which (if any) of the outcomes seem related to skills you learned in high school? Which do you think will be applicable to courses outside of English 101? Which do you need to work on most as an individual writer? Explain your responses.

3. Your instructor will ask you to break into small groups and will assign each group one of the English 101 outcomes. In your group, work to define what you think the outcome means and to provide an example. Your instructor will visit each group to offer assistance, but begin with your own definition and interpretation, backed up by evidence from the syllabus, course materials, or this textbook. Be prepared to report on your assigned outcome and its meaning, either in a short written text or a brief presentation to the class.

4. The expectations of your English 101 course are spelled out in a formal institutional genre, the syllabus, which functions as an agreement between you and your instructor. After examining your 101 syllabus, explain what it tells you about the goals and objectives of the course, the structure of the course, the reading and writing you will be doing, and the ways your writing will be evaluated. What questions do you have, or what terms or information are you uncertain about? Bring any questions you have back to the larger class for discussion.

Reading Rhetorically

2

Academic writing, reading, and inquiry are inseparably linked; and all three are learned by not doing any one alone, but by doing them all at the same time.

—James Reither

We have designed this book to help you succeed at the writing, reading, and inquiry tasks that James Reither refers to above. College students are often surprised, even overwhelmed, by the heavy reading they are assigned and by the challenge of integrating material from that reading in their own writing. Along with textbook chapters and other assigned readings in a course, your college reading will include specialized Web sites, books, articles, and abstracts that you will examine in order to prepare research papers for a wide variety of classes, not only for English but for natural science, social science, and pre-professional classes such as introductory courses in accounting or nursing. Throughout this chapter, we will be describing and explaining how the techniques of **reading rhetorically** will help you do all this successfully.

Imagine the following scenario: It's early evening on Thursday, and you are planning your weekend's study schedule. Besides an assignment to read a chapter in your chemistry textbook for Monday, you have some writing assignments due next week. Consider this hypothetical list of reading and writing assignments that you need to get started on over the weekend:

- Find and analyze a local newspaper editorial for your political science class according to concepts laid out in a textbook chapter titled "Interest Groups and the Media."
- Summarize and write a critical reflection on a recent *Atlantic* online Web "Dispatch" assigned for your Environmental Studies class.
- Identify points of difficulty in a Platonic dialogue for your humanities seminar and formulate questions about them for discussion.
- Begin developing a research question for a major paper for your African history class, due next month.

Chapter 2, Reading Rhetorically, is taken from John C. Bean, Virginia A. Chappell, and Alice M. Gilliam's *Reading Rhetorically*, pp. 1–15 (Chapter 1, Reading to Write: Strategies for College Reading).

For many students, a list like this seems daunting simply because it lays out many different kinds of reading and writing tasks that all must be done in the same relatively short period of time. This challenge of what some people call "alla-tonceness" is what this book is designed to help you with. The techniques of reading rhetorically—the central concept of this book—will help you sort through and develop the varied reading and writing skills called for in college courses.

For each assignment on our hypothetical list, your ability to meet your instructor's goals would depend not only on your ability to craft clear, grammatical sentences, but also on your ability to read insightfully and analytically. Note that each one calls upon students to read in a particular way. This variety occurs because professors design assignments to help students learn not just the subject matter but the academic methods central to their disciplines. Thus, assignments often necessitate reading with different purposes and types of awareness. In these four cases, students need to

- Comprehend political science textbook concepts about interest groups well enough to tie them to an editorial
- Distill the key ideas in a popular Web article and reflect upon how they apply (or not) to ideas being discussed in a course
- Spot ambiguities and formulate discussion questions that zero in on them
- Scan through class notes and library databases to locate issues that will focus on an individual research question

For the most part, students adapt to these new demands and gradually learn what academic reading entails, so that by the time they are juniors and seniors within their major fields, they know how to do the reading and writing demanded in their disciplines and future professions. But the process is often slow and frustrating, marked by trial and error and the panicky feeling that reading for different purposes is like hacking through a jungle when there might be a path nearby that could make the journey easier.

We hope that learning to read rhetorically, a concept that informs every chapter of this book, will help you find that path and thus accelerate your growth as a strong academic reader and writer.

What Do We Mean by "Reading Rhetorically"?

To read rhetorically is (1) to read with attention to how your purposes for reading may or may not match an author's purposes for writing and (2) to recognize the methods that authors use to try to accomplish their purposes. Remember this: All authors have designs on their readers. Authors want their readers to see things their way so that readers will adopt their point of view. But rhetorical readers know how to maintain a critical distance from a text and thus determine carefully the extent to which they will go along with the author.

As you move into your college majors, new writing assignments will ask you to write about your reading in a way that shows that you are "doing" a discipline, for example, ***doing*** political science or ***doing*** philosophy. That is why we stress throughout these chapters the importance of interacting with a text beyond just understanding what it says. In college, reporting about what you have read will be only a beginning point. You will be asked to find meaning, not merely information, in books and articles. You will be asked to respond to that meaning—to explain it, to use it, to analyze it, to critique it, to compare it to alternative meanings that other writers have created or that you create yourself as you write.

To fulfill such writing and reading assignments, you will need to analyze not just *what* texts say but *how* they say it. This double awareness is crucial to reading rhetorically. By analyzing both the content and the technique of a given text, a rhetorical reader critically considers the extent to which he or she will accept or question that text.

The Demands and Pleasures of Academic Reading

Once you become immersed in academic life—caught up in the challenge of doing your own questioning, critical thinking, analysis, and research—you'll discover that academic reading has unique demands and pleasures. If you ask an experienced academic reader engaged in a research project why she reads, her answer may be something like this: "I'm investigating a problem that requires close analysis of several primary sources. I also need to read secondary sources to see what other researchers are saying about this problem. Then I can position myself in the conversation."

This may seem a curious answer—one that you might not fully understand until you have had more experience writing papers that require analysis or research. To help you appreciate this answer—and to see how it applies to you—consider that in most college courses, you will have two underlying goals:

Goal 1. Learning conceptual knowledge.   You need to learn the body of information presented in the course—to master the key concepts and ideas of the course, to memorize important facts, to learn key definitions or formulas, to understand the discipline's theories, and understand how they seek to explain certain data and observations. Cognitive psychologists sometimes call this kind of learning **conceptual knowledge**—that is, knowledge of the course's subject matter. Transmitting conceptual knowledge is the primary aim of most college textbooks. Ironically, even textbooks designed for beginners present challenging reading assignments because their pages are packed with specialized terminology that students need to know if they are to follow lectures, pass exams, and, more generally, understand how chemists (for example) think about, label, and measure the physical world.

Goal 2. Learning procedural knowledge.   Most college courses are designed to help you learn the discipline's characteristic ways of applying conceptual knowledge to new problems. What questions does the discipline ask? What are its methods of analysis or research? What counts as evidence? What are the discipline's shared or disputed assumptions? How do you write arguments in this discipline, and what makes them convincing (say in literature, sociology, engineering, or accounting)? Thus, in addition to learning the basic concepts of a course, you need to learn how experts in the discipline pose problems and conduct inquiry. Cognitive psychologists call this kind of learning **procedural knowledge**—the ability to apply conceptual knowledge to new problems by using the discipline's characteristic methods of thinking.

When teachers assign readings beyond the typical textbook—newspaper or magazine articles, scholarly articles, or primary sources such as historical documents or literary texts—they are asking you to use procedural knowledge by analyzing or using these readings in discipline-specific ways. Consider the political science assignment in our opening scenario. The professor who assigned analysis of a local newspaper editorial undoubtedly wants students to learn what the textbook says about interest-group politics (conceptual knowledge), and then to apply those concepts to analyze current events (procedural knowledge). As you read a variety of editorials looking for one to analyze, you would need to read them through the lens of your political science textbook. A different kind of challenge is presented by the Platonic dialogue. Not only does it contain complex ideas, but it also demonstrates a form of discourse and a philosophical way of thinking that has had a lasting impact on European traditions. The professor's decision to start by asking students to raise questions about difficult passages provides a way for students to start exploring the text without being intimidated by it.

As you read the various kinds of texts assigned in your courses and write different kinds of papers, you will discover that academic disciplines are not inert bodies of knowledge but contested fields full of uncertainties, disagreements, and debate. You will see why college professors want you to *do* their discipline rather than simply study it. They want you not just to study chemistry or political science or history, but to *think like a chemist or a political scientist or an historian*. As you learn to read rhetorically, you will learn to recognize different authors' purposes and methods, the ways that claims are typically asserted and supported in different disciplines, and the types of evidence that are valued by those disciplines. For example, historians value primary sources such as letters and diaries, government records, and legal documents. Psychologists gather quite different kinds of research data, such as empirical observations of an animal's learning behaviors under different diet conditions, statistical data about the reduction of anxiety symptoms in humans after different kinds of therapy, or "think-aloud" transcripts of a person's problem-solving processes after varying amounts of sleep. Your accumulating knowledge about disciplinary discourses will teach you new ways of thinking, and you will learn to use those methods in your own writing.

It is important to realize that even people with considerable background knowledge and high interest in a subject will probably find course readings daunting when they are dense with new concepts, vocabulary, and information. With so much unfamiliar material, each new sentence can seem just as important as the one before, causing you to think, "I've got to know all of this—how will I ever write anything about it?" Reading rhetorically can help you separate key concepts from supporting details.

Reading and Writing as Conversation

Consider again how our experienced researcher at the beginning of the last section answered the question, "Why do you read?" It is obvious that she is immersed in *doing* her discipline and that she sees reading as central to her work. But she also says that she is reading "to position myself in the conversation." What does she mean by that? How is reading part of a "conversation"?

To understand this metaphor of conversation, think of writers as talking to readers—and think of readers as talking back. For example, suppose our researcher's investigation leads her to new insights that she would like to share with others. If she is a professional scholar, she may write an academic article. If she is an undergraduate, she may write a research paper. In both cases, her intended audience would be academic readers interested in a particular problem or question. Motivated by the belief that she has produced something new or controversial to add to the conversation, she aims to present the results of her research and try to persuade readers to accept her argument and claims.

Thinking of yourself as joining a conversation will be helpful whenever you read or write so that you can consider not only the text you are reading, but also the conversation that it joins. Think of this conversation as multi-voiced. The first voice is that of the text's author; a second voice (actually a set of voices) is the network of other writers the author refers to—previous participants in the conversation. The third voice is yours as you respond to the text while you read, and later when you write something about it.

This broad view of readers and writers interacting via texts extends the metaphor of "conversation" to say that texts themselves are in a conversation with previous texts. Each text acts in relationship to other texts. It asserts a claim on a reader's attention by invoking certain interests and understandings, reminding readers of what has been previously written about the subject. For example, articles in scientific journals typically begin with a **literature review**; that is, a summary of important research already conducted on the question at hand. Similarly, political commentators will summarize the views of others so that they can affirm, extend, or take issue with those views. In the arts, reviewers of music, film, and books are likely to refer to (and, on the Web, perhaps link to) not just the work under review but discussions about the given artist's reputation, which, of course, was established not just by word of mouth but also by other texts or performances with which the current reader may not be familiar.

Joining the Conversation

The reasons any of us engage in conversation, oral or written, will vary widely according to the occasion and our individual needs. In academic and workplace settings, we read so that we can make informed contributions to a conversation that is already in progress. Indeed, we are expected to join in.

Entering an oral conversation can sometimes be a simple process of responding to a question. ("Have you seen the new film at the Ridgemont?") But if a conversation is already well under way, finding an opening can sometimes be a complex process of getting people's attention and staking claim to authority on a subject. ("Um, you know, I've seen all of John Woo's films, and I think. . . .") The challenge is even greater if the goal is to redirect the conversation or contradict the prevailing opinion. ("Yes, but listen! The reading I've done for my cinematography class tells me that his action films are not as innovative as the ads claim.") When we take up writing as a way of entering the conversation, we don't have to worry about interrupting, but we do have to review the conversation for our readers by laying out introductory background.

To explore the similarities between your motives for joining a conversation and your motives for reading, consider how the influential twentieth-century rhetorician and philosopher Kenneth Burke uses conversation as a metaphor for reading and writing:

> Imagine you enter a parlor. You come late. When you arrive, others have long preceded you, and they are engaged in a heated discussion, a discussion too heated for them to pause and tell you exactly what it is about. In fact, the discussion had already begun long before any of them got there, so that no one present is qualified to retrace for you all the steps that had gone before. You listen for a while, until you decide that you have caught the tenor of the argument; then you put in your oar. Someone answers; you answer him; another comes to your defense; another aligns himself against you, to either the embarrassment or gratification of your opponent, depending upon the quality of your ally's assistance. However, the discussion is interminable. The hour grows late, you must depart. And you do depart, with the discussion still vigorously in progress.[1]

■ ■ ■ FOR WRITING AND DISCUSSION

To explore the implications of Burke's parlor metaphor for your own reading processes, consider the following questions.

ON YOUR OWN

1. In what ways does Burke's parlor metaphor fit your experience? Freewrite for a few minutes about an oral conversation in which you managed to assert your voice—or "put in your oar," as Burke says—after listening for a while, or about a situation where reading helped you gather a sense of the general flow of ideas so that you could have something to say about a topic.
2. Consider a community that you belong to where you feel that you can quickly catch the drift of an in-progress conversation (e.g., other triathlon athletes, or regulars on *Farmville*). What are some "hot topics" of conversation in these communities? What might exclude someone from these conversations? If you wanted to address a general audience about this issue, how much background information would you need to supply?
3. Now let's reverse the situation. Have you ever listened to a conversation in which you were a baffled outsider rather than an insider? Describe an experience where you had to work hard to get inside an ongoing conversation. Then consider how that experience might be an appropriate analogy for a time when you were frustrated by trying to read a book or article addressed to an insider audience rather than to someone with your background.

WITH YOUR CLASSMATES

Share your responses with other members of your class. See if others have had experiences similar to yours. What have been the topics of conversations where they were in "insider" and "outsider" roles? Help each other appreciate the concepts of insider and outsider audiences and of reading as joining a conversation.   ■ ■ ■

---

[1]Kenneth Burke, *The Philosophy of Literary Form: Studies in Symbolic Action*, 3rd ed. (Berkeley: U of California P, 1973), 110–11. Print.

Reading and Writing as Acts of Composing

The give and take of oral conversation connects naturally to our second metaphor, reading as an act of composing. The idea that writing is an act of composing is probably familiar to you. Indeed, the terms *writing* and *composing* are often used interchangeably. Originally associated with fine arts such as painting, music, or literary writing, the term *composing* still carries with it the idea of originality or creativity, even though it has come to mean the production of any kind of written text, from a memo to a prize-winning novel. Unlike the term *writing,* the word *composing* suggests more than the mere transcription of a preexisting meaning or idea. Instead, it suggests a creative putting together of words and ideas to make a new whole. Except for the act of literally recopying what someone else has written, all writing, even memo writing, is a matter of selecting and arranging language to accomplish a purpose that is unique to a particular situation and audience.

However, the idea that reading is an act of composing may be less familiar. The ancients thought of reading as a passive activity in which the author, via the text, deposited meaning in a reader—the text was metaphorically (or even literally) "consumed." The Old Testament prophet Ezekiel, for example, has a vision in which he is instructed by the Lord to open his mouth and literally consume a book that gives him the knowledge he needs to speak to the rebellious Israelites. Commenting on the consumption metaphors associated with reading, Alberto Manguel, in *A History of Reading,* notes the parallels between the cooking metaphors associated with writing—the author "cooks up" a plot or "spices" up her introduction—and the eating metaphors associated with reading—the reader "devours" a book, finds "nourishment" in it, then "regurgitates" what he has read.[2] Although the image of Ezekiel's eating of a text seems fantastic, the mistaken idea persists that reading is a one-way transaction: author → text → reader. To illustrate the flaws in this model of the reading process, let's try a simple experiment described by reading researcher Kathleen McCormick. Read the following passage and jot down your interpretation of its meaning:

> Tony slowly got up from the mat, planning his escape. He hesitated a moment and thought. Things were not going well. What bothered him most was being held, especially since the charge against him had been weak. He considered his present situation. The lock that held him was strong but he thought he could break it. . . . He was being ridden unmercifully. . . . He felt that he was ready to make his move.[3]

There are two common interpretations: readers assume that Tony is either in jail or in a wrestling match. Unless you are familiar with wrestling, you likely thought Tony was a prisoner planning a jailbreak. However, if this paragraph appeared in a short story about a wrestler, you would immediately assume that "mat," "escape," "charge," "being held," and "lock" referred to wrestling even if you knew very little about the sport. This experiment demonstrates two important aspects of the reading process: (1) readers use

---

[2]Alberto Manguel, *A History of Reading* (New York: Penguin, 1997), 170–71. Print.
[3]Kathleen McCormick, *The Culture of Reading and the Teaching of English* (Manchester, England: Manchester UP, 1994), 20–21. Print.

their previous experiences and knowledge to create meaning from what they read; and (2) context influences meaning.

Research such as McCormick's shows that readers make sense of a text not by passively receiving meaning from it, but by actively composing a reading of it. This composing process links the reader's existing knowledge and ideas with the new information in the text. What the reader brings to the text is as important as the text itself. In other words, reading is not a process in which an author simply transfers information to the reader. Rather, it is a dynamic process in which the reader's worldview interacts with the writer's worldview. The reader constructs meaning from the text, in effect creating a new "text" in the reader's mind. The new text is the reader's active interpretation of the text being read.

When college writing assignments ask you to explain and support your reading (or interpretation) of a text, whether verbal or visual, it is important to distinguish between *private* associations that are only loosely related to the text and interpretations that are *publicly* defensible in terms of textual evidence. Private associations are one-way responses in which a certain word, image, or idea in a text sends you off into your own world, causing you to lose track of the network of cues in the text as a whole. Although such private responses are natural, and indeed one of the pleasures of reading, if you are to offer a public interpretation, you must engage in a two-way interaction with a text, attending to both its network of cues and your personal responses and associations with it. In short, "good" or sound interpretations are those that are supported by textual evidence and thus are understandable as well as persuasive to other readers, whose experiences and beliefs are probably different from yours.

Reading Rhetorically as a Strategy for Academic Writing

The metaphors of conversation and composing bring out the essential rhetorical nature of reading and writing. By **rhetorical**, we mean "related to an intended effect." Invoking the term "rhetoric" always draws attention to a writer's relationship to and intentions toward an audience. Consider Aristotle's definition of rhetoric as the art of discovering the available means of persuasion in a given situation. Although the word "persuasion" focuses on an audience, Aristotle's definition highlights **discovery** along with **persuasion**. From this pairing, we can understand that writers must thoroughly understand their subject in order to discover the best methods for presenting their material to others. By "best," we mean the most ethically responsible as well as the most persuasive. Rhetoric's partnership of discovery and persuasion makes it clear why reading rhetorically is a powerful academic strategy in all disciplines. When you read rhetorically, you read with awareness of both the purposes of the author whose text you are reading and your own purposes as a reader and writer.

The Purposes of the Author Whose Text You Are Reading

When we introduced the term *reading rhetorically* early in this chapter, we described authors as having designs on their readers. That phrasing underscores the fact that writers want to change readers' perceptions and thinking, and that they use both direct and indirect means to do so. Typically, a writer's goal is to change a reader's understanding of subject matter in some way. Sometimes the change might simply confirm what the reader thought beforehand—readers typically enjoy music and film reviews that affirm their own opinions and political columns that echo their views. At other times, the change might involve an increase in knowledge or in clarity of understanding (an article explaining how bluenose dolphins use whistling sounds to converse with each other might increase your awe of sea mammals). Sometimes the change might radically reconstruct a reader's whole view of a subject (an article reporting new scientific evidence might convince you to reverse your position on legalization of medical marijuana). How much change occurs as a result of reading? The reader decides.

Your Own Purposes as an Active Reader/Writer

When an assignment asks you to respond in some way to texts that you have read, you must take on the role of an active reader who composes meanings. Your responses might range from writing marginal notes on the text itself (something that expert readers do) to posting an entry on your class online discussion forum to writing a major research paper. Your decisions about the way you will read a text and think critically about it will depend upon your own purposes as a writer.

Questions Rhetorical Readers Ask

You can begin the practice of reading rhetorically by asking the eight analytical questions that follow when you encounter new texts. Whether you are reading the abstract of a scientific article or comments posted on a forum about R&B styling, these questions will help you discover how a writer's purpose and worldview become evident in a text. These insights, in turn, will help you analyze how a given text works so that you can decide how you want to respond to it and use it in your own writing.

1. What questions does the text address, explicitly or implicitly? (Why are these significant questions? What community cares about them?)
2. Who is the intended audience? (Am I part of this audience or an outsider?)
3. How does the author support his or her thesis with reasons and evidence? (Do I find this argument convincing? What views and counterarguments are omitted from the text? What counterevidence is ignored?)
4. How does the author hook the intended reader's interest and keep the reader reading? (Do these appeals work for me? Do they make me suspicious of the author's motives?)
5. How does the author make himself or herself seem credible to the intended audience? (Is the author credible for me? Are the author's sources reliable?)
6. Are this writer's basic values, beliefs, and assumptions similar to or different from my own? (How does this writer's worldview accord with mine?)
7. How do I respond to this text? (Will I go along with or challenge what this text is presenting? How has it changed my thinking?)
8. How do this author's evident purposes for writing fit with my purposes for reading? (How will I be able to use what I have learned from the text?)

■ ■ ■ FOR WRITING AND DISCUSSION

The Questions Rhetorical Readers Ask can be useful for analyzing visual texts as well as verbal texts. To demonstrate the power of rhetorical reading, we invite you to use the eight questions to analyze how the Web page depicted in Figure 2.1 attempts to influence the thinking of viewers/readers.

Working alone or with classmates, use the eight questions to consider first, how the various visual and verbal elements work to project a corporate image for Chevron, and second, how you respond to that image.

Some background: The page shown in Figure 2.1 came up via a click on "We Agree" (depicted as a red rubber stamp) on the Chevron home page. It was part of a major advertising campaign on this theme that included both print and television. If you are not able to find the site online, here is a brief summary: The video presents 30 seconds of overlapping statements in which the young teacher in the right frame calls for speeding up the development of renewable energy ("We've got to get on this now!") while the Chevron environmental operations specialist in the left frame speaks enthusiastically about the millions of dollars Chevron is investing in solar and biofuel technologies, "Right now!"   ■ ■ ■

An Extended Example: Researching the Promise of Biofuels

Imagine that your instructor in a geography or political science class assigns a major research paper that will require you to find and select your own sources. These potential sources (there may be hundreds of possibilities) will pose reading challenges different from those of your course textbooks because these sources will be written for many

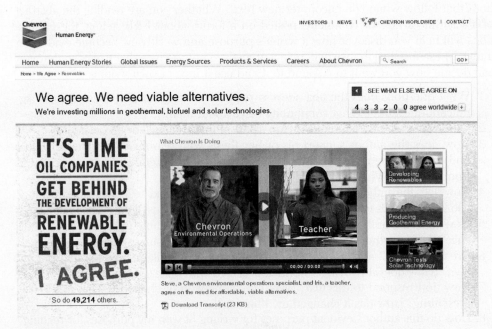

FIGURE 2.1 Screen capture from Chevron Web statement about developing renewable energy

different audiences and purposes by authors with varied credentials on the subject. On any given topic—let's take the development of biofuels as a broad example—it's likely your research will turn up scholarly articles, popular magazine articles, news reports, a few books, and a range of politically charged editorials, op-ed columns, blogs, and Web sites. All of them will have been published in different contexts for readers with a range of different concerns: experts and nonexperts, theorists and researchers, farmers and automakers, politicians of every stripe, and ordinary citizens trying to figure out the best car to buy, or which politician to vote for. As a reader who is planning to write, you will need to determine what, among all this material, suits *your* needs and purposes.

Your purposes may grow out of personal interests and questions. Let's take as an example a first-year student we'll call "Jack," who has become interested in biofuels because holiday dinners with relatives who farm in the Midwest have produced many heated arguments about corn ethanol. One uncle produces feed corn to be sold not to cattle farmers, but to ethanol producers. Another uncle grows corn for people food. He is certain that the market for corn ethanol will disappear within a couple of years because cleaner and more efficiently produced biofuels will be developed. Both of these men support environmental causes, and each feels that his choice about what kind of corn to grow will be better for the environment. Additionally, one uncle argues that producing corn ethanol contributes to U.S. energy independence; the other argues that using good farmland to produce fuel rather than food will have negative consequences. These dinner-table conversations became even more intense after Congress ended federal tax breaks for companies that produce gasoline mixed with ethanol.

Motivated by curiosity about which of his uncles might be making the better choice, Jack decides to write a paper for his political science class about the pros and cons of growing corn for ethanol production. During class discussion, he gains and shares insights with a classmate who grew up in a big city and is writing about corn ethanol from the perspective of consumers who are environmentalists, asking whether it really is a clean fuel. They are both aware of intense debates around these issues, as reflected in the visual arguments represented in Figures 2.2 and 2.3, and they agree that their goals are to gather information for their papers, not controversial arguments.

Despite a wealth of readily available materials on the subject, both students eventually find themselves hard pressed to provide definite answers to their questions. Searches of periodicals databases uncover a wealth of materials on ethanol and other biofuels, but the conclusions seem almost contradictory. Published reports indicate that despite the end of federal tax subsidies for ethanol producers, the amount of corn grown for ethanol continues to increase. Meanwhile, university professors and oil companies receive press coverage for their research about the practicality of using other biofuels to run gasoline engines.

Web searches turn up a wide range of perspectives on ethanol, from industry groups supporting expanded corn ethanol production, to oil companies boasting of their commitment to alternative fuels, to environmental organizations opposing the use of farmland for biofuel development. Furthermore, Jack's classmate discovers that environmental groups have been arguing not only that the fuel is not particularly clean or efficient but also that ethanol production is actually bad for the environment. Between them, they discover that, as yet, there is no clear answer about the wisdom of

FIGURE 2.2 Illinois billboard advertising corn seed hybridized for ethanol production from Pioneer Hi-Bred International, Inc.

FIGURE 2.3 Editorial cartoon by Robert Ariail

developing corn ethanol for automotive fuel, nor about the trade-offs of using agricultural land for developing biofuels.

In other words, Jack and his friend learn that there is not one "ethanol debate." There are many, depending on the interests and values of the debaters. Jack discovers that he must recognize and investigate the perspectives not only of farmers like his uncles, but also of environmental organizations, producers of ethanol and gasoline, investors in alternative fuels, scientists (who want hard evidence), government agencies (who rely on the scientists' research), manufacturers of gasoline engines—and ordinary consumers shopping for a car that fits their values and pocketbook.

Jack's experience illustrates our larger point that only careful reading will lead to a good academic paper on a complex subject. Reading rhetorically is a powerful academic skill that will help you recognize the persuasive strategies built into many different kinds of texts. Inevitably, no text tells the whole story. A reader needs to focus not only on what a given text says but on its rhetorical strategies for making its case. To promote an argument, some texts will distort opposing perspectives; others will make certain perspectives invisible. A headline on the Web about "Biofuels' Potential to Revolutionize the Global Economy" may primarily be a pitch to interest investors in a start-up company. The organization behind a headline announcing an article about the "Pros and Cons of Ethanol" might be a trade association that lobbies for (or against) corn ethanol, or it could be a lone environmental blogger repackaging reports of unknown reliability. Eventually, after you (like Jack) have read enough materials from sources you have learned to trust, by writers you learn to respect (in part by checking their credentials), you will be able to fill in background that you perhaps did not even notice was missing when you first started reading in a given subject area.

How can you tell whether a text seeks to give you a full picture in a fair and reliable manner or is simply making another one-sided argument about a hotly contested issue? By learning to read rhetorically. Doing so will enable you to read—and then write—successful college papers.

Analyzing Rhetorical Situations: Purpose, Genre, and Context

3

It is like the rubbing of two sticks together to make a fire,
the act of reading, an improbable pedestrian task that leads
to heat and light.

—Anna Quindlen

Here is this chapter's point in a nutshell: Writers write for a purpose to an audience within a genre. Together, these three factors—purpose, audience, and genre—create what we call "**rhetorical context**." The more aware you are of these factors, the more efficient you will be as a reader and the more effective you will be as a writer. Analyzing a text's rhetorical context as you read will enable you to frame a response in terms of your own rhetorical context: What will be your purpose, audience, and genre? Your answers will influence not only what you write but also the way you read and use additional texts.

Rhetorical Context: Purpose, Audience, and Genre

Recognizing the influence of rhetorical context helps rhetorical readers reconstruct the strategy behind an author's choices about content (for example, what to include and exclude), structure (for example, what to say first, when to reveal the thesis, how to arrange the parts, how to format the document), and style (whether to use big words or ordinary words, complex or easy sentence structure, lots of jargon or no jargon, and so forth).

Analyzing an Author's Purpose

In Chapter 2 we noted that writers have designs on readers—that is, writers aim to change a reader's view of a subject in some way. They might aim to enlarge a reader's view of a subject, clarify that view, or restructure that view. This motive to reach out to an audience through language inevitably stems from some problem or perceived misunderstanding or gap in knowledge that an author wishes to remedy. Rhetorician Lloyd F. Bitzer used the term **exigence**

Chapter 3, Analyzing Rhetorical Situations: Purpose, Genre, and Context, is taken from John C. Bean, Virginia A. Chappell, and Alice M. Gilliam's *Reading Rhetorically*, pp. 17–37 (Chapter 2, Analyzing Your Reading and Writing Context).

for a flaw that an author believes can be altered by a text presented to an audience.[1] This flaw might be a circumstance that is other than it should be, a situation in need of attention, or perhaps an occasion in need of special recognition. Your ability as a reader to pinpoint an author's sense of a flaw, a problem, or some other situation in need of change will enable you to zero in on that author's purpose. Furthermore, when you are ready to write about what you have read, thinking of your purpose as writing in order to remedy a flaw will help you focus sharply. Such "flaws" or problems may be as simple as the need to provide information or as complex as the need to advocate for standardizing a set of medical procedures in order to reduce infections. (You will see surgeon Atul Gawande make this argument in the reading at the end of Chapter 4.) For example, you might need to inform a potential employer of your availability and qualifications for a particular job, so you submit a letter and résumé. Or you could need to demonstrate to a history professor that you do, indeed, have a good grasp of the economic system that dominated during China's Ming dynasty, so you answer an exam question with careful detail.

A set of categories for conceptualizing the ways that writers aim to change readers' minds is summarized in Table 3.1. Based on a scheme developed by rhetoricians to categorize types of discourse in terms of a writer's aim or purpose, the table identifies eight **rhetorical aims** or purposes that writers typically set for themselves. This framework offers a particularly powerful way of thinking about both reading and writing because each row zeroes in on how a writer might envision a purpose that connects subject matter to audience in a given rhetorical situation. In the table, we describe how texts in each category work, what they offer readers, and the response their authors typically aim to bring about. The table illustrates the differences among the aims with examples of texts that a college student might compose in response to assignments in a variety of courses.

We have labeled the table's third column "Desired Response" because we want to emphasize that a writer can only *desire* a certain response from a reader; they cannot assume or force that response. The reader is in charge because it is the reader who decides whether to accede to the writer's intentions or to resist them. Because writers try to persuade an intended audience to adopt their perspective, they select and arrange evidence, choose examples, include or omit material, and select words and images to best support their perspective. But readers are the ones who decide—sometimes unconsciously, sometimes deliberately—whether the presentation is convincing. Your awareness of how a text is constructed to persuade its intended audience will enable you to decide how you want to respond to that text and use it in your own writing.

■ ■ ■ ■   **FOR WRITING AND DISCUSSION**

To explore the spectrum of aims presented in Table 3.1, choose an issue or situation that interests you and fill in the grid of a similar table with sample writing scenarios and purposes for each of the table's eight rows of rhetorical aims. Working alone or

---

[1]Bitzer's concept of an exigence within a *rhetorical situation*, modified over the years, was first described in his essay, "The Rhetorical Situation," *Philosophy and Rhetoric* 1.1 (1968): 1–14. *EbscoHost*. Web. 3 June 2012.

TABLE 3.1   A Spectrum of Purposes

Rhetorical Aim	Focus and Features	Desired Response	Examples
Express and Reflect **Offers Readers:** Shared emotional, intellectual experience	**Focus:** Writer's own life and experience **Features:** Literary techniques such as plot, character, setting, evocative language	**Readers** can imagine and identify with writer's experience. **Success** depends on writer's ability to create scenes, dialog, and commentary that engage readers.	Nursing student reflects on her semester of Service Learning at a school for young children with developmental delays and disabilities.
Inquire and Explore **Offers Readers:** Shared intellectual experience, new information, new perspectives	**Focus:** Puzzling problem seen through narration of writer's thinking processes **Features:** Delayed thesis or no thesis; examination of subject from multiple angles; writer's thinking is foregrounded.	**Readers** will agree question or problem is significant, identify with writer's thinking, and find new insights. **Success** depends on writer's ability to engage readers with question or problem and the exploration process.	Students in an honors seminar taught by a physicist and philosopher write papers that explore the question: "What makes study of the origins of the universe significant to daily life in the twenty-first century?"
Inform and Explain (also called *expository writing*) **Offers Readers:** Significant, perhaps surprising, new information; presentation tailored to readers' interest and presumed knowledge level	**Focus:** Subject matter **Features:** Confident, authoritative stance; typically states point and purpose early; strives for clarity; provides definitions and examples; uses convincing evidence without argument	**Readers** will grant writer credibility as expert, and be satisfied with the information's scope and accuracy. **Success** depends on writer's ability to anticipate readers' information needs and ability to understand.	Economics intern is assigned to track 10 years of the rise and fall of mortgage interest rates and report on experts' current explanations of the trends.
Analyze and Interpret **Offers Readers:** New way of looking at the subject matter	**Focus:** Phenomena that are difficult to understand or explain **Features:** Relatively tentative stance; thesis supported by evidence and reasoning; new or unsettling analyses and interpretations must be convincing; doesn't assume that evidence speaks for itself	**Readers** will grant writer credibility as analyst and accept insights offered, or at least acknowledge value of approach. **Success** depends on writer's ability to explain reasoning and connect it with phenomena analyzed.	Literature student analyzes the definition of *justice* employed by various characters in Sophocles' play *Antigone* with the goal of interpreting the author's understanding of the concept.

(continued)

TABLE 3.1   A Spectrum of Purposes (Continued)

Rhetorical Aim	Focus and Features	Desired Response	Examples
Persuasion: **Take a Stand** **Offers Readers:** Reasons to make up or change their minds about a question at issue	**Focus:** Question that divides a community **Features:** States a firm position, provides clear reasons and evidence, connects with readers' values and beliefs, engages with opposing views	**Readers** will agree with writer's position and reasoning. **Success** depends on writer's ability to provide convincing support and to counter opposition without alienating readers.	For an ethics class, an architecture student decides to write an argument in favor of placing certain buildings in his community on the historic preservation register, thus preserving them from demolition or radical remodeling.
Persuasion: **Evaluate and Judge** **Offers Readers:** Reasons to make up or change their minds about a focal question regarding worth or value	**Focus:** Question about worth or value of a phenomenon **Features:** Organized around criteria for judgment and how phenomenon matches them	**Readers** will accept writer's view of the worth or value of the phenomenon. **Success** depends on writer's ability to connect subject to criteria that readers accept.	Political theory students are asked to evaluate and choose between the descriptions of an ideal ruler embodied in Plato's philosopher king and Machiavelli's prince.
Persuasion: **Propose a Solution** **Offers Readers:** A recommended course of action	**Focus:** Question about what action should be taken **Features:** Describes problem and solution, then justifies solution in terms of values and consequences; level of detail depends on assumptions about readers' knowledge	**Readers** will assent to proposed action and do as writer suggests. **Success** depends on readers' agreement that a problem exists and/or that the recommended action will have good results.	A group of seniors majoring in social welfare collaborates on a grant proposal to a community foundation interested in improving health education in a rural area.
Persuasion: **Seek Common Ground** **Offers Readers:** New perspectives and reduced intensity regarding difficult issues	**Focus:** Multiple perspectives on a vexing problem **Features:** Lays out the values and goals of the various stakeholders so that others can find commonalities to build on; does not advocate	**Readers** will discover mutuality with opponents; conflict may not be resolved; discussion could lead to cooperative action. **Success** depends on readers' discovery of mutual interests.	An environmental studies student designs a thesis project to interview advocates and stakeholders who are divided over a proposal to remove a dam from a major river; her goal is to find and highlight points of agreement.

with others, fill in as many cells in the example column as you can. Choose from the following hypothetical writers or another writer-reader combination that intrigues you in connection with the topic you choose.

- College students in a variety of courses
- A single writer (perhaps an entertainment columnist or a sports writer) seeking publication in a variety of venues, including the Web, about the same subject matter
- People in a variety of roles writing with different aims about the same topic (perhaps a family matter such as pets or divorce, or a public matter such as green energy or human rights)

Identifying an Author's Intended Audience

Audience plays a major role in guiding an author's choices. As you analyze a text, watch for cues in the author's language and use of detail that reveal assumptions about the intended audience.

For example, suppose a writer wants to persuade legislators to raise gasoline taxes in order to reduce fossil fuel consumption. Her strategy might be to persuade different groups of voters to pressure their congressional representatives. If she writes for a scientific audience, her article can include technical data and detailed statistical analyses. If she addresses the general public, however, her style will have to be less technical and more lively, with storylike anecdotes rather than tabular data. If she writes for an environmental publication, she can assume an audience already supportive of her pro-environment values. However, if she writes for a business publication such as the *Wall Street Journal*, she will have to be sensitive to her audience's pro-business values—perhaps by arguing that what is good for the environment will be good for business in the long run.

Analyzing an Author's Designs on Your Thinking

One way to analyze an author's purpose is to consider the kind of change the author hopes to bring about in readers' minds. Try using this formula to quiz yourself about the author's desire to change your mind:

At the beginning of the text, the writer assumes that the reader believes _____.

By the end of the text, the writer hopes that the reader believes _____.

These questions will help you, as a rhetorical reader, to analyze your own response to the text—whether you are going to think or do what the writer apparently hopes you will.

Analyzing a Text's Genre

As writers respond to rhetorical situations by adapting content, structure, and style to different purposes and audiences, they must also adapt to the conventions of a text's **genre**, a term that refers to a recurring category or type of writing based on identifiable features such as structure (for example, a thesis-driven argument or an informal reflection) and document design (for example, the format of academic papers, Web pages, or promotional brochures). These genre-based decisions about format include whether to add visual images, and, if so, what kind will be appropriate and effective. Because particular textual features are expected in particular situations, a writer's effort to follow or modify genre conventions can become a valuable tool for engaging readers and moving them toward desired responses such as those indicated in Table 3.1.

You may be familiar with the concept of genre from literature classes where you studied an assortment of genres, such as plays, novels, and poems. Within each of these broad literary genres are subgenres such as the sonnet and haiku or tragedy and comedy. Similarly, workplace writing has a number of subgenres (memos, marketing proposals, financial reports, progress reports) as does academic writing (laboratory reports, field notes, article abstracts, literature reviews). As the descriptions of typical college writing assignments later in this chapter show, even familiar academic assignments have subgenres (informal response papers, essay exams, article summaries, or researched arguments that present a semester's worth of work).

Consider one commonly encountered genre: the **inverted pyramid** of a news article, in print or online. These reports begin with the key facts of a news event—*who, what, when, where, why,* and *how*—before offering background information and details. As Figure 3.1 shows, a similar structure is recommended for Web writing, where it is necessary to capture readers' attention quickly, in the limited amount of space immediately visible on a screen.

In both cases, someone in a hurry or with only a passing interest in the subject matter should be able to glean the gist of the news or of the Web site's purpose by reading just the initial sentences. Furthermore, on Web sites, putting the essential facts first makes it easier for search engines to spot and report on the page's content.

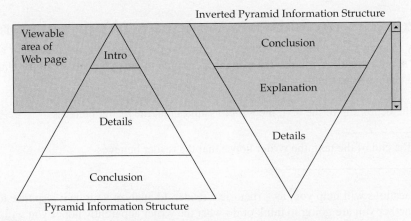

FIGURE 3.1 Diagram of inverted pyramid structure recommended for organizing Web content

Genre differences in written texts frequently become evident through visual cues, and these cues in turn create reader expectations. The Web site of the *New York Times* uses typefaces and layout that resemble those of its paper edition, but the home page of a veterinary clinic (interested in inviting new patients) will likely be different from the home page of an advice blog about caring for exotic birds. Similarly, genre differences influence the look of print documents. If you were browsing publications in the current periodicals rack at a library, you could quickly distinguish popular magazines such as *Popular Science* and *Business Week* from scholarly journals such as the *American Journal of Human Genetics* or the *Journal of Marketing Research*. The glossy covers of the magazines, often adorned with arresting photographs, distinguish them from sober-looking scholarly journals, the covers of which typically display a table of contents of the articles within. As you develop your ability to recognize genres and the ways that their conventions shape content, you will also sharpen your ability to decide whether and how to use particular texts for your own purposes.

As illustration, consider the distinctive differences between the genres of the two articles introduced by the images in Figures 3.2 and 3.3. As the captions indicate, the first is taken from the scholarly journal *Appetite* and the second was originally published in a monthly health newsletter, the *UC Berkeley Wellness Letter*. A quick glance makes evident the differences in these texts' rhetorical contexts, from the different page layouts to the contrasts between casual language and formal vocabulary.

The article from *Appetite* depicted in Figure 3.2 is one of two studies from the October 2011 issue that were used by a staff writer for the *Wellness Letter* to produce "Chew on This"—a short, easy-to-read summary of recent research on gum-chewing (presented in full in Figure 3.3). This piece was written to catch the attention of casual readers whose curiosity might be piqued by the clever title and the questions about the effects of chewing gum placed in bold-face headings, questions that readers will discover do not have definitive answers. Contrast this informal article with the formality and detail evident on the first page of the *Appetite* article in Figure 3.2. Despite the playful wording in the title—"Cognitive Advantages of Chewing Gum. Now You See them, Now You Don't"—the overall presentation of the opening page signals that it is a scholarly research report, including the label at the upper left labeling it as such. Scholarly elements highlighted by the labels and circles in the figure include the names of four authors (with an asterisk indicating the one to whom correspondence may be sent), a history of the article's submission to the journal, an abstract, a keywords list, and an introduction reviewing the literature from previous studies on the topic. The article's remaining seven pages describe in detail the methodology of two studies about gum-chewing and test-taking behaviors, present charts and graphs of the results, and discuss the significance of those results.

Casual readers are likely to respond positively to the newsletter's brief summary of the research, but the readers of the scholarly journal are looking for more than lighthearted advice about gum-chewing. The *Appetite* article's intended audience is other researchers, not the general public. The keywords list will help those researchers find this article so that they can read about both its findings and methodology. As is customary, the article's last page suggests what work needs to be done by subsequent researchers: "In summary, the current study demonstrates that the discrepancies in research

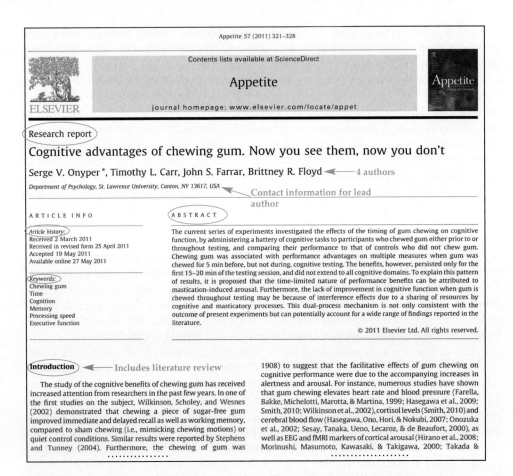

FIGURE 3.2 Image from page 1 of a research report the scholarly journal *Appetite* about the fleeting cognitive benefits of gum-chewing

findings of the burgeoning literature on the effect of gum chewing on cognitive function can be attributed to the timing of chewing....further studies are needed to provide a more complete picture of the relationship between physiological changes and cognitive functioning due to the chewing of gum." (Onyper et al., 327—see full citation below).[2]

From dense scientific research reports like this, the unnamed author of "Chew on This" used expert reading skills to dig out key points of information—and ambiguity—and transform them into a lively little article designed to spark a few smiles as well.[3] This reader-writer might have been trained as a journalist, or might be a graduate

---

[2]Serge V. Onyper, et al., "Cognitive Advantages of Chewing Gum. Now You See Them, Now You Don't." *Appetite* 57.2 (2011): 321–328. *Science Direct.* Web. 9 June 2012.

[3]The *Appetite* article about gum-chewing and snacking is by Marion M. Hetherington and Martin F. Regan, "Effects of Chewing Gum on Short-Term Appetite Regulation in Moderately Restrained Eaters." *Appetite* 57.2 (2011): 475–482. *Science Direct.* Web. 9 June 2012.

Chew on This — Punning Title

Most people chew gum for pleasure or out of habit; others to freshen breath or stop a food or cigarette craving. Does gum provide any real benefits? There have been lots of studies on gum over the years, including two recent ones.

The best evidence concerns gum's ability to prevent cavities by boosting saliva flow and neutralizing acid produced by mouth bacteria. Sugar-free gums are best for this, notably those with the sugar alcohol xylitol, which suppresses the growth of cavity-producing bacteria. Still, gum can't replace brushing and flossing.

Can gum make you thinner? Gum chewing burns only about 11 calories an hour. But if it keeps you from eating a candy bar, that's a big plus. Studies on whether gum reduces appetite have produced conflicting findings. The latest study, in the journal *Appetite*, found that when women chewed gum (15 minutes, once an hour, for three hours), they ate about 30 fewer calories when subsequently offered a snack compared to when they hadn't chewed gum. The women also said they felt less hungry and fuller after chewing the gum. Gum manufacturers have helped publicize these results. But each piece of gum had 5 to 10 calories, so the women didn't actually cut down on calories significantly. Would sugarless gum have had the same effect? Maybe, maybe not.

Informal language in attention-getting questions

Closes with scholarly quote followed by joking paraphrase.

Make you smarter? Some early research found that gum chewing improved performance on memory tests, perhaps by boosting blood flow to the brain and stimulating a part of the brain where information is processed. But more recent studies have failed to find any brain benefit—or have noted that gum sometimes worsens performance.

Another recent study in *Appetite* found that gum improved performance on certain cognitive tests, but only when it was chewed before, not during, the tests. The benefit lasted just 15 to 20 minutes. According to the researchers, gum doesn't help thinking—and possibly even impairs it—during a task because of "interference due to a sharing of metabolic resources by cognitive and masticatory processes." In other words, some people can't think (or walk) and chew gum at the same time.

FIGURE 3.3 Text of the "Last Word" column on the last page (p. 8) of the *UC Berkeley Wellness Letter*, Feb. 2012. Note that the journal that published the original research, *Appetite,* is mentioned only briefly (as highlighted in the figure).

student in psychology or public health who will go on to build a career by publishing in journals like *Appetite*. In the pages ahead, we suggest strategies for you as both reader and writer for developing your own abilities to work with and for a variety of audiences, purposes, and genres.

■ ■ ■ **FOR WRITING AND DISCUSSION**

Both of the scholarly articles about gum-chewing from the October 2011 issue of *Appetite* (see full citations in footnotes 2 and 3) should be available through your school library, probably electronically. We invite you to explore in more detail the genre differences between them and the newsletter article in Figure 3.3. If your library also subscribes to the *UC Berkeley Wellness Letter,* you will have an opportunity to note contrasting genre features in that publication as well.

Analyzing Your Own Rhetorical Context as Reader/Writer

When you are assigned to read texts of any type (a textbook, a scholarly article, data on a Web site, historical documents, or other kinds of readings), think not only about the authors' rhetorical context, but also about your own.

Determining Your Purpose, Audience, and Genre

When you write about various texts or use them in your own arguments, you will be writing for a purpose to an audience within a genre. In college, your purpose will be determined by your assignment. (See the final section of this chapter, "Typical Reading-Based Writing Assignments Across the Curriculum.") Your audience may range from yourself to your professor and your classmates, to readers of a certain newspaper or blog, even to participants in an undergraduate research conference. Your assigned genre might come from a wide range of possibilities: summary, Web posting, rhetorical analysis, reader-response reflection, source-based argument, or a major research paper.

Identifying your purpose at the outset helps you set goals and plan your reading accordingly. Your purpose for reading may seem like a self-evident matter—"I'm reading Chapter 1 of this sociology book because it was assigned for tomorrow." That may be, but what we have in mind is a more strategic consideration of your purpose. Ask yourself how the reading assignment ties in with themes established in class. How does it fit with concepts laid out on the course syllabus? Is this your first course in sociology? If so, you might set a purpose for yourself of gathering definitions of the foundational concepts and specialized vocabulary used by sociologists. These basic but strategically stated goals might lead you to allow extra time for the slowed-down reading that students usually need in order to get their bearings at the beginning of introductory courses.

To illustrate the importance of establishing purposes for your reading, let's move farther into the semester and assume you are skimming articles to select some for closer reading and possible use in an annotated bibliography for this first course in sociology. Further, imagine that your assignment is to choose and summarize articles that demonstrate how sociological research can shed light on a current public controversy. An important first step in an assignment like this is to identify a clear and compelling **research question**. A strong research question will enable you to know what you're looking for, and it will guide you to read more purposefully and productively. Let's say you are interested in whether pop culture has a negative effect on family values. You want to think that it doesn't, but from sometimes intense discussions among family and friends, you realize that the answer might be "it depends." Maybe sociological research has laid out some systematic ways of thinking about this issue, and a more productive question would be "How does pop culture impact family values?" or "What is known about how pop culture impacts family values?"

Following the demands of your research question, you will need to define both "pop culture" and "family values" and narrow your focus as you find articles related to your controversy. Some sources will report research findings contrary to your own views; others will tend to confirm your views. To summarize them fairly, you will have to pay careful attention to the way these authors articulate their own research questions and present their results. Setting goals ahead of time for both your writing and your reading will help you know what to look for as you select and read articles.

Matching Your Reading Strategies to Your Purpose as Reader/Writer

Although all readers change their approach to reading according to their audience, purpose, and the genre of the text at hand, most readers do so without thought or reflection, relying on a limited set of strategies. By contrast, experienced readers vary their reading process self-consciously and strategically. To see how one accomplished undergraduate, Sheri, contrasts her "school" reading with her "reading-for-fun" process, see the box on the next page. You will no doubt notice that her strategies combine idiosyncratic habits (the blue pen and cold room) with sound, widely used academic reading habits (looking over chapter headings, checking for study guide questions, and so on).

What personal habits or rituals do you combine with your more purposeful reading behaviors? The awareness and flexibility evident in the way Sheri talks about her reading are valuable because planning as she does would enable you to work efficiently and maximize the use of your time. Furthermore, thinking about your purpose as Sheri does will help you maintain a sense of your own authority as you read, a notion that is very important for college writing.

Sheri's self-awareness and deliberate reading strategies are not typical. When we ask students to describe the behaviors of good readers, many initially say "speed" or "the ability to understand a text in a single reading." Surprisingly, most experienced readers don't aim for speed reading, nor do they report that reading is an easy, one-step process. On the contrary, experienced readers put considerable effort into reading and rereading a text, adapting their strategies and speed to its demands and to their purpose for reading. Because your purposes for reading academic assignments will vary considerably, so must your academic reading strategies. You will read much differently, for example, if your task is to interpret or analyze a text than if you are simply skimming it for its potential usefulness in a research project. Contrary to popular myth, expert readers are not necessarily "speed" readers. Experienced readers pace themselves according to their purpose, taking advantage of four basic reading speeds:

- *Very fast:* Readers scan a text very quickly if they are looking only for a specific piece of information.
- *Fast:* Readers skim a text rapidly if they are trying to get just the general gist without worrying about details.

Preparing to Read: Sheri's Process

"When I am reading for class, for starters I make sure that I have all of my reading supplies. These include my glasses, a highlighter, pencil, blue pen, notebook paper, dictionary, and a quiet place to read, which has a desk or table. (It also has to be cold!) Before I read for class or for research purposes I always look over chapter headings or bold print words and then formulate questions based on these. When I do this it helps me to become more interested in the text I am reading because I am now looking for answers.

"Also, if there are study guide questions, I will look them over so that I have a basic idea of what to look for. I will then read the text all the way through, find the answers to my questions, and underline all of the study guide answers in pencil.

"When I read for fun, it's a whole other story! I always take off my shoes and sit on the floor/ground or in a very comfortable chair. I always prefer to read in natural light and preferably fresh air. I just read and relax and totally immerse myself in the story or article or whatever!"[4]

- *Slow to moderate:* Readers read carefully in order to get complete understanding of an article. The more difficult the text, the more slowly they read. Often difficult texts require rereading.
- *Very slow:* Experienced readers read very slowly if their purpose is to analyze a text. They take elaborate marginal notes and often pause to ponder over the construction of a paragraph or the meaning of an image or metaphor. Sometimes they reread the text dozens of times.

As your expertise grows within the fields you study, you will undoubtedly learn to vary your reading speed and strategies according to your purposes, even to the point of considering "efficient" reading of certain texts to involve slowing way down and rereading.

How Expert Readers Use Rhetorical Knowledge to Read Efficiently

This section illustrates two strategies used by expert readers to apply rhetorical knowledge to their reading processes.

Using Genre Knowledge to Read Efficiently

Besides varying reading speed to match their purpose, experienced readers also adjust their reading strategies to match the genre of a text. It is clear that the articles represented in Figures 3.2 and 3.3 call for different kinds of reading strategies, but you may

---

[4]Sheri's description of her reading process is quoted in Paula Gillespie and Neal Lerner, *The Allyn and Bacon Guide to Peer Tutoring* (Boston: Allyn & Bacon, 2000), 105. Print.

be surprised to learn that many scientists wouldn't read the scholarly article straight through from beginning to end. Instead, depending on their purpose, it is likely that they would read different sections in different order. The material in the following box describes how a group of physicists were guided both by their purpose for reading and by their familiarity with the genre conventions of scientific research reports. We invite you to read the material in the box before proceeding to the next paragraph.[5]

Considering how scientists with different interests read specialized articles in their discipline, we can surmise that some researchers would read the results section of the *Appetite* article very carefully, whereas others would concentrate on the methodology section. Still another reader, perhaps a graduate student interested in finding a dissertation topic, might read it to see what research the authors say still needs to be accomplished. With sharply narrow interests and purposes, these readers would probably not find the article difficult to read. In contrast, nonspecialists might find it daunting to read, but as experienced readers, they would recognize that it is not necessary to understand all the details in order to understand the article's gist. They might read the abstract, then skip directly to the discussion section, where the authors analyze the meaning and the significance of their results.

Using a Text's Social/Historical Context to Make Predictions and Ask Questions

Recognizing that a text is part of a larger conversation about a particular topic, experienced readers can also use textual cues—such as format, style, and terminology—as well as their own background knowledge to speculate about the original context of a text, make predictions about it, and formulate questions.

Physicists' Techniques for Efficient Reading

Researchers who studied the way that physicists read articles in physics journals found that the physicists seldom read the article from beginning to end but instead used their knowledge of the typical structure of scientific articles to find the information most relevant to their interests. Scientific articles typically begin with an abstract or summary of their contents. The main body of these articles includes a five-part structure: (1) an introduction that describes the research problem, (2) a review of other studies related to this problem, (3) a description of the methodology used in the research, (4) a report of the results, and (5) the conclusions drawn from the results. The physicists in the study read the abstracts first to see if an article was relevant to their own research. If it was, the experimental physicists went to the methodology section to see if the article reported any new methods. By contrast, the theoretical physicists went to the results section to see if the article reported any significant new results.[5]

---

[5]Research reported by Cheryl Geisler, *Academic Literacy and the Nature of Expertise* (Hillsdale, NJ: Erlbaum, 1994), 20–21. Print.

These strategies for actively engaging with a text's social or historical context are illustrated in Ann Feldman's report of interviews with expert readers reading texts within their own areas of expertise. For example, Professor Lynn Weiner, a social historian, describes in detail her behind-the-scenes thinking as she prepared to read a chapter entitled "From the Medieval to the Modern Family" from Philippe Aries's *Centuries of Childhood: A Social History of Family Life*, written in 1962. Quotations from Professor Weiner's description of her thinking are shown in the box below. As Professor Weiner reads, she continues to elaborate this context, confirming and revising predictions, asking new questions, evaluating what Aries has to say in light of the evidence he can provide, and assessing the value of his ideas to her own work as a social historian. She concludes by saying, "A path-breaking book, it was credited with advancing the idea that childhood as a stage of life is historically constructed and not the same in every culture and every time. In my own work I might refer to Aries as I think and write about families as they exist today."

Professor Weiner's description of creating a context for understanding the Aries book suggests that the ability to recognize what you do not know and to raise questions about a text is as important as identifying what you do know and understand. Sometimes readers can reconstruct context from external clues such as a title and headings; from a text's visual appearance; from background notes about the author, including the date and place of publication; or from what a book's table of contents reveals about its structure and scope. But readers often have to rely on internal evidence to get a full picture. A text's context and purpose may become evident through some quick spot reading (explained in the next chapter), especially in the introduction and conclusion. Sometimes, however, the full rhetorical and social context can be reconstructed only through a great deal of puzzling as you read. It's not unusual that a whole first reading is needed to understand exactly what conversation the writer is joining and how she or he intends to affect that conversation. Once that context becomes clear, rereading of key passages will make the text easier to comprehend.

Building a Context for Reading

"This work isn't precisely in my field and it is a difficult text. I also know it by its reputation. But, like any student, I need to create a context in which to understand this work. When the book was written, the idea of studying the family was relatively new. Before this time historians often studied kings, presidents, and military leaders. That's why this new type of social history encouraged us to ask, 'How did ordinary people live?' Not the kings, but the families in the middle ages. Then we have to ask: 'Which families is [Aries] talking about? What causes the change that he sees? . . . For whom is the change significant?' . . . I'll want to be careful not . . . to assume the old family is bad and the new family is good. The title suggests a transition so I'll be looking for signs of it." [6]

---

[6]Ann Feldman, *Writing and Learning in the Disciplines* (New York: Harper, 1996), 16–17, 25–29. Print.

Typical Reading-Based Writing Assignments Across the Curriculum

In college, a reading assignment is often only the first step in a complex series of activities that lead toward writing something that will be graded. In many cases, the material you are asked to read and respond to may include visual elements that demand attention, such as charts and graphs, photographs, drawings, or specific features of document or Web design. What you write will naturally vary according to the situation, ranging from a quick answer on an essay exam to an extensive source-based paper. In this section, we discuss five types of common college assignments in which reading plays a major role:

1. Writing to understand course content more fully
2. Writing to report your understanding of what a text says
3. Writing to practice the conventions of a particular type of text
4. Writing to make claims about a text
5. Writing to extend the conversation

The role that reading plays in connection with these different purposes for writing can be placed along a continuum, starting at one end with assignments in which the ideas in the texts you read predominate and moving to assignments in which the content is subordinate to your own ideas and aims. The first two assignment types ask you to write in order to learn course subject matter and to practice careful listening to texts. The last three ask you to compose your own analyses and arguments for specific audiences. Writing teachers sometimes distinguish these two categories of assignment goals by referring to them as "writing to learn" and "learning to write."

Writing to Understand Course Content More Fully

"Writing-to-learn" assignments aim to deepen your understanding of materials you read by asking you to put the author/creator's ideas into your own words or to identify points of confusion for yourself. The primary audience for writing in this category is often yourself, although teachers may sometimes ask you to submit them so that they can check on your understanding and progress. The style is informal and conversational. Organization and grammatical correctness are less important than the quality of your engagement with the content of the reading. These assignments typically take one of the following forms.

In-Class Freewriting   The point of freewriting is to think rapidly without censoring your thoughts. It is often assigned in class as a way to stimulate thinking about the day's subject. A typical in-class freewrite assignment might be this:

> Choose what for you personally is the single most important word in what we read for today. You need not speculate about which word the author or your instructor or any other classmate would choose. Just choose the word that seems most important to you, and then explore in writing why you chose it. This word may occur only once or many times.[7]

---

[7]We thank Joan Ruffino, an instructor at the University of Wisconsin–Milwaukee, for this freewriting assignment.

Reading or Learning Logs   Reading or learning logs are informal assignments, usually organized chronologically, in which you record your understanding, questions, and responses to a reading or image. Some teachers give specific prompts for entries, whereas others just ask that you write them with a certain regularity and/or of a certain length. A typical prompt might be "How would you describe the author's voice in this essay?" If a teacher asks you simply to write your own reflections in a log, you might use some of the questions rhetorical readers ask to examine the text's method and your response to it.

Double-Entry Journals   Double-entry journals are like reading logs but formatted so that you may conduct an ongoing dialogue with your own interpretations and reactions to a text. Once again, the audience is primarily yourself. Although the double-entry system was originally designed for lined notebook paper, it can work equally well—or even better—on screen. Here is how the system works: Divide a notebook page with a line down the middle, or set up a two-column layout in your word processing program. On the right side of the page, record reading notes—direct quotations, observations, comments, questions, objections. On the left side, record your later reflections about those notes—second thoughts, responses to quotations, reactions to earlier comments, answers to questions or new questions. Skip lines as necessary so that your dialogue on the left lines up with your original notes on the right. Another option is to use a commenting function to create a sidebar column for your responses to your original notes; but in our experience, students find the spatial alignment difficult to track. Rhetorician Ann Berthoff, who popularized the double-entry approach, says that it provides readers with a means of conducting a "continuing audit of meaning."[8] In a double-entry journal, you carry on a conversation with yourself about a text.

Short Thought Pieces or Postings to a Discussion Board   Sometimes written for an instructor, sometimes for a specified group of peers, short (250–300 words) response papers or "thought" pieces are somewhat more formal than the assignments discussed so far, but they are still much more informal than essay assignments. They call for a fuller response than the previous types of writing, but the purpose is similar—to articulate an understanding of a particular text by identifying significant points and offering a personal response or interpretation of them. Teachers will often provide a specific prompt for these assignments, sometimes as a way to generate a series of short pieces that will build to a larger paper. When the piece is written for a discussion forum, instructors may ask that you include a question or respond to a classmate's questions.

Here is a sample response piece that was posted to an online class forum. The teacher asked the students to write about the insights they gleaned regarding obsessive-compulsive disorder (OCD) from reading Lauren Slater's essay "Black Swans," in which the author narrates the onset of her ongoing battle with it.

---

[8]Ann Berthoff, *The Making of Meaning* (Montclair, NJ: Boynton Cook, 1981), 45. Print.

Student Posting to a Class Forum

Reading "Black Swans" taught me some basic information about OCD, but more importantly, it taught me how terrifying this disease can be. It begins with a single obsessive thought that leads to a cycle of anxiety, repetitive behaviors, and avoidance of situations that produce the obsessive thoughts. In severe cases, like Slater's, the person completely avoids life because the obsessive thoughts invade every aspect of life.

What impressed me most about this essay, however, was Slater's ability to put me in her shoes and make me feel some of the terror she felt. She vividly describes her experience at being stricken with this condition without warning. A single thought—"I can't concentrate"—suddenly blocked out all other thoughts. Even her own body seemed foreign to her and grotesque: "the phrase 'I can't concentrate on my hand' blocked out my hand, so all I saw was a blur of flesh giving way to the bones beneath, and inside the bones the grimy marrow, and in the grimy marrow the individual cells, all disconnected." I see why Max says it was the most terrifying aspect of the disease to him. I can't imagine being disconnected from my own body. More horrifying to me, though, was her sense of being completely unable to control her mind: "My mind was devouring my mind." I will be interested to see what others think.

Writing to Report Your Understanding of What a Text Says

Another common reading-based assignment asks you to report your understanding of what a text says. Here, your goal is to summarize the text rather than respond to it. Reports like this are necessary, for example, when essay exam questions ask students to contrast the ideas of several authors. Another example would be an **annotated bibliography** summarizing sources related to a particular topic or question, or a literature review at the beginning of a report for a science class. A summary can be as short as a single sentence (when, for example, you want to provide context for a quotation in a paper) or longer and more detailed (when, for example, you are summarizing an opposing view that you intend to refute in your own argument.) Although summaries or reports of your understanding of a text will vary in length and purpose, they are always expected to be accurate, fair, and balanced.

Writing to Practice the Conventions of a Particular Type of Text

Assignments that ask you to practice the conventions of a particular type of writing—its organizational format, style, ways of presenting evidence, and so on—use readings as models. Such assignments are common in college courses. In a journalism class, for example, you would learn to write a news report using the inverted pyramid structure;

in a science course, you would learn to write up the results of a lab experiment in a particular scientific report format. Novices in a discipline learn to write in specialized genres by reading examples and practicing their formats and rhetorical "moves."

Generally, using readings as models of a genre or subgenre involves the following activities:

- Identifying the features that characterize a particular type of text
- Noting the ways in which a rhetorical situation affects the features identified in model texts
- Deciding on your own topic and reason for writing this particular type of text
- Using the features of the model text (or texts) and your own rhetorical situation to guide your writing

Let's say, for example, that you've been asked to write a **proposal argument**. Proposals typically include three main features: description of the problem, proposal of a solution, and justification of that solution. As you read sample proposals, you will find that in different contexts, authors deal with these features differently, depending on their audience and purpose. In some cases, for example, there is a great deal of description of the problem because the intended audience is unfamiliar with it or doesn't recognize it as a problem. In other cases, it is presumed that the intended reading audience already recognizes the problem. The key to success is to adapt a model text's structural and stylistic characteristics to your own rhetorical purpose, not to follow the model slavishly.

In courses across the curriculum, your ability to analyze and adopt the conventions particular to a given discipline's ways of writing will help you write successful papers. For example, when you are asked in a philosophy class to write an argument in response to Immanuel Kant's *Critique of Pure Reason,* you are primarily being asked to engage with the ideas in the text. But secondarily, you are also being asked to practice the conventions of writing a philosophical argument in which counterexamples and counterarguments are expected. Thus, in any field of study, it pays to be alert not only to the ideas presented in material you are assigned to read, but also to its structure and style.

Writing to Make Claims About a Text

Assignments in this category ask you to analyze and critique texts, including texts in which images and layout are key elements of rhetorical effect. Such papers must go beyond a summary of what a text says to make claims about that content and how it is presented. Many academic writers take as their field of study the texts produced by others. Literary critics study novels, poems, and plays; cultural critics analyze song lyrics, advertisements, cereal boxes, and television scripts; historians analyze primary source documents from the past; theologians scrutinize the sacred texts of different religions; lawyers analyze the documents entered into court proceedings, the exact wording of laws and statutes, and the decisions of appellate courts. In all these cases, the analysis and critique involve examining small parts of the whole to understand, explain, and perhaps object to, overall points and success.

Many college composition courses ask students to write rhetorical analyses of texts. To **analyze**—a word that at its root means "take apart"—a text, you need to identify specific rhetorical methods and strategies used by the author, show how these rhetorical choices contribute to the text's impact, and evaluate those elements in light of the author's evident purpose. In assignments like this, the text and your ideas about it are of equal importance. These assignments asking for analysis are not invitations for you to refer briefly to the text and then take off on your own opinions about the topic, nor are they invitations merely to summarize or rehearse what the text has said. Rather, analysis assignments expect you to engage critically with a specific text. On the one hand, you will be expected to represent what the text said accurately and fairly. On the other hand, you will be expected to offer your own analysis, interpretation, or critique in a way that enables readers to see the text differently.

Writing to Extend the Conversation

These assignments treat texts as voices in a conversation about ideas. They typically ask writers to read and synthesize material from several sources. Here, your own ideas and aims take center stage; your source texts play important but less prominent backup roles. The most familiar form this assignment takes is the research or seminar paper. A key difference between these assignments and high school research papers is that college instructors expect the paper to present your own argument, not simply to report what others have said. In other words, you are expected to articulate a significant question or problem, research what published authors have said about it in print or on the Web, and formulate your own argument. To write these multisource papers successfully, you must use your source texts primarily to position yourself in the conversation and to supply supporting data, information, or testimony. The argument—your main points—must come from you.

A helpful way to approach these assignments is to treat the texts you have read as springboards for further research and discovery. Think of the readings you encounter in your research as voices in a conversation that your essay will join. By giving you the opportunity to define your own purposes for writing in dialog with other texts, such assignments prepare you for the research assignments typical of many college courses, where your goal is to synthesize material from a number of sources and then produce your own paper, inserting another voice—your own—into the ongoing conversation.

Writing Rhetorical Analyses

4

A good question is never answered. It is not a bolt to be tightened into place but a seed to be planted and to bear more seed toward the hope of greening the landscape of idea.

—John Ciardi

Learning to question a text is central to your academic success in college. Your professors will ask you to engage with texts in ways that you may not be used to. They expect you to do more than just "bank" the knowledge you glean from reading; they expect you to use this knowledge to do various kinds of intellectual work—to offer your own interpretations or evaluations, to launch a research project of your own, to synthesize ideas from a number of readings, and to draw independent conclusions. Such thoughtful reading of texts begins with your questions addressed to the text and its author. Academics sometimes refer to the questioning process as interrogation of a text, an apt metaphor that likely brings to mind scenes from television shows where police officers or attorneys grill suspects and witnesses (metaphoric stand-ins here for a text that requires examination).

Importantly, questioning does not necessarily mean fault-finding, and it certainly doesn't mean dismissing an author's ideas wholesale. Rather, it entails carefully interrogating a text's claims and evidence and its subtle forms of persuasion so that you can make sound judgments and offer thoughtful responses. Your job in critiquing a text is to be "critical." However, the meanings of the term *critical* include "characterized by careful and exact evaluation and judgment," not simply "disagreement" or "harsh judgment." In questioning a text, you bring your critical faculties to bear on it along with your experience, knowledge, and opinion. But you must do so in a way that treats the author's ideas fairly and makes judgments that can be supported by textual evidence.

Chapter 4, Writing Rhetorical Analyses, is taken from John C. Bean, Virginia A. Chappell, and Alice M. Gilliam's *Reading Rhetorically*, pp. 69–76 and 92–100 (Chapter 4, Questioning a Text). The section "Writing About What Texts Say and Do" is excerpted from John C. Bean, Virginia A. Chappell, and Alice M. Gilliam's *Reading Rhetorically*, pp. 56–58 (Chapter 3, Listening to a Text).

The close, even-handed examination of a text's content and persuasive strategies is greatly facilitated by using the three classical rhetorical appeals identified by Aristotle:

- *Ethos:* the persuasive power of the author's credibility or character
- *Logos:* the persuasive power of the author's reasons, evidence, and logic
- *Pathos:* the persuasive power of the author's appeal to the interests, emotions, and imagination of the audience

Although these three appeals interconnect and sometimes overlap—for example, a writer may use a touching anecdote both to establish credibility as an empathetic person (*ethos*) and to play on the reader's emotions (*pathos*)—we introduce them separately to emphasize their distinct functions as means of persuasion.

"I don't just record ideas when I read, I contend with the ideas the book presents; I work with them, engage in combat with them, synthesize them into concepts I already know, and then come up with my own ideas. I engage with the world and develop an original vision. This is the process that writers use."[1]

—Maxine Hong-Kingston

Examining a Writer's Credibility and Appeals to *Ethos*

To change readers' minds about something, writers must make themselves credible by projecting an image of themselves that will gain their readers' confidence. In most cases, writers want to come across as knowledgeable, fair-minded, and trustworthy. To examine a writer's credibility, ask yourself, "Do I find this author believable and trustworthy? Why or why not?"

Strong academic readers always try to find out as much as possible about an author's background, interests, political leanings, and general worldview. Sometimes they have independent knowledge of the writer, either because the writer is well known or has been discussed in class, or because an article has a headnote or footnote describing the author's credentials. Often, though, readers must discern a writer's personality and views from the text itself by examining content, tone, word choice, figurative language, organization, and other cues that help create an image of the writer in their minds. Explicit questions to ask might include these:

1. Does this writer seem knowledgeable?
2. What does the writer like and dislike?
3. What are this writer's biases and values?
4. What seems to be the writer's mood? (Angry? Questioning? Meditative? Upset? Jovial?)
5. What is the writer's approach to the topic? (Formal or informal? Logical or emotional? Distant and factual, or personal? Mixed in attitude?)
6. What would it be like to spend time in this writer's company?

---

[1]Maxine Hong-Kingston, in *Speaking of Reading*, ed. Nadine Rosenthal (Portsmouth, NH: Heinemann, 1995), 178. Print.

■ ■ ■ **FOR WRITING AND DISCUSSION**

ON YOUR OWN

1. To help you consider an author's image and credibility, try these activities the next time you are assigned a reading. Describe in words your image of the author as a person (or draw a sketch of this person). Then try to figure out what cues in the text produced this image for you. Finally, consider how this image of the writer leads you to ask more questions about the text. You might ask, for example, "Why is this writer angry? Why does this writer use emotionally laden anecdotes rather than statistics to support his or her case? What is this writer afraid of?"

2. Try these activities with the **op-ed article** by Atul Gawande at the end of this chapter. What kind of an image does he create for himself in this text? How would you describe him in words or portray him in a drawing? Take a few minutes to find and jot down the cues in the text that create this image for you.

WITH YOUR CLASSMATES

Compare your impressions of Gawande with those of your classmates. Do any contradictory impressions come up? That is, do some people in the group interpret the textual cues differently? Some people, for example, might see a comment as "forthright" and "frank" while others might see it as "antagonistic" or "hyperbolic." What aspects of his character (as represented in the text) do you as a group agree on? What aspects do you disagree about?

■ ■ ■

Examining a Writer's Appeals to Reason or *Logos*

Perhaps the most direct way that writers try to persuade readers is through logic or reason. To convince readers that their perspective is reasonable, skilled writers work to anticipate what their intended readers already believe and then use those beliefs as a bridge to the writer's way of thinking. These writers seek to support their claims through a combination of reasons and evidence.

For example, imagine a writer arguing for stricter gun control laws. This writer wants to root his argument in a belief or value that he and his readers already share, so he focuses on concerns for the safety of schoolchildren. The line of reasoning might go something like this: Because the easy availability of guns makes children no longer safe at school, we must pass strict gun control laws to limit access to guns. Of course, readers may or may not go along with this argument. Some readers, although they share the writer's concern for the safety of schoolchildren, might disagree at several points with the writer's logic: Is the availability of guns the main cause of gun violence at schools or are there other, more compelling causes? Will stricter gun control laws really limit the availability of guns? If this same writer wished to use evidence to strengthen this argument, he might use statistics showing a correlation between the rise in the availability of guns and the rise in gun violence in schools. Here, the writer would be operating on the assumption that readers believe in facts and can be persuaded by these statistics that increased gun violence in schools is linked to the availability of firearms.

Explanation of Op-Ed Articles

Gawande was writing as a guest columnist for the **New York Times**. Such articles are called **"op-eds,"** or "op-ed articles," referring to newspapers' traditional placement of signed opinion columns on the page opposite the editorial page, which presents unsigned editorials approved by an editorial board, editorial cartoons, and letters to the editor.

Experienced readers are alert to the logical strategies used by authors, and they have learned not to take what may appear as a "reasonable" argument at face value. In other words, they have learned to question or test this reasoning before assenting to the position the author wants them to take. To examine a writer's reasoning, you need to be able to identify and examine carefully the basic elements of an argument—claims, reasons, evidence, and assumptions. The following questions will help you examine a writer's reasoning:

1. What perspective or position does the writer want me to take toward the topic?
2. Do the writer's claims, reasons, and evidence convince me to take this perspective or position?
3. Do I share the assumptions, stated or unstated, that authorize the writer's reasoning and connect the evidence to the claim?

Claims

The key points that a writer wants readers to accept are referred to as **claims**. For example, Kirk Savage's initial claim in the selection at the end of Chapter 5 is that the Vietnam Veterans Memorial was Washington, D.C.'s "first true victim's monument," a term that he immediately defines as "a monument that existed not to glorify the nation but to help its suffering soldiers heal." Or take another example: In the reading at the end of this chapter, Atul Gawande begins his fourth paragraph by calling a decision of the federal Office for Human Research Protections "bizarre and dangerous." Both of these assertions seem contestable, so readers are smart to raise questions, especially about the wording and scope. Is the meaning of key words in the claims clear? Can particular words be interpreted in more than one way? Is the claim overstated? One might ask of Gawande, "Bizarre? How so?" "Dangerous? In what way?" Likewise, one might ask Savage why he does not consider earlier monuments, such as the Tomb of the Unknown Soldier, to be victim monuments.

Reasons

To support a main claim, writers must provide **reasons**. A reason can usually be linked to a claim with the subordinate conjunction "because." Consider the gun control argument mentioned earlier, which we can now restate as a claim with a reason: "We must pass gun control laws that limit access to guns [claim] because doing so will make children safer at school [reason]." This argument has initial appeal because it ties into the audience's likely belief that it is good to make children safe at school. However, as we discussed earlier, the causal links in the argument are open to question. Thus, we see that the "reason" that "doing so will make children safer at school" is a subclaim that itself needs to be supported with reasons and evidence.

Once you've identified the reasons that an author offers for various claims, then you can proceed to examine the adequacy of these reasons. Do they really support the claim? Is the assertion in the reason in need of further support and argument? Do the reasons tie into values, assumptions, and beliefs that the audience shares?

Evidence

The facts, examples, statistics, personal experience, and expert testimony that an author offers to support his or her view of the topic are referred to as **evidence**. To examine an author's use of evidence, consider whether the supporting material is reliable, timely, and adequate to make the case. Ask also whether there is more than one way the evidence can be interpreted.

For example, Gawande is quite convincing as he recounts what he calls the government's "blinkered" reasoning, arguing that although the reasoning may be logical, it is shortsighted. But he does not offer direct statements from the officials with whom he disagrees so that readers can judge for themselves whether the reasoning is "blinkered" or led to a "bizarre" decision. Readers skeptical of his argument might question his rendition of the rationale behind the government ruling. Similarly, in our gun control example, skeptics could question whether the statistical correlation between rising availability of guns and rising gun violence in schools is in fact a causal relationship. The fact that A and B happened at the same time does not mean that A caused B.

Assumptions

In an argument, the often unstated values or beliefs that the writer expects readers to accept without question are referred to as **assumptions**. You can interrogate an argument by questioning, even casting doubt upon, those assumptions. For example, in paragraphs 5 and 6 of his op-ed, Gawande attacks the assumptions underlying the Office for Human Research's reasoning that the checklist for inserting IV lines and the use of an experimental drug are comparable interventions in medical care. Similarly, part of the hypothetical gun control argument presented earlier is based on an assumption that the proposed legislation will in fact limit the availability of guns. You can question this assumption by pointing to the existence of black markets.

■ ■ ■ **FOR WRITING AND DISCUSSION**

ON YOUR OWN
Find a newspaper or magazine opinion piece (an editorial or an individual opinion piece) and identify its claims, reasons, evidence, and assumptions. You may find that some of these elements are missing or only implied.

WITH YOUR CLASSMATES

1. Briefly summarize the opinion piece you found and explain your analysis of it to a small group of classmates.
2. After each group member has presented his or her editorial, discuss which group member's editorial involves the most persuasive reasoning and why. Try to focus on the writer's reasoning rather than your own opinions about the matter. Present the results of your group discussion to the rest of the class. If there is disagreement about which piece uses the best reasoning, present more than one to the class and explain the differences in your evaluation.

Examining a Writer's Strategies for Engaging Readers, or *Pathos*

The third of the classical rhetorical appeals is to an audience's interests and emotions—the process of engaging readers. How does a writer hook and keep your interest? How does a writer make you care about the subject? How does a writer tweak your emotions or connect an argument with ideas or beliefs that you value?

Rhetoricians have identified four basic ways that writers engage readers at an emotional or imaginative level—by influencing the reader to identify (1) with the writer; (2) with the topic or issue, including people mentioned in the text; (3) with a certain group of fellow readers; or (4) with particular interests, values, beliefs, and emotions. Let's look at each in turn.

In the first approach, writers wanting readers to identify with them might use an informal conversational tone to make a reader feel like the writer's buddy. Writers wanting to inspire respect and admiration might adopt a formal scholarly tone, choose intellectual words, or avoid "I" altogether by using the passive voice—"it was discovered that... ." In the second approach, writers wanting readers to identify with the topic or issue might explain the importance of the issue or try to engage readers' emotions. In urging community action against homelessness, for example, an author might present a wrenching anecdote about a homeless child. Other methods might be the use of vivid details, striking facts, emotion-laden terms and examples, or analogies that explain the unfamiliar in terms of the familiar. In the third approach, writers try to get readers to identify with a certain in-group of people—fellow environmentalists or feminists or Republicans or even fellow intellectuals. Some writers seek to engage readers by creating a role for the reader to play in the text. For example, the author of "Chew on This" puts readers in the role of wondering if there are benefits to chewing gum, and Savage invites readers to consider the appeal of Maya Lin's "antimonument" concept to Vietnam veterans' experiences of alienation from American society. In the fourth approach, writers appeal to readers' interests by getting them to identify with certain values and beliefs. For example, a politician arguing for radical Social Security reform might appeal to young voters' belief that there will be no Social Security available to them when they retire. Awareness of how all of these appeals work will enable you to distance yourself from arguments sufficiently to examine them critically.

■ ■ ■ **FOR WRITING AND DISCUSSION**

Examine in detail the ways in which Gawande works to engage readers in his opinion piece at the end of this chapter. On what basis do his opening sentences engage your attention? What kind of a relationship does he try to establish with readers? How does he try to make you care about his topic? What interests and values does he assume his audience shares? Do you consider yourself part of his intended audience? Why or why not? ■ ■ ■

Writing About What Texts Say and Do

Descriptive outlining enables you to extend your understanding of what a text or visual image *says* into how it is working rhetorically (what it *does*).[2] Some people call these "*says/does* outlines.*"* In them, a ***says*** statement summarizes the content of a stretch of text (a sentence, a paragraph, a group of paragraphs), and a ***does*** statement sums up how that particular piece of text functions within the whole. It might *describe* or *explain* or *argue,* for example. For help with conceptualizing what texts can *do,* see the list of Verbs That Describe What Texts Do on the next page.

Does statements should not repeat content but should focus instead on the purpose or function of that content in relation to the overall purpose of the larger text. Here are some sample *does* statements:

- Offers an anecdote to illustrate previous point
- Introduces a new reason for adopting policy
- Provides statistical evidence
- Summarizes the previous section

Using *does* and *says* statements to create a descriptive outline will help you see how a text works at the micro level, paragraph by paragraph, section by section. This kind of analysis is particularly useful as a way to begin a summary as well as to focus an analysis or critique of an author's rhetorical methods.

Sample Does-Says Statements

To illustrate, we offer the following sample *does* and *says* statements for the three opening paragraphs of the Savage selection printed at the end of chapter 5. We begin each set with a *does* statement to keep the focus on the function of a given paragraph within the unfolding structure of the larger text. Notice that the implicit subject of the *does* and *says* verbs is the text itself.

> **Paragraph 1:** *Does:* Announces a new way of understanding Maya Lin's accomplishment with the Vietnam Veterans Memorial (VVM). *Says:* VVM is first true victim monument, designed to help soldiers heal
>
> **Paragraph 2:** *Does:* Places VVM in context with other war memorials. *Says:* VVM is "first" in a number of categories
>
> **Paragraph 3:** *Does:* Discusses VVM in relation to monument traditions preceding it. *Says:* VVM is "fundamental" break with tradition because it delivers no message

---

[2]We first learned about descriptive outlining from Kenneth Bruffee's work in *A Short Course in Writing,* 3rd ed. (Boston: Little Brown, 1985), 103. Print.

VERBS THAT DESCRIBE WHAT TEXTS DO

Each of these verbs might be used to complete a phrase such as "this paragraph [or section] _____."

adds (e.g., adds detail)	evaluates	proposes
analyzes	explains	qualifies
argues	expresses	questions
asks	extends	quotes
cites	generalizes	reasons
compares	illustrates	rebuts
connects	informs	reflects
continues	interprets	repeats
contradicts	introduces	states
contrasts	lists	speculates
demonstrates	narrates	suggests
describes	offers	summarizes
details	opposes	supports
dramatizes	predicts	synthesizes
elaborates	presents	traces
	projects	uses

Descriptive outlining will give you analytical distance that will prove to be not only a powerful tool for rhetorical analysis, but also a valuable aid for your own writing. When you are revising, asking yourself what specific sections of your text are doing and saying—and what you want them to do and say—will help you focus on both content and organization as you compose or revise. Even during composing, asking yourself what you want your text to *do* next will often help you figure out what to *say* next.

At first you may find that creating a descriptive outline is more difficult than you expect because it forces a slow rereading of a text's distinct parts. But that slowed-down analysis is the purpose of the technique. It is designed to prompt thought that goes beyond scooping up surface meaning. Rereading this way will take you to a clearer understanding of the argument and structure of the text you are examining. Trust us!

■ ■ ■ **FOR WRITING AND DISCUSSION**

ON YOUR OWN

Make a paragraph-by-paragraph descriptive outline of a book chapter or article that you have been assigned to read in one of your other courses (or of another text as your teacher directs), providing one *does* sentence and one *says* sentence for each paragraph. Then, from the set of *does* and *says* statements, create an idea map that represents visually the relationship or hierarchy of ideas in the article or chapter.

WITH YOUR CLASSMATES
Working in small groups, compare your idea maps and descriptive outlines. Each group can then draw revised idea maps and put them on the board or an overhead for discussion. ■ ■ ■

Writing a Rhetorical Analysis Paper: Guidelines

A rhetorical analysis paper is the written counterpart of rhetorical reading. Writing this kind of paper gives you the opportunity to draw together and apply all the listening and questioning strategies discussed in this and the previous chapter for a twofold purpose: (1) articulating your own insights about how a text seeks to influence its readers, and (2) communicating those critical insights to other readers. Here, we offer general guidelines for writing a rhetorical analysis paper, followed by a student example.

Guidelines for Writing a Rhetorical Analysis

Getting Started   We suggest you prepare for your rhetorical analysis by undertaking the following preliminary activities:

1. Write a summary of the text you are going to analyze to make sure that you understand it well enough to represent its meaning accurately and fairly.
2. Make a descriptive outline as a way of scrutinizing distinctions between what the text says and what it does to develop those ideas.

Selecting a Focus for Your Analysis   To write an effective rhetorical analysis, you will need to focus on some aspect of the text's rhetorical methods, an aspect that merits close examination or critique. We suggest one of two approaches. You can start deductively with the effect the text had on you as a reader—a strong positive or negative response, a tension or contradiction you found in the text, or some aspect of the text that confused or surprised you. If you begin with your response, you will need to analyze the text to discover the rhetorical features that account for this response. How do they work? Why are these features effective or ineffective? Alternatively, you can start inductively by identifying and then analyzing particularly striking rhetorical features.

Abby's Assignment

Write an essay of approximately 750 words (3 pages) in which you examine the key rhetorical strategies used by Atul Gawande in "A Lifesaving Checklist" to engage readers and convince them to adopt his perspective. Assume that members of your own **audience** are familiar with the rhetorical concepts discussed in this and earlier chapters, and that they have read the text you are analyzing, but have not thought carefully about it. Your **purpose** is to offer these readers insights about how the text works rhetorically. Present a perspective that might not be obvious upon someone's first reading of the piece but that you have gleaned from your analysis of the text.

If you begin inductively, you will need to consider how these features work and to what effect. What new understanding of the text does your analysis reveal?

Whether you begin deductively or inductively, you will need to select specific rhetorical features to write about. Choose features that you consider particularly effective or ineffective, or in which you detect inconsistencies or tensions between two different appeals. To frame your analysis, choose among the questions about texts' rhetorical methods suggested throughout this chapter.

Drafting Your Paper Once you have determined a focus, reread the text carefully to find specific examples of these features, taking notes on how they contribute to the effect you have identified. Use these notes to draft a working thesis that states the gist of the insights your rhetorical analysis will offer about the text's meaning and methods. You can revise and refine this working thesis after you draft the whole paper. In your final draft, the thesis should clearly introduce the new understanding that results from your analysis and indicate what that analysis says about the text's effectiveness or ineffectiveness.

The full draft of your paper should have the following elements:

1. An introduction that includes (a) a brief summary of the text, (b) contextual information about the text, and (c) your thesis about the text's rhetorical effect
2. A series of body paragraphs that develop the thesis by (a) discussing specific rhetorical features that produce the rhetorical effect and (b) providing specific textual evidence to back up your points
3. A conclusion that makes clear (a) why the new understanding that your paper presents is important, and (b) why the insights of your analysis are significant to other readers

An Annotated Rhetorical Analysis of "A Lifesaving Checklist"

Earlier in this chapter, we presented some of Abby's early writing as she explored how she would approach analysis of Atul Gawande's 2007 *New York Times* op-ed column calling for federal rule changes that would permit resumption of research on the effectiveness of medical checklists designed to regularize anti-infection procedures. We now present the paper in which she applies many of the questioning techniques presented in this chapter. In addition, we have annotated the paper to highlight her analytical and organizational strategies.

A Surprising Checklist

For many *New York Times* readers, it must have been somewhat 1 surprising to encounter Atul Gawande's December 30, 2007, op-ed article criticizing a little known U.S. government

Abby begins with brief information about the article and asserts her response of "surprise." Abby has chosen a deductive focus for her analysis.

office for endangering lives when it ordered a halt to research on the effectiveness of a medical checklist. We expect *Times* op-eds to be about urgent aspects of politics and foreign policy, not checklists. But this article presents the surprising information that medical doctors need to be reminded to wash their hands before they put intravenous lines into patients, something that might be urgent after all. Gawande uses clear reasoning and direct language to convince readers that it is. The combination creates an effective argument that is full of energy and difficult to argue against.

Details here support her point about surprise, and forecast the other two major points she will develop: clear reasoning and direct language.
Asserts thesis about why the argument is effective.

2   The medical checklist, which has five steps, was designed by researchers who wanted to see if using it on a regular basis would reduce infection. Gawande's primary claim is that the federal Office for Human Research Protections (OHRP) made a bad decision when it ordered doctors in Michigan to stop researching the effectiveness of the checklist. He wants the research resumed, and ultimately suggests that Congress may need to step in.

First body paragraph provides foundation for her analysis, with a factual summary of the argument and background about the checklist.

3   Gawande comes across with a strong *ethos*, partly because of the biographical note indicating that he's a surgeon, a *New Yorker* staff writer, and a book author. Appearing on the *New York Times* op-ed page lends him plenty of credibility, too. This authority grows through the concise, down-to-earth way that he presents facts, including lots of statistics. He starts out almost casually, setting the scene as if to tell a story. He mentions an obscure building where OHRP does its assigned work to protect people. "But lately you have to wonder," the doctor calmly notes (par. 1).[3] It may not seem like a serious life-or-death matter is coming up, but it is.

Second body paragraph examines Gawande's credibility as author and his establishment of a "down-to-earth" *ethos*.

4   Gawande gains momentum when he reports the "stunning" (positive) results of using the checklist: a large decrease in infections and thus a big increase in saved lives and saved money (par. 3). Then, the beginning of the next paragraph is just as stunning. We learn that OHRP stopped the study. The problem, it said, was that any research project involving humans requires everyone involved (patients and health care providers alike) to sign a consent form. But not everyone had, or could.

Abby's organization follows the flow of the op-ed, pointing out the strength of the reasoning within Gawande's unfolding argument.

---

[3]Instead of using page references in her parenthetical citations of quotations, Abby is following her teacher's request to use the paragraph numbers in the reprint at the end of this chapter.

Here is the core of both the government's argument and Gawande's rebuttal. OHRP says that doing research without informed consent violates scientific ethics. Gawande suggests, but never quite says exactly, that stopping the research on the checklist's usefulness violates scientific ethics. In his final paragraph, he almost says it when he asserts that the OHRP authorities are "in danger of putting ethics bureaucracy in the way of actual ethical medical care" (par. 11). His next assertions are even more direct. First, he calls for the research to continue "unencumbered." Then, in his final sentence, he says that if the agency won't allow this to happen, "Then Congress will have to" (par. 11). It almost sounds like a threat of punishment.

5 Abby pinpoints Gawande's central claim as a rebuttal of the government claim.

Gawande's rhetorical purpose is to inform the general public and draw it to his cause. His target audience seems to be a combination of experts (and policymakers) with different levels of awareness and concern about the stopped research, and ordinary readers who want hospitals to be safer places.

6 Having worked through the article, Abby briefly states her understanding of Gawande's purpose and audience, points 3 and 4 in the rhetorical précis structure.

Gawande reaches out to the interests and values of both groups in this audience not only through reasoning, or *logos*, but by grabbing our attention through casual, conversational language. He got my nonexpert attention in the second paragraph with the surprising information that the checklist leads doctors to "actually wash their hands." It's shocking, yet it clicks with common knowledge that hospitals can make you sicker because they are home to so many dangerous germs. Soon the reader comes upon colloquial zingers such as "the results were stunning" (par. 3) and Gawande calling OHRP's decision "bizarre and dangerous" (par. 5). At first, this strong language may seem easy for a reader to resist. After all, we are taught in school to be suspicious of arguments that come on too strong. But the clarity of Gawande's reasoning is convincing.

7 Abby now steps back to analyze the way Gawande uses pathos to draw in the audience. Here, she analyzes the impact of Gawande's language on readers, especially nonexperts.

Labeling as "blinkered logic" the government's claim that informed consent was needed for research about the checklist (par. 5), Gawande proceeds to take apart the OHRP reasoning. (The phrase "blinkered logic" brought to my mind the image of big draft horses wearing those big leather contraptions that keep them from seeing sideways. They can only see in one direction.) Gawande shows that the reasoning by analogy that considers testing a checklist to be ethically the same as testing a drug is just wrong. According to him,

8 Based on her analysis of ethos, pathos, and language, Abby unpacks Gawande's key moves in countering the OHRP position.

Abby points to "reasoning by analogy" as the core of Gawande's argument.

testing a checklist falls into the category of establishing minimum standards for the sake of safety, not the risky category of developing something new. The research on checklists is important, he continues, "not merely because it poses lower risks [than experimental drugs], but because a failure to carry it out poses a vastly greater risk to people's lives" (par. 6).

Gawande's careful rebuttal is all the more effective because 9 he places it between strong assertions about the improvements that occurred when checklist standards were followed (par. 2–3) and the dire consequences of doctors not following minimum standards (par. 7–9). Early in the article, he uses everyday language to describe results: "they actually wash their hands and don a sterile gown and gloves" (par. 2). After he prevsents his argument that the government's reasoning is wrong, the language is much stronger: "a large body of evidence … has revealed a profound failure by health care professionals to follow basic steps proven to stop infection" (par. 7). Paragraph 2 takes readers into the reality of a hospital room; paragraph 7 passes judgment on what goes wrong.

Much of Abby's analysis has been based on the flow of reading the essay, preparing her own readers to see the strategic importance of organization in Gawande's argument, which she brings up explicitly in this paragraph.

10. By the end of this short article, a matter that seemed 10 unlikely to concern an ordinary college student like me became surprisingly urgent, something that perhaps I should email Congress about. Gawande's success in the piece illustrates how effective an argument can be when it speaks in plain language directly to the interests of an audience, even an initially unconcerned audience. After all, evidence of "profound failure" in the health care system is difficult for anyone to brush away as insignificant.

Concluding paragraph ties the analytic threads together by commenting on how Gawande convinced this writer of his argument's importance.

A Lifesaving Checklist

ATUL GAWANDE

Surgeon and writer Atul Gawande is a widely known advocate of using checklists for complex projects in a wide variety of fields. He is Professor of Surgery at Harvard Medical School and Professor in the Department of Health Policy and Management at the Harvard School of Public Health. He serves as director of the World Health Organization's (WHO) Global Challenge for Safer Surgical Care, and in that capacity guided development of a safe surgery checklist that was published by WHO in June 2008. It was modeled on the checklist designed to reduce hospital infections that he discusses in the article below that was modeled after aviation procedures. The surgical protocol, distributed as a laminated card, was featured in a celebrated reunion episode of the television show *ER* in March 2009. Dr. Gawande served as a consultant to the script writers.

Dr. Gawande is also a staff writer for the *New Yorker* and the author of three acclaimed books: *Complications: A Surgeon's Notes on an Imperfect Science* (2002); *Better: A Surgeon's Notes on Performance* (2007), a *New York Times* bestseller; and *The Checklist Manifesto: How to Get Things Right* (2010), also a major bestseller. The son of two medical doctors, Dr. Gawande was born in 1965 in Brooklyn, New York. This op-ed piece was published in the *New York Times* on Sunday, December 30, 2007.

1 In Bethesda, Md., in a squat building off a suburban parkway, sits a small federal agency called the Office for Human Research Protections. Its aim is to protect people. But lately you have to wonder. Consider this recent case.

2 A year ago, researchers at Johns Hopkins University published the results of a program that instituted in nearly every intensive care unit in Michigan a simple five-step checklist designed to prevent certain hospital infections. It reminds doctors to make sure, for example, that before putting large intravenous lines into patients, they actually wash their hands and don a sterile gown and gloves.

3 The results were stunning. Within three months, the rate of bloodstream infections from these I.V. lines fell by two-thirds. The average I.C.U. cut its infection rate from 4 percent to zero. Over 18 months, the program saved more than 1,500 lives and nearly $200 million.

4 Yet this past month, the Office for Human Research Protections shut the program down. The agency issued notice to the researchers and the Michigan Health and Hospital Association that, by introducing a checklist and tracking the results without written, informed consent from each patient and health-care provider, they had violated scientific ethics regulations. Johns Hopkins had to halt not only the program in Michigan but also its plans to extend it to hospitals in New Jersey and Rhode Island.

5 The government's decision was bizarre and dangerous. But there was a certain blinkered logic to it, which went like this: A checklist is an alteration in medical care no less than an experimental drug is. Studying an experimental drug in people without federal monitoring and explicit written permission from each patient is unethical and illegal. Therefore it is no less unethical and illegal to do the same with a checklist. Indeed, a checklist may require even more stringent oversight, the administration ruled, because the data gathered in testing it could put not only the patients but also the doctors at risk—by exposing how poorly some of them follow basic infection-prevention procedures.

6   The need for safeguards in medical experimentation has been evident since before the Nazi physician trials at Nuremberg. Testing a checklist for infection prevention, however, is not the same as testing an experimental drug—and neither are like-minded efforts now under way to reduce pneumonia in hospitals, improve the consistency of stroke and heart attack treatment and increase flu vaccination rates. Such organizational research work, new to medicine, aims to cement minimum standards and ensure they are followed, not to discover new therapies. This work is different from drug testing not merely because it poses lower risks, but because a failure to carry it out poses a vastly greater risk to people's lives.

7   A large body of evidence gathered in recent years has revealed a profound failure by health-care professionals to follow basic steps proven to stop infection and other major complications. We now know that hundreds of thousands of Americans suffer serious complications or die as a result. It's not for lack of effort. People in health care work long, hard hours. They are struggling, however, to provide increasingly complex care in the absence of effective systematization.

8   Excellent clinical care is no longer possible without doctors and nurses routinely using checklists and other organizational strategies and studying their results. There need to be as few barriers to such efforts as possible. Instead, the endeavor itself is treated as the danger.

9   If the government's ruling were applied more widely, whole swaths of critical work to ensure safe and effective care would either halt or shrink: efforts by the Centers for Disease Control and Prevention to examine responses to outbreaks of infectious disease; the military's program to track the care of wounded soldiers; the Five Million Lives campaign, by the nonprofit Institute for Healthcare Improvement, to reduce avoidable complications in 3,700 hospitals nationwide.

10   I work with the World Health Organization on a new effort to introduce surgical safety checklists worldwide. It aims to ensure that a dozen basic safety steps are actually followed in operating rooms here and abroad—that the operating team gives an antibiotic before making an incision, for example, and reviews how much blood loss to prepare for. A critical component of the program involves tracking successes and failures and learning from them. If each of the hundreds of hospitals we're trying to draw into the program were required to obtain permissions for this, even just from research regulators, few could join.

11   Scientific research regulations had previously exempted efforts to improve medical quality and public health—because they hadn't been scientific. Now that the work is becoming more systematic (and effective), the authorities have stepped in. And they're in danger of putting ethics bureaucracy in the way of actual ethical medical care. The agency should allow this research to continue unencumbered. If it won't, then Congress will have to.

Understanding and Summarizing Others' Arguments

5

The process of reading is not just the interpretation of a text but the interpretation of another person's worldview as presented by a text.

—Doug Brent

In this chapter, we focus specifically on the nuts and bolts of reading the kinds of texts you will be assigned in college. You will learn to integrate the strategies used by experienced readers into your own reading repertoire.

Our discussion in this chapter as well as the next extends the metaphor of reading as conversation by using the terms "listening" and "questioning" to describe specific reading techniques. The **listening strategies** we discuss will help you read attentively so that you can understand a text in the way the author intended and then represent the text fairly when you write about it.

To illustrate the strategies presented in the rest of this chapter we will refer to three texts: the *UC Berkeley Wellness Letter* article, "Chew on This," found in Chapter 2; an excerpt from art historian Kirk Savage's chapter on the Vietnam Veterans Memorial in *Monument Wars,* "The Conscience of the Nation," printed at the end of this chapter; and Atul Gawande's argument for "A Life-Saving Checklist," presented at the end of Chapter 4. We use "Chew on This" as an example of the lively popular pieces you are likely to encounter when doing research on contemporary culture. Savage's text illustrates the sophisticated scholarly reading you are likely to be assigned in a variety of disciplines. Gawande's text exemplifies the tightly argued opinion pieces you will find when you research public policy issues or when you read news and opinion articles in the ordinary course of being an informed citizen.

Writing as You Read

Rhetorical readers "listen" by reading with pen in hand in order to interact with the text and record their ideas-in-progress. When they read on screen, they use a text highlight tool or keep a second file open for note-taking.

Chapter 5, Understanding and Summarizing Others' Arguments, is taken from John C. Bean, Virginia A. Chappell, and Alice M. Gilliam's *Reading Rhetorically,* pp. 39–40, 46–49, 54–55, and 59–68 (Chapter 3, Listening to a Text).

You will find that writing as you read will transform your reading process from passive receptivity into active meaning-making.

You may have heard of "active listening," a technique by which listeners use eye contact and body language to convey that they are listening carefully to someone. Writing as you read is **active reading**. Skilled rhetorical readers might write in the margins of a text (unless it is a library book), or they might keep a reading log or journal in which they record notes—on paper or in a designated "ideas" file on their computer. Sometimes they stop reading in the middle of a passage and freewrite their ideas-in-progress. When a text stimulates their own thinking, writing down those ideas captures that thinking for future reference and stimulates further thought. To put it another way, rhetorical reading strategies focus on both **comprehension** (a reader's understanding of a text) and **invention**—the ideas a reader generates in response to a text. Thus, writing while you read helps you generate ideas, as well as interact more deeply with a text.

Not surprisingly, then, most of the rhetorical reading strategies that we present in this book require you to write. To foster the reading-writing connection, we recommend that you, too, keep a reading log, paper or electronic, in which you practice the strategies described in this chapter. Doing so will help you develop powerful advanced reading skills, as well as generate a wealth of ideas for essay topics.

Listening as You Read Initially

Just as good listeners attend carefully to what their conversational partners say, trying to give them a fair hearing, so, too, do good readers "listen" carefully to what a text says, trying to consider its ideas carefully and accurately before rushing to judgment. College reading assignments put a particular premium on giving an impartial hearing to ideas and positions that are new and sometimes radically different from your own. Moreover, in class discussions, examinations, and paper assignments, you will frequently be asked to demonstrate that you have listened well to assigned texts. Professors want to know that you have comprehended these texts with reasonable accuracy before you proceed to analyze, apply, or critique the ideas in them. In the language of Kenneth Burke's metaphor of the conversational parlor, you might think of this listening phase of the reading process as the phase where you try to catch the drift of the conversation and give it the fullest and fairest hearing before "putting in your oar."

Listening strategies help you understand what to listen for, how to hear what the text is saying, and how to track your evolving understanding of the text. The first time through a text, reading with its grain, you are trying to understand a text's overall gist and compose a "rough-draft interpretation" of its meaning and your own response. As we discuss later in this chapter, after you have a sense of the gist, a second reading will enable you to confirm and deepen your understanding, and revise it if necessary.

We have urged you to read with a pen or pencil in hand, to adopt experienced readers' practice of marking passages, drawing arrows, and making notes. (You can do this with electronic highlighting and annotating, too.) Active use of your hands as well as your eyes will be necessary to undertake the four strategies for an efficient initial reading that we recommend in the next four sections.

Note Organizational Signals

Headings and transition words serve as organizational signals that help you anticipate and then track a text's overall structure of ideas. Experienced readers use these signals to identify the text's central ideas, to distinguish major ideas from minor ones, to anticipate what is coming next, and to determine the relationship among the text's major ideas. Organizational signals and forecasting statements (which directly tell you what to expect) function like road signs, giving you information about direction, upcoming turns, and the distance yet to go. For example, experienced readers note words that signal a change in the direction of thought, such as *however, in contrast,* or *on the other hand.* Likewise, they take advantage of the guidance provided by words such as *first, second,* and *third* that signal a series of parallel points or ideas; words such as *therefore, consequently,* or *as a result* that signal logical relationships; and words such as *similarly, also,* or *likewise* that signal additional support for the current point. Circling or otherwise marking these terms will make it possible for a quick glance back to remind you of the structure of ideas.

Mark Unfamiliar Terms and References

As you read, it is important to mark unfamiliar terms and references because they offer contextual clues about the intended audience and the conversation of which a given text is a part. The very unfamiliarity of these terms and references may tell you that the text is written for an insider audience whose members share a particular kind of knowledge and concerns. To become part of the conversation, you need to learn such terms. We suggest that you mark them with a question mark or write them in the margins and return to them after you finish your initial reading. Stopping to look them up as you read will break your concentration. By looking them up later, after you have that "rough-draft" sense of the text's overall purpose, you will gain insight into how key terms function and how they represent major concerns of a particular field or area of study.

"Read as though it made sense and perhaps it will."

—I. A. Richards

Identify Points of Difficulty

One of the most important traits of experienced readers is probably their *tolerance for ambiguity and initial confusion.* They have learned to read through points of difficulty, trusting that confusing points will become clear as they continue to read. When you are reading about new and difficult subject matter, you will inevitably encounter passages that you simply do not understand. A valuable reading strategy is to identify explicitly what you don't understand. We recommend that you bracket puzzling passages and keep reading. Later, you can come back to them and try to translate them into your own words or to frame questions about them to ask your classmates and professor.

Annotate

When you annotate a text, you underline, highlight, draw arrows, and make marginal comments. Annotating is a way of making the text your own, of literally putting your mark on it—noting its key passages and ideas. Experienced readers rely on this common but powerful strategy to note reactions and questions, thereby recording their in-process understanding of a text. By marking the page, they are able to monitor their evolving construction of a text's meaning.

Annotations also serve a useful purpose when you return to a text to reread or review it. Not only can they remind you of your first impressions of the text's meaning, but they also can help you identify main points and come to new levels of understanding—clearer answers to earlier questions, new insights, and new questions. Indeed, we recommend that you annotate each time you read a text, perhaps using different colors so that you have a record of the new layers of meaning you discover. Of course, you would not do this in a library book, and there's one additional caveat: annotating can become counterproductive if you underline or highlight too enthusiastically. A completely underlined paragraph tells you nothing about its key point. To be useful, underlining must be selective, based both on your own purposes for reading and on what you think the writer's main points are. In general, when it is time to review the text and recall its main ideas, notes in the margin about main ideas, questions, objections, and connections will be far more useful than underlining or highlighting.

To illustrate this listening strategy, at the end of this chapter, we have annotated part of the excerpt from Kirk Savage's *Monument Wars* about the Vietnam Veterans Memorial at the end of this chapter. The annotations were made from the perspective of the student we asked you to imagine who is working on a project about public art and memorials and who decided to buy a personal copy of the book in order to make annotations like these. These notes demonstrate one student's efforts to understand Savage's points about the memorial as an "antimonument." We invite you to turn to the selection now and read carefully through both the passage and the annotations. Consider how these or other annotations would help you understand the passage more fully—and think about what uses you or another student might make of these annotations.

Listening as You Reread

Rhetorical reading often requires careful rereading. Of course, not every text requires rereading; however, whenever detailed analysis is required or whenever a text is particularly difficult, a careful second (and sometimes a third) reading is needed. Experienced academic readers will often use the techniques we lay out in this section as a way of keeping track of complex texts that they will need to use as a basis for their own writing, perhaps as foundational evidence for their own assertions, perhaps as a taking-off point for a critique.

In the remainder of this chapter, to help you acquire the mental habits of strong academic readers and to give you practice with the types of writing you will use frequently as part of college-level analysis and research, we offer strategies for approaching texts in ways that go beyond skimming for content: idea maps, summaries, and rhetorical précis.

Mapping the Idea Structure

Idea maps provide a visual representation of a text's major ideas and the relationships among those ideas. In many college courses, it is important to get a sense of how an assigned text works as a whole, not just pieces of its concepts or data. An excellent way to establish this sense of the whole is to reread the text with the goal of creating an idea map. This process will enable you to distinguish main points from subordinate ones; then, as you connect them in a visual diagram, the process will help you understand how the text establishes relationships among those primary and secondary ideas. These relationships are akin to a hierarchy in a power structure: particular explanations and sets of details chunk together to support particular overarching points that in turn flesh out a thesis. You might think of idea maps as X-rays of the text's idea structure.

The time to map a text's idea structure is after you have finished reading it and are sitting back to review its main ideas. To create a map, draw a circle in the center of a page and write the text's main idea inside the circle. Then record the text's supporting ideas on branches and subbranches that extend from the center circle. In Figure 5.1, we offer a sample idea map of the excerpt from Savage's "The Conscience of the Nation," found at the end of this chapter. If you tend not to be a visual thinker, creating an idea map can

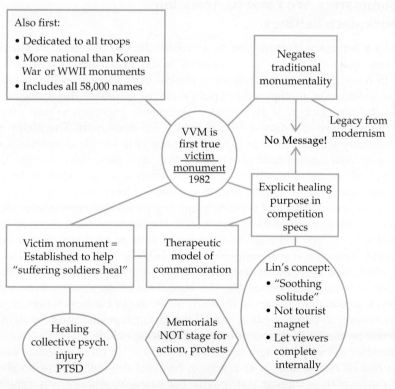

FIGURE 5.1 Idea map for Kirk Savage's discussion of the Vietnam Veterans Memorial of *Monument Wars,* reprinted at the end of this chapter

be challenging because it forces you to think about the text's main ideas in a new way; indeed, that is the advantage of doing an idea map. You may even find that creating a map reveals inconsistencies in the text's organizational structure or puzzling relationships among ideas. This, too, is important information and may be an issue you should bring up in class discussion or in your written responses to the text. In any case, creating an idea map is a way to understand a text at a deeper level and thus to understand and evaluate its importance in relation to course content or to a writing project of your own.

Writing About How Texts Work: Guidelines and Two Examples

Probably the best way to demonstrate that you have "listened" carefully to a text is to compose a **summary**—a condensed version of a text's main points written in your own words, conveying the author's main ideas but eliminating supporting details. When your goal is to describe not only the content of a text but *how* that text makes its points, a still more powerful technique is to write a **rhetorical précis**.

How Summaries Are Used in Academic and Workplace Settings

Composing a summary requires you to articulate the gist of a text. Summaries take many forms and fulfill a variety of functions in the workplace as well as academic courses. In research papers, you will often present brief summaries of sources to give readers an overview of another writer's perspective or argument, thus bringing another voice into the conversation. If the source is particularly important to your project, you might write a longer summary—perhaps even a full paragraph. The ability to write a good summary will be valuable for any number of academic assignments that ask you to report your understanding of what a text says, particularly for the literature reviews typically required in science classes. Summaries are also likely to be useful in a persuasive "take-a-stand" paper: first, to provide evidence that supports your view, and second, to present fully and accurately any arguments that oppose your view (after which you will try to counter these arguments). Furthermore, for a paper in the social or physical sciences, you will often be expected to write an **abstract** of your own work (a summary), because it is conventional in these fields to begin a published work with a highly condensed overview in case busy readers don't have time to read the whole text. In business and professional life, the equivalent of an abstract is an **executive summary**, a section that appears at the front of any major business report or proposal. Summary writing, in other words, is one of the most frequently used forms of writing that you will encounter in your academic and professional life.

Summaries will vary in length according to purpose. At times, you may summarize a text in one or two sentences as a way of invoking the authority of another voice (probably an expert) to support your points. For example, suppose you wanted to use Savage's concept of the therapeutic model of commemoration to contrast the Vietnam Veteran's Memorial with a statue of a nineteenth-century general mounted on a horse. You might write something like the following:

> Unlike the statue of the general on his horse, which is intended to commemorate the general's heroism, the Vietnam Veterans Memorial (VVM) has what Kirk Savage calls a "therapeutic" purpose. In his book Monument Wars, Savage lays out the advantages of the "therapeutic model of commemoration" that is embodied in Maya Lin's design for the VVM. Elements of this model include a healing purpose, absence of a "message," and an overall setting that will allow viewers to explore the meaning of the monument internally.

After this brief summary introducing the concept, you could go on describe the extent to which the heroic monument you are considering possesses these or contrasting qualities, perhaps calling upon Savage's discussion of hero monuments elsewhere in his book. (Its index has multiple references to the topic.)

At other times, summaries may be one of your main purposes for writing. A typical college assignment might ask you to summarize the arguments of two writers and then analyze the differences in their views. In the summary part of such an assignment, your professor will expect you to demonstrate your understanding of what might be quite complex arguments. The guidelines that follow will help you do so.

Guidelines for Writing a Summary

Writing a fair and accurate summary requires that you (1) identify a text's main ideas, (2) state them in your own words, and (3) omit supporting details. For efficiency and thoroughness, the best first step is to create a descriptive outline of the text you need to summarize, using *does* statements to clarify its structure and *says* statements to put in your own words the main point of each paragraph. (A first draft of your summary could be simply your sequencing of all your *says* statements.) Making a descriptive outline will help you see the text's different sections and organizational strategies. Almost all texts—even very short ones—can be divided into a sequence of sections in which groups of paragraphs chunk together to form distinctive parts of the argument or discussion. Identifying these parts or chunks and how they function within the whole text is particularly helpful because you can write a summary of each chunk, then combine the chunks.

We present a step-by-step process for summary writing in Box 5.1. To illustrate the process, we present a summary written by a student we'll call "Jaime" of the *UC Berkeley Wellness Letter*'s "Chew on This" article. Because this article is so brief, it may at first seem that it would be difficult to summarize, but that shortness makes it a good example of the process of omitting details in order to boil a text down to its essence.

Sample Summary with Attributive Tags   In the following summary of "Chew on This," notice that Jaime regularly refers back to the article itself by using what are called "attributive tags" or "signal phrases," such as, "the author reports," "it presents," "the article suggests," and so forth. These phrases serve as signals that Jaime is summarizing someone else's ideas rather than stating his own. Using phrases like these will help you avoid one of the big mistakes that novice writers make when summarizing: making the original author invisible.

BOX 5.1 COMPOSING A SUMMARY

Step 1: Read the text first for its main points.

Step 2: Reread carefully and make a descriptive outline.

Step 3: Write out the text's thesis or main point. (Suppose you had to summarize the whole argument in one sentence.)

Step 4: Identify the text's major divisions or chunks. Each division develops one of the stages needed to make the whole main point. Typically, these stages or parts might function as background, review of the conversation, summary of opposing views, or subpoints in support of the thesis.

Step 5: Try summarizing each part in one or two sentences.

Step 6: Now combine your summaries of the parts into a coherent whole, creating a condensed version of the text's main ideas in your own words.

We invite you to read over Jaime's summary and evaluate it against the checklist in Box 5.2. What might you say or do differently to make this a better summary? Could you make it shorter still, perhaps by just one line, without cutting important information?

Jaime's Summary of "Chew on This"

[1]"Chew on This," published as a Last Word feature in the February 2012 UC Berkeley Wellness Letter, briefly updates readers about recent research regarding whether gum-chewing is beneficial and suggests that any benefits are minor or do not last for long. [2]The article's unnamed author reports that the most likely benefit of gum chewing is increased saliva flow, which prevents cavities, especially with sugar-free gum containing xylitol. [3]But regular brushing and flossing are more important. [4]The article reports in somewhat more detail about studies published recently in

---

BOX 5.2 CHECKLIST FOR EVALUATING SUMMARIES

Good summaries must be fair, accurate, and complete. Use this checklist to evaluate drafts of a summary.

- Is the summary economical and precise?
- Is the summary neutral in its representation of the original author's ideas, omitting the current writer's own opinions?
- Does the summary reflect the proportionate coverage given various points in the original text?
- Are the original author's ideas expressed in the summary writer's own words?
- Does the summary use attributive tags (also called "signal phrases"), such as "Savage describes," to remind readers whose ideas are being presented?
- Does the summary quote sparingly (usually only key ideas or phrases that cannot be said precisely except in the original author's own words)?
- Will the summary stand alone as a unified and coherent piece of writing?
- Is the original source cited so that readers can locate it?

the scholarly journal Appetite. [5]Regarding the possibility that gum-chewing helps prevent weight gain, one study found that the main weight-control benefit comes not from burning calories but from chewing gum instead of snacking on something with higher calories. [6]Another study published in Appetite focused on the possibility of improved cognitive performance from gum-chewing and reported that recent studies show that the benefits are brief and that not everyone experiences them.

Guidelines for Writing a Rhetorical Précis

A **rhetorical précis** (pronounced *pray-SEE*) provides a structured model for describing the rhetorical strategies of a text, as well as for capturing the gist of its content. It differs from a summary in that it is less neutral, more analytical, and comments directly on the method of the original text. ("Précis" means "concise summary.") Highly structured, it is designed for presentation of insights about a text from the perspective of a rhetorical reader. If you think of a summary as primarily a brief representation of what a text says, then you might think of a rhetorical précis as a brief representation of what a text both says and does. Although less common than a summary, a rhetorical précis is a particularly useful way to sum up your understanding of how a text works rhetorically.

Part summary and part analysis, the rhetorical précis is also a powerful skill-building exercise often assigned as a highly structured four-sentence paragraph (see Box 5.3).[1] As explained in the box, these sentences provide a condensed statement of a text's main point (the summary part), followed by brief statements about its essential rhetorical elements: the methods, purpose, and intended audience (the analytical part). Note the ways in which Jaime's four-sentence rhetorical précis of the *Wellness Letter* article is similar to and different from his six-sentence summary of the article.

Jaime's Rhetorical Précis

[1]A UC Berkeley Wellness Letter article, "Chew on This" (Feb. 2012), summarizes recent research on the possible benefits of gum-chewing and reports that so far, this research shows only small or brief benefits. [2]The author notes first that gum-chewing may increase saliva flow that prevents cavities (but should not replace

---

BOX 5.3 HOW TO STRUCTURE A RHETORICAL PRÉCIS

Sentence 1: Name of author, genre, and title of work, date in parentheses; a rhetorically accurate verb (such as *claims, argues, asserts, suggests*); and a "that" clause containing the major assertion or thesis statement in the work
Sentence 2: An explanation of how the author develops and supports the thesis, usually in chronological order
Sentence 3: A statement of the author's apparent purpose
Sentence 4: A description of the intended audience and/or the relationship the author establishes with the audience

---

[1]Our rhetorical précis assignment and illustration are based on the work of Margaret K. Woodworth, "The Rhetorical Précis," *Rhetoric Review* 7 (1988): 156–65. Print.

brushing and flossing), but then takes a "maybe" approach when reporting that gum-chewing's possible benefits for both weight maintenance and brain stimulation are limited and short-lived. [3]The fact that this article fills the newsletter's customary spot for brief research reports establishes the author's purpose as informative, but its informal tone suggests that it is written to amuse as well as to inform. [4]The author assumes an audience of well-educated readers who have high interest in health and wellness issues but a cautious attitude toward research findings, and thus is able to use a humorous tone as well as a clever, punning title that implicitly warns that what is being reported is something to "chew on" but not to be taken as certain.

A Brief Writing Project

This assignment asks you to apply what you've learned about reading rhetorically in this chapter by listening carefully to a text and writing about what you "hear." Working with a text identified by your instructor, use the strategies suggested in this chapter to prepare two short assignments, each of which will help you move on to the next.

1. A 150- to 200-word summary of the text
2. A four-sentence rhetorical précis of the text

The Conscience of the Nation

KIRK SAVAGE

Kirk Savage is professor of the History of Art and Architecture at the University of Pittsburgh and active in public discussions about monuments and memorials, including the planned Eisenhower Memorial in Washington, D.C., and the 9-11 Memorial in New York City. *Monument Wars* (2009), from which the following selection has been excerpted, received rave reviews in both the popular and scholarly press and was awarded the 2010 Charles C. Eldredge Prize for Distinguished Scholarship in American Art from the Smithsonian American Art Museum. *Washington Post* commentator Philip Kennicott describes Savage as "a monument optimist."[2] His first book, *Standing Soldiers, Kneeling Slaves: Race, War, and Monument in Nineteenth-*

---

[2]"'Monument Wars' Puts Eisenhower Memorial Controversy in Context." *Washington Post*. Washington Post Co., 18 June 2012. Web. 29 June 2012.

Century America, published by Princeton University Press in 1997, examined the representation of race and slavery in monuments. In his faculty biography Savage describes himself as interested generally in the concepts of "traumatic memory" and "therapeutic memorial," concepts he discusses regarding the VVM, the Oklahoma City National Memorial, and plans for the World Trade Center memorial(s) in an essay in *Terror, Culture, Politics: Rethinking 9/11,* ed. Daniel Sherman and Terry Nardin (2006). His blog can be found on his University of Pittsburgh Web page.

From Chapter 6 of *Monument Wars*[3]

The VVM [Vietnam Veterans Memorial] was the capital's first true victim monument—a monument that existed not to glorify the nation but to help its suffering soldiers heal. Maya Lin's design has bequeathed to us a therapeutic model of commemoration that has become the new common sense of our era but has also opened up difficult questions that have yet to be resolved, or even considered.

> Victim monument—Key term and definition
>
> Track this concept Use for our presentation!

The VVM was a first in many respects. It was the capital's first comprehensive war memorial, dedicated to all U.S. troops who served in a national war rather than a subset from a particular branch, division, or locality. The memorial was more profoundly national in scope than any of the previous memorials erected to the heroes of the Civil War or the world wars. Even the Tomb of the Unknown Soldier in Arlington Cemetery, which included remains of the dead from World War I, World War II, Korea, and Vietnam and served as a national focal point for ritual services on Memorial Day and Veterans Day, did not satisfy the felt need for comprehensive recognition of the nation's servicemen.[4] The VVM was the first—and is still the only—war memorial in the capital and the nation that claims to include the names of all the U.S. dead. Maya Lin's sunken black granite walls were designed, first and foremost, with this intention—to carry the names of the fifty-eight thousand U.S. servicemen who lost their lives in the war. The explicit healing purpose of the monument drove this logic of comprehensiveness. Once

> Note: "explicit healing purpose"

---

[3]Kirk Savage, *Monument Wars.* (Berkeley, CA: U California P, 2009), 266–70. Print. Note: Our footnotes to this excerpt summarize rather than repeat Savage's footnotes.

[4]Savage's footnote here notes an author who has also made this point.

born, though, the new type could be adapted to other purposes. The Korean War Veterans Memorial and the World War II memorial are also comprehensive, though quite different in tone and content from Lin's prototype; neither one attempts the reproduction of individual names at the heart of her design.

Dedicated in 1982, Lin's walls have since become the most talked-about, most written-about monument in American history. The memorial is now so popular a fixture on the Mall that we can forget how radical her proposal once was and how close her critics came to stopping it altogether. Lin herself has called her work an antimonument—a negation of traditional monumentality. She brought into material form an attitude that had long been articulated in modernist circles. The British art historian Herbert Read, writing in the late 1930s in the aftermath of the catastrophes of World War I and the Spanish Civil War, had declared that in the modern world "the only logical monument would be some sort of negative monument." A negative monument, he assumed, would have to be "a monument to disillusion, to despair, to destruction."[5] Lin, however, found a way to break this logic that conflated negation and disillusion. She did not intend her memorial to deliver a message of protest against war (as did Picasso's huge mural *Guernica*, about which Read was writing). The break with tradition was more fundamental: her memorial avoided delivering *any* message. The meaning was to be generated by the viewers themselves, in their experience of the place.

If this sounds vaguely familiar, that is because the "antimonument" idea tapped into an old American tradition of iconoclasm that long predated modernist ideas of negation. After all, it was in 1800 that John Nicholas had proposed a "blank tablet" for Washington on which "every man could write what his heart dictated." Like the blank tablet, Lin's simple wall of names awaits completion by individual viewers and indeed the notes and other memorabilia visitors have left at the wall make manifest that internal process, like the act of writing Nicholas contemplated. On the one hand, Lin's design was a work of high conceptual art totally alien to the veterans who

Margin notes:

!

"modernist circles"?

No message in the VVM ++ Import! NOT a protest [Find Guernica online—just curious] ☆

Uh-oh. Not familiar to me! Ask Prof. R. re using this background
Look up iconoclasm

Connects to the above ☆

Maybe find article or video about memorabilia—maybe 30-year anniversary

---

[5]Savage inserts a footnote here indicating the sources of both Lin's and Read's remarks.

sponsored the monument; on the other, it represented an aspiration toward "living memory" that must have resonated with the antiauthoritarian, democratic impulses of many in their constituency.

As many have already pointed out, the idea of a nontraditional, nondidactic war memorial was not Lin's alone. She submitted a design in response to an open competition, whose program specified that the memorial must list the names of all the American war dead; must avoid political interpretations of the war, pro or con; and must harmonize with its tranquil park setting in the new Constitution Gardens. The memorial's statement of purpose, while affirming that it would "provide a symbol of acknowledgment of the [soldiers'] courage, sacrifice, and devotion to duty," ended in this way: "The Memorial will make no political statement regarding the war or its conduct. It will transcend those issues. The hope is that the creation of the Memorial will begin a healing process."[6] Lin's genius lay in her ability to create a simple and beautiful solution to this novel and difficult program.

← "nondidactic"?

← Healing explicitly in statement of purpose

← Note: "Lin's genius"!

Thus the nation's first "therapeutic" memorial was born—a memorial made expressly to heal a collective psychological injury. It is surely no coincidence that the monument campaign that led to Lin's selection began at about the time that "posttraumatic stress disorder" entered the official psychiatric diagnostic manual.[7] The man who hatched the campaign, Jan Scruggs, was a Vietwtraumatic stress. Scruggs wanted the monument to serve a dual healing function: for the veterans themselves, who had endured not only the trauma of combat but a crushing rejection from society afterward, and for the nation that had been so bitterly divided over the justice of the cause. The last thing he and his fellow veterans in charge of the monument campaign wanted was to reignite the political conflicts that were still fresh in everyone's mind, in part because they had been so dramatized in protests on the Mall itself. The monument was intended to rally Americans around the simple idea that the veterans of the war needed recognition and support[.]…

---

[6]Savage's lengthy footnote here cites the source of the quote and refers to other references to the VVM as "therapeutic" and "healing," including a book published after his was in production.
[7]Savage's footnote here refers readers to discussions about veterans and trauma.

… Lin … soothing solitude in mind when she designed her entry for the west end of Constitutional Gardens. Her proposal did not envision the memorial as a crowded tourist magnet like the Lincoln Memorial. Whereas that memorial was sited conspicuously on a high platform at the end of the east-west axis [of the Mall], the VVM site was screened by trees, and Lin hid the memorial even further by situating the walls below grade. The approach through Constitution Gardens created a moment of surprise: visitors would happen upon the walls unfolding in front of them, a revelation reminiscent of those [that 19th century landscape designer Andrew Jackson] Downing had had in mind for the Mall.[8]

This quiet, secluded experience seemed the opposite of the collective marches and assemblies held out in the open, which had defined the image of the Mall in the period from the civil rights movement to the antiwar struggle. Nevertheless, Lin's design was an outgrowth of that recent history. The experience she wanted to create developed organically from the Mall's twentieth-century psychology with its introspective quality already evident in the Lincoln Memorial and the axis to the Capitol. Lin wanted to turn that introspective experience further inward. "I thought the experience of visiting the memorial," she said later, "should be a private awakening, a private awareness of [individual] loss." For her, memorial spaces were not "stages where you act out, but rather places where something happens within the viewer."[9] Although her emphasis on the subjectivity of viewer response was already inherent in the spatial turn public monuments began to take in the early twentieth century, her understanding of that subjective process as fundamentally private belonged to a more recent cultural turn away from political activism and ritual and toward self-exploration.

---

[8]Savage's footnote here refers readers to another author's discussion of Lin's intentions when she entered the competition.

[9]Savage uses a footnote here to source the quote in comments from Lin at a 1995 symposium.

Mapping an Ongoing Debate

6

Every subject which contains in itself a controversy to be resolved . . .
involves a question about a fact, or about a definition, or about
the nature of an act, or about . . . processes.

—Cicero, De
Inventione I iii 7

Students who want a systematic way of asking questions about rhetorical situations can use the ancient **stases**, which help rhetors determine exactly what any argument is about; use of the stases also ensures that rhetors investigate an issue fully. The term *stasis* (Latin *status* or *constitutio*) is derived from a Greek word meaning "a stand." Thus a stasis can refer to the place where one rhetor takes a stand. If two rhetors disagree, the stasis marks the place where they come to rest, where they can agree that they disagree. Hence the appropriateness of the Latin *constitutio,* which can be translated as a "co-standing" or a "standing together." But although finding the point of stasis is an important first step, this resting place is temporary, suspended as it is between conflicting movements until a writer or speaker begins the actual argument.

The most satisfactory modern equivalent for stasis seems to be the term **issue**, which we define as the point about which all parties to an argument can agree that they disagree: this is what is at issue. This point of agreement is important because all parties to an argument must know the precise issue on which they disagree; otherwise, they may just talk past one another. This failure to agree on the point of disagreement often results in frustration for all concerned parties, and thus it may be one reason why people don't like to argue.

Determining the point of stasis is crucial to any rhetorical argument. However, figuring out the stasis is sometimes more difficult than it may seem at first glance. Most people who are engaged in arguments want to advance their own position as quickly and forcefully as possible. Thus they do not want to take the time to find all the available arguments, as ancient means of invention require. However, this hasty approach can lead to stalemate (or shouting or violence), as has happened in public arguments over abortion.

Chapter 6, Mapping an Ongoing Debate, is taken from Sharon Crowley and Debra Hawhee's *Ancient Rhetorics for Contemporary Students*, pp. 56–72 and 86–87 (Chapter 3, Achieving Stasis by Asking the Right Questions).

Happily, the stases also provide rhetors with a set of questions that, when asked systematically, can help them to determine the arguments that are available in a given rhetorical situation. Rhetors who do take the time to find all the available arguments can be assured both that their position is defensible and that they have found the best evidence to support it. The very old systematic investigative procedures described in this chapter were used for thousands of years to help rhetors figure out what arguments are available to them, and we hope that they will help you to determine the issues you want to argue, as well.

On Inventing: How to Proceed

We recommend that you begin your work with the stases by trying to answer the questions outlined next. Consider all the statements you generate to be potential propositions. If you work systematically and thoroughly, you should produce a full and useful analysis of the issue you have chosen to examine. Doing all this intellectual work has several advantages. Rhetors who work through the questions raised by this heuristic in systematic fashion will find that

1. It clarifies their thinking about the point in dispute.
2. It forces them to think about the assumptions and values shared by members of their targeted audience.
3. It establishes areas in which more research needs to be done.
4. It suggests which proofs are crucial to the case.
5. It may point the way toward the most effective arrangement of the proofs.

What this or any heuristic will not provide, however, is a draft of a paper or speech. Ancient rhetors spent a good deal of time in preparation for writing or speaking, trying out one method of invention or another. They did not mind if these trials produced false starts because they knew that the false starts turned up in one case could most likely be used in some other rhetorical situation. Contemporary debaters work in a similar fashion, preparing all relevant arguments in advance in case they ever need to use them, and to limit the chance that a skilled opponent will use an argument they are not prepared to answer. It is important to remember, then, that practice with this (or any heuristic) also supplies the rhetor with *copia*. Proofs generated in practice with any heuristic may prove useful at some other time.

One additional caution: heuristics do not work as reliably as mathematical formulas do. In many cases, you will continue to refine the issue and to develop nuances of your proposition as you work through each of the rhetorical canons. In fact, invention can begin all over again during late stages of the composing process—arrangement, revision or even editing. However, attention to the heuristics described in this book will certainly enrich your stock of arguments—your verbal *copia*. And systematic, thoughtful consideration of the issue at hand just may provide you with precisely the proposition you are looking for, as well as arguments you can use to support it.

The Importance of Achieving Stasis

Contemporary public discourse about abortion provides a good example of an argument that has been sustained for many years but that shows no sign of being resolved. Public debate on this issue began in earnest nearly forty years ago, when the Supreme Court legalized the practice in 1973. Ever since that time, those who oppose the availability of abortion, usually on moral grounds, have employed a number of tactics to get the procedure banned, while at the same time, those who support the availability of abortion have fought to keep the practice, as they say, "safe, legal, and rare." Those who oppose abortion are called "pro-life" because of their belief that abortion is murder; those who support it are called "pro-choice" because they believe that women should be able to choose their methods of controlling reproduction.

Ever since *Roe v. Wade,* the 1973 Supreme Court decision that legalized abortion, proponents and opponents of abortion have battled one another in both the judicial and legislative arenas. In 2005, for example, the state legislature of South Dakota passed a bill making it a felony for a doctor to perform an abortion anywhere in the state. The legislation allowed no exceptions whatever: abortions were not permitted when a mother's health was at stake (unless her life was in danger), and citizens of South Dakota who had suffered rape or incest were denied this option as well. The law had been expressly designed by its advocates to produce a test case that would challenge *Roe v. Wade.* Then, in 2006, abortion rights activists succeeded in placing a resolution on the ballot that would strike down the 2005 legislation, and the people of South Dakota supported it. Legislation similar to the 2005 bill that banned nearly all abortions appeared on the ballot again in 2008, and once again voters in South Dakota defeated it.

Clearly this issue is hotly contested in South Dakota, as well as in other states. One reason that the argument over abortion has not been resolved is that it cannot be, as long as the central propositions put forward by those involved in it are not in stasis. People who oppose the legalization of abortion ordinarily offer the following statement as their major proposition: Abortion is murder. People who argue that abortion should maintain its current status as a legal operation put the following statement forward as their major proposition: Women have the right to control their reproductive practices. Keeping in mind that reaching stasis means finding the place where opponents agree to disagree, even a cursory examination of these statements shows that they are not in stasis. A rhetor who wishes to find stasis with someone who believes that abortion is murder should argue (a) that abortion is not murder, or (b) that abortion is legal so therefore it cannot be murder because murder is illegal in America, or (c) that abortion is not murder because a fetus is not a human being, or some other proposition that defines abortion in such a way that it can be excluded from the category "murder."

Stasis Achieved: Rhetors Can Now Agree to Disagree

A. Abortion is murder.

B. Abortion is not murder.

A rhetor who wishes to find stasis with someone who believes that women have the right to control their own reproductive practices, on the other hand, must argue that (a) women do not have that right, at least when they are pregnant, or (b) that the right to life of a fetus outweighs a woman's right to choose what happens to her body, or (c) that the right to life extends to fetuses and takes primacy over any other human right, or some other similar proposition about the priority ordering of human rights.

Stasis Achieved: Rhetors Can Now Agree to Disagree

  A. Women have the right to decide what happens to their bodies, including terminating a pregnancy.

  B. Women do not have the right to decide what happens to their bodies when they are pregnant because a potential life is at stake.

Although the propositions we turned up in our stasis analysis do appear in contemporary discourse about abortion, they are seldom offered in the systematic, head-to-head way we have listed them here; that is, they are seldom put in stasis. But the act of putting them in stasis establishes that the participants in this argument are usually arguing right past each other. That is to say, the major propositions they put forward do not address the same issue.

Interestingly enough, the statements that would achieve stasis in this argument are not very persuasive to opponents: pro-choice advocates do not often directly address the pro-life position by saying, "Abortion is not murder." Nor do pro-life advocates often say in public forums that "women do not have the right to determine what happens to their bodies." This reluctance to state the implications of its propositions may be another reason why the argument is not in stasis. Those who frame the abortion issue as a question of murder are compelled to argue that abortion, defined as murder, outweighs a woman's right to determine when or if she will have children. They frequently support their position by making reference to religious, moral, or natural laws. Those who support legal abortion, on the other hand, must either argue or ignore the claim that abortion is not murder, and to do so they have recourse to the political discourse of rights, arguing that individuals have a right to conduct private business without interference from the state. This argument assumes further that deciding to have an abortion is a private, not a public, matter.

Another way to articulate this failure to achieve stasis is to say that people who oppose abortion are arguing from philosophical or theological assumptions about the point at which life begins; people who defend women's rights are arguing from political grounds about the rights of individuals and the relation of those rights to the good of the community. The point to be made here, however, is that as long as the major propositions in this discourse remain out of stasis, the argument will continue. To date, those who argue about this issue in these terms have ordinarily been unwilling to meet one another on the same ground.

Theoretical versus Practical Questions

Ancient rhetoricians divided questions into two kinds: theoretical and practical. Some questions concern what people should do (action), but these are always related to questions about why people should do something (theory). Cicero gave this example of a theoretical question in his treatise called *Topics* (xxi 82): Does law originate in nature or in some agreement and contract between people? This is the sort of abstract theoretical question that is discussed today by law school professors and their students when they talk about what grounds or centers the law. It is an important question because certain practical actions follow from any answer that may be given. If law is grounded in nature it cannot easily be changed; for instance, it is futile to argue that the law of gravity is wrong, or ill-suited to the times, or that it supports one party to the detriment of another. A rhetor's only option in this case is to argue that the law in question is unnatural. To get an idea of how difficult this is, imagine yourself arguing in court that gravity is unnatural. The theoretical argument from nature is used on occasion: motorcycle riders who opposed legislation requiring them to wear helmets argued—without much success—that such laws violate the natural human desire for freedom from restraint.

If law results from human contract, on the other hand, it is much easier to justify alterations to laws because a rhetor can appeal to the expressed opinions or desires of the majority as support for her argument that a law should be changed. Someone who advocates against a helmet law for motorcycle riders, then, can simply provide as proof a survey showing that some percentage of riders (preferably more than 50%) prefer to ride unprotected by a helmet; someone who advocates the practice of abortion can cite polls showing that the majority of Americans want *Roe v. Wade* to stand (which can be tricky because the percentage of Americans who support or disapprove of abortion changes from poll to poll, depending, in part, on who is taking the poll).

Unlike theoretical questions, which address the origins and natures of things, practical questions always concern proposed actions, what people should do. Cicero gave this example of a practical question: Should a philosopher take part in politics? Notice that this question asks what people who study philosophy ought to do; it does not raise questions about the nature or aim of philosophy or politics, as a theoretical question would. The English word *theory* derives from a Greek word (*theorein*), which literally meant "to sit in the highest row of the theatre." More freely translated, the term meant something like "to observe from afar." A theoretical question, then, allows rhetors to view questions "from afar," as though they had no immediate relevance for daily affairs and putting aside for the moment their practical effects. Many times theoretical investigations will provide positions on more practical issues. But they also take rhetors far afield from everyday events. Take this very practical (and very specific) question, for instance:

should i drop engineering and major in history instead?

To answer this question, a rhetor needs to consider the reasons why he decided to study engineering (interest, good job opportunities) and why he now might prefer to study history (interest, he wants to become a teacher or archivist). He also needs to consider the consequences attached to each choice (If I change majors, will it take me longer to graduate? What sort of work is available to a history major? and so on). Another way to think about the difference between theoretical and practical questions is to consider the **level of generality** at which an issue may be addressed. Greek rhetoricians used the term *hypothesis* to name a specific question that involved actual persons, places, or events. They used the term *thesis*, on the other hand, to name general questions having wide application—matters suited to political, ethical, or philosophical discussion—which don't refer to actual persons or events. The classic example of a general question was:

Should anyone marry!

The classic specific question was:

Should Cato marry?

Here are some contemporary examples of general and specific questions:

1. *General:* Is it legal to protest at funerals?

   Specific: Should members of the Westboro Baptist Church be allowed to protest at funerals for soldiers killed in the line of duty?

2. *General:* Should people convicted of murder be put to death?

   Specific: Should Timothy McVeigh have been put to death for blowing up the Murrah Building in Oklahoma City on April 19, 1995, an act that resulted in the deaths of 168 people?

3. *General:* Should the sexual orientation of couples who want to marry be taken into account?

   Specific: Should our state legalize gay marriage?
   More Specific: Should Joan and Annette be allowed to marry?

The ancient distinction between a theoretical question and a question of action is a binary distinction—that is, it allows for only two possibilities. However, as the last example demonstrates, general and more specific questions are more helpfully thought of as lying along a spectrum or range from very general to very specific. There are many levels of generality and specificity at which any issue can be stated. Hence the generality or specificity of a given claim is never absolute; it follows that statements of a question are general or specific only in relation to each other. For example:

General: Is conservation of the environment more important than economic development? (*This is a theoretical as well as a very general question—stated this way, the question raises issues for contemplation and discussion rather than action*).

More Specific: Should the United States sacrifice industries that negatively affect its environment—logging, manufacture of certain chemicals and plastics, nuclear power plants—to conserve the environment? (*This question, although still general, is no longer simply theoretical; answers to it imply actions to be taken by the United States.*)

Even More Specific: Should the City Council of Ourtown reject an application to build a large discount department store if this requires clear-cutting five acres of forest?

Very Specific: Should I take time to recycle plastics, paper, and aluminum even though to do so costs money and time? (*The last three versions of the claim raise practical questions, insofar as they imply human actions, but each successive claim involves fewer people, so each is more specific than the one preceding it.*)

The level of generality at which a question or issue is stated determines the amount of research needed and the kinds of proofs that must be composed to argue it persuasively. More general questions require broader knowledge, and they usually require a longer and more complex treatment. To answer the general question about conservation given here, for example, would require at least a book-length discussion. On the other hand, the very specific question, involving a personal decision, at minimum requires some private reflection and a bit of hands-on research. To answer the very specific and very practical question whether I should take time to recycle only requires me to recycle plastics, glass, paper, and aluminum for awhile to see how much time and/or money is required to recycle these substances and to compare these results to the time and money required in having unsorted garbage hauled away by the city. A paper or speech answering this question could simply state a proposition ("Recycling is expensive and time-consuming for me") and report the results of this research. As you can see, though, answers given to this very specific question depend on answers given to more generally stated questions, including the first, very general, question stated earlier. Whether you recycle or not depends, ultimately, on your values: Is preservation of the environment more important to you than your time or your budget? (Here we've restated the very specific question just a bit more generally).

The relation of general to specific issues was a matter of debate among ancient rhetoricians. As Quintilian pointed out, every special issue presupposes a general one: for example, the question of whether Cato ought to marry really couldn't be answered satisfactorily unless the general question, "Should a person marry?" had also been considered (III v 13). Too, there are questions that hover somewhere between the very general and the very specific: for example, "Should an older person marry?" For ancient rhetoricians, questions like these were ethical ones, having to do with a person's character and the right course of conduct for certain characters. Ethical questions still concern us, of course. We regularly read or hear arguments about whether young people ought to marry, for example, or whether gay people ought to be allowed to marry. Often these arguments are cast as personal or financial choices, but they have ethical aspects, too, because decisions about marriage and reproduction affect many people, not just those who make them.

Of course any decision you make about the level of generality at which you will pursue an issue is always affected by the rhetorical situation for which you are composing. Who is the audience for the paper or speech? What is the setting? How does the audience feel about the issue? What do they know already, and what will the rhetor have to tell them?

The Four Questions

The process of asking questions does not conclude once the point of stasis has been identified. Ordinarily, the determination of the question for debate will give rise to other questions. Ancient rhetoricians devised a list of four questions or stases that would help them refine their grasp on the point at issue.[1]

1. CONJECTURE (*stasis stochasmos*)—"Is there an act to be considered?"
2. DEFINITION (*stasis horos*)—"How can the act be defined?"
3. QUALITY (*stasis poiotes*)—"How serious is the act?"
4. POLICY (*stasis metalepsis*)—"Should this act be submitted to some formal procedure?"

If someone is accused of theft, for example, the first question that must be raised is **conjecture:** "Did she do it or not?" If all parties agree that she took the property in question, the stasis moves to a question of **definition:** "Was it theft?" (She might have borrowed it). And if everyone agrees that the act can be defined as theft, the stasis becomes: "Was it right or wrong?" (The theft might be justified on any number of grounds—she took liquor from the house of a friend who is an alcoholic, for instance). Some ancient teachers called this stasis "quality," and we will use this term as well. Last, if the question of quality is agreed on, the stasis then becomes: "Should she be tried for the offense?" This last stasis is the question of procedure or **policy.**

THE FOUR QUESTIONS

Conjecture: Does it exist? Did it happen?

Definition: What kind of thing or event is it?

Quality: Was it right or wrong?

Policy: What should we do?

Cicero and Quintilian insisted that only the first three questions were necessary to the preparation of arguments to be used outside the courtroom. Nevertheless, the fourth stasis, policy, is sometimes useful in nonlegal settings. People who deliberate in city councils or student assemblies often have to decide how to regulate practices: Should we put a crosswalk on Elm Street to eliminate jaywalking there? Should we lobby the administration for faculty library privileges for graduate students?

Cicero recommended that speakers and writers work through the questions in order. This approach has several advantages: the process of working through questions of conjecture, definition, and quality, in order, will help rhetors to find the points about which they and their audience agree; it will also establish the point from which they must begin the argument—the point where they disagree.

---

[1] The system of questions given here does not appear in the work of any ancient thinker. We have generalized the four questions we feature out of primary and secondary classical sources (for an illuminating if complex account of competing ancient traditions of stasis, see Quintilian's painstaking discussion in the third book of the *Institutes*). Our system is a hybrid, although it is the same one that George Kennedy reconstructs for Hermagoras' lost treatise (307–08). In particular, our consideration of policy along with the other three stases is a departure from ancient thought because the ancients usually classed policy with questions of law (forensic rhetoric), whereas the first three stases we discuss were ordinarily associated with deliberative rhetoric.

In the first stasis, conjecture, the rhetor determines whether or not he and his audience agree about the existence of some being or thing or act or idea. If they do, this stasis is no longer relevant or useful, having been agreed to—waived—by both parties.

In the second stasis, definition, the rhetor determines whether or not he and his audience agree about the classification of the being or thing or idea or the act; if so, the stasis of definition may be passed by.

In the third stasis, quality, the rhetor determines whether he and his audience agree about the value of the thing or idea or being or act. That is, what is its importance to the community as a whole? Cicero explained the function of the third stasis as follows: this stasis comes into play when there is both agreement on what has been done and certainty about how the act should be defined, but there is a question nevertheless about how important it is or about its quality: for example, was it just or unjust, profitable or unprofitable? (*De Inventione* I viii 12). Use of this stasis required rhetors to think hard about values that are widely held in their community, values such as loyalty and responsibility, thriftiness and benevolence, heroism or self-control.

In the fourth stasis, policy, there is controversy about what should be done in a given situation: Should citizens pass a property tax increase? Should the students at State University establish policies opposing the expression of bigotry? Should I drop engineering and major in art instead? As you can probably guess, the point of agreement is often much easier to establish in the first and second stases than in the third and fourth.

A Simple Example

During the midterm elections in 2010, citizens of Florida were asked to vote on a proposition that would raise class sizes in Florida's public schools. Here is an article from the Fort Myers *News-Press* about voters' decision, written by Dave Breitenstein:

> Florida's public schools must adhere to strict class-size caps after a provision to relax standards couldn't muster enough support.
>
> Statewide, 55.3 percent of voters wanted to calculate class size by using schoolwide averages, as opposed to individual classroom limits. However, the constitutional amendment needed 60 percent to become law.
>
> The rejection of Amendment 8 means core classes—math, English, science and social studies—still cannot exceed 18 children in pre-kindergarten through third grade, 22 students in grades four through eight and 25 in high schools. Caps do not apply to art, music or physical education classes . . . .
>
> Class-size reduction has been a costly initiative. In Lee [County] alone, the district spent $535.5 million through last year to hire more teachers and build additional classrooms, and $92.4 million was budgeted this year.
>
> Lee estimates the negative vote will cost an extra $30.3 million annually to create overflow classrooms for extra students. School districts can be fined if they're not in compliance.
>
> In 2002, 52.4 percent of Florida voters approved class-size limits. Initially, the state used district averages, then school averages, and individual classroom caps were implemented in August. The amendment proposed capping classes at 21, 27 and 30 students for the three grade levels, respectively.

Obviously, when a ballot proposition receives just over 50% of the vote, an issue exists. That is, the people of Lee County disagree about the importance of class sizes in public schools. Some possible arguments about this dispute emerge when we consider the four questions of stasis in regard to it:

Is there a question of fact or conjecture? Yes. In 2002 Florida voters approved class-size limits, and then in 2010 they rejected a proposal to raise those limits. Does anyone disagree that these events occurred? Probably not. So this question can be agreed to, or waived, and participants in this discussion can move to the second question.

Is there a question of definition? That is, what kind of thing, idea, or act is at issue here? The stasis of definition is clear in this dispute: What is at issue is a previous vote to limit class sizes; that is, a ballot proposition. It is doubtful that any party to the discussion would deny this definition of the act, although the minority who voted against it might object to its having been placed on a ballot at all. But this objection is not relevant under the head of definition; it is instead a policy question and should be raised under the fourth stasis.

As is often the case, the third and fourth stases yield more interesting, and more controversial, arguments. Even a cursory examination of the third stasis, questions of value, suggests that there are at least two values at stake in this dispute. The first is educational excellence: all parties to the discussion must agree that limiting class size is a good thing. Those who do not agree must offer evidence that counters the many studies supporting this point, or, they may take issue with this claim on some other ground. It appears, for instance, that some school districts have had difficulty raising enough money to support the extra classrooms and teachers that are required by smaller classes. It is, after all, cheaper to assign 30 or 40 students to a single teacher using one room than it is to find space and teachers for more, smaller, groups of 18 students each. People who voted against the ballot proposition in 2010 apparently valued educational quality over economy; that is, they believed that limits on class size improved educational quality sufficiently to offset the additional cost. So the values at stake here include at least quality of education and economic expediency. We have chosen a relatively simple case for illustrative purposes, so rhetors will ordinarily find more than two competing values at work within the complex issues that people face in their daily lives.

Let us move on to the fourth stasis. Is there a question of procedure? Yes. The ballot proposition itself is a proposal to eliminate a program that was established eight years earlier. No doubt the legislators who struggled with this issue in 2010 examined alternative policy suggestions, which could include raising class sizes only in high schools, where students can be expected to need less help than do elementary students. Or they might have proposed a tax increase to pay for the reduction in class size. Or, they might have offered a different kind of proposition that required only a majority vote to pass, rather than trying to amend the Florida constitution, which requires 60% support. When the four questions are expanded and specified, as recommended by ancient teachers, they ordinarily create additional propositions like these.

Expanding the Questions

Each of the four questions can be expanded into other sets of questions. According to Cicero, there are four ways of dealing with a question of conjecture (*Topics* xxi 82). One can ask

Whether the thing exists or is true

What its origin is

What cause produced it

What changes can be made in it

Some modern rhetoricians call the issue of conjecture "the question of fact." However, the Greek term *stochasmos* is more literally translated as "a guess" or "an inference." Today the term *fact* connotes hard physical evidence, but this reading is misleading here (see the chapter on extrinsic proofs for more information about factual evidence). The stasis of conjecture does not establish anything at all about the truth or fact of the matter under discussion; rather, it represents an educated guess about what might be, or what might have occurred. And because reality may be perceived very differently by people who occupy different social and political positions, people may paint very different pictures of that reality. For example, people who opposed federal legislation about health care in 2010 worried that it mandated "death panels"—committees of doctors that would condemn elderly people to die without medical care. Proponents of the measure, on the other hand, pointed out that the legislation only contained a provision providing insurance for anyone who wanted to make a living will in consultation with a doctor. People on both sides of this issue offered conjectures about the way the legislation would work, or how people would behave were it to pass. In these examples of conjecture, each party to the dispute has some stake or **interest** in picturing the legislation in the way that they do. Their disagreement about these facts is what renders conjecture rhetorical.

Questions of Conjecture

Does it exist? Is it true?

Where did it come from? How did it begin?

What is its cause?

Can it be changed?

For example, let's say that a rhetor named Lisa Simpson wants her city, Springfield, to pass a dark-sky ordinance. Under the question of conjecture, she can ask:

Does light pollution exist in Springfield?

What is the origin of the pollution?

What causes it?

What will change it?

When she tries to answer these questions, Lisa learns that she will probably need to provide evidence that light pollution does indeed exist. She will also need to provide evidence that the pollution is not natural (that is, that it doesn't originate from moonlight or starlight). She will have to establish that the pollution is caused by billboards and streetlights, and she will need to establish further that elimination of these two sources will produce a level of light that will make astronomic observation possible.

Use of the stasis of conjecture is often productive in just this way—that is, it demonstrates to rhetors what evidence they need to mount their arguments. Sometimes, use of the stasis of conjecture also establishes that there is no issue, or that a rhetor has framed the issue incompletely, or that he wants to change his mind about the issue. Because heuristics often produce surprises—that is what they are for, after all—rhetors must be prepared for shifts in their thinking. When using the stases—or any means of invention—rhetors should always remain aware that invention may cause them to change their minds about an issue.

If all parties to the discussion agree about the conjecture—the description of the state of things—the search for stasis moves on to matters of definition.

Questions of Definition

What kind of thing or event is it?

To what larger class of things does it belong?

What are its parts? How are they related?

Definitions are rhetorical because they can determine on whose ground the question will be taken up (see the chapter on the sophistic topics for advice about composing definitions). In this case, Lisa Simpson can take advantage of the rhetorical aspect of definition to compose one that suits her interest. Lisa and the astronomers at the local observatory are probably the only parties, other than thieves and lovers, who have an interest in diminishing light pollution.

Definition requires that Lisa name the particular or proper quality of light pollution and divide that quality into its constituent parts. Let's say that she defines light pollution as "those levels of light that are sufficient to interfere with astronomical observations." She might then divide such light levels into

Light caused by billboards

Light caused by streetlights

Light caused by home lighting

Light caused by natural sources such as the moon

This **division** demonstrates to her that she needs evidence that establishes the level of pollution caused by each of these sources. It tells her further that if the evidence demonstrates that natural light is not an important factor in creating light pollution, she can concentrate her major arguments on the other sources of light, all of which can be mitigated by a dark-sky ordinance. As it does here, the stasis of definition will sometimes produce a way of dividing up the discourse—producing what ancient rhetoricians called the **partition**.

Other parties concerned about this issue might return to the question of conjecture to assert that there is no such thing as light pollution, in an attempt to render Lisa's definition irrelevant. If they succeed in this, she too will be forced to return to the stasis of conjecture if all parties wish to continue the discussion. If they accede to her definition, on the other hand, the argument is in stasis, and all parties can turn to the next stasis: quality.

If, on the other hand, they do accept that light pollution exists, and that it can be defined as she asserts, Lisa has been able to set up the discussion in terms that favor her interest.

Questions of Quality: Simple or Complex

Simple questions of quality attempt to determine the worth of the issue—its justice or rightness or honor—or how much the community desires it. Comparative questions of quality put the issue in the context of other qualities, comparing it with other values to determine its priority among the community's values. If asked simply, then, the question of quality is, "Is light pollution a good or a bad thing?" If asked comparatively in this case, the question could become, "Is the safety of citizens more important than the needs of astronomers?"

According to Cicero, there are three kinds of simple questions of quality:

what to seek and what to avoid,

what is right and what wrong,

what is honorable and what base (*Topics* xxi 84).

Simple Questions of Quality:

Is it a good or a bad thing?

Should it be sought or avoided?

Is it right or wrong?

Is it honorable or dishonorable?

Comparative Questions of Quality

Is it better or worse than something else?

Is it more desirable than any alternatives?

Is it less desirable than any alternatives?

Is it more or less right than something else?

Is it more or less wrong than something else?

Is it more honorable than something else?

Is it less honorable than something else?

Is it more base than something else?

Is it less base than something else?

Thus Lisa might ask the following simple questions of quality:

Should lower levels of light pollution be sought, or should they be avoided?

If the lower levels of light affect other situations, like citizens' safety, should they then be avoided?

> Is it right or wrong to ask for lower levels of light?
> Is it honorable to put the needs of astronomers above those of ordinary citizens?
> Is it dishonorable to deprive citizens of a source of safety?

Thinking comparatively, the rhetor compares the importance of her issue to other related issues. In Lisa's case, for example, a general comparative question of quality is

> Should the present state of affairs, which includes light pollution, be preferred to a state of affairs in which light pollution has been lessened?

A comparative specific question is

> Should the present state of affairs in Springfield, which includes lighted billboards, be maintained in preference to an imagined state of affairs (or the actual state of affairs in the town down the road), where lighted billboards have been eliminated so that astronomers can see better?

Because questions of comparison are of two kinds—similarity and difference—Lisa can ask herself what differences will be brought about in her observations of the night sky if light pollution is reduced. She can argue from similarity that astronomers in the town down the road enacted legislation to control light pollution, and the quality of their observations of the night sky improved.

If she is systematic in her use of the stases, Lisa must produce all the available arguments, even those that oppose her position. She can be sure that those who disagree with her will produce these arguments, and so she must be prepared to answer them. For example, her use of the stasis of comparative difference may produce this question: Will the reduction of light pollution alter our previous descriptions of the night sky because it gives us a clearer view? In other words, will astronomers be forced to revise our earlier work if we can see better?

As this example makes clear, the stases of quality are ordinarily very productive. Using them, Lisa has generated some questions that can show her which arguments are available in a given situation. In some cases the stases may force rhetors to articulate assumptions they previously held more or less unconsciously, and which may be controversial to others. For example, any astronomer might simply assume, without giving the issue much thought, that other citizens value a dark sky as much as he does. Other citizens, however, will not take this proposition for granted. The police will be concerned about safety, and billboard companies will be concerned about possible loss of revenue if they cannot light their advertising signs at night. Use of the stases, then, demonstrates that a rhetor must prepare arguments that defend his proposition, should it become necessary to do so.

Questions of Policy

The fourth stasis, policy, is relevant to Lisa's case as well. In questions of policy, the rhetor proposes that some action be taken (or not) or that some action be regulated (or not) by means of a policy or law. Questions of policy are usually twofold: they are both **deliberative** and **forensic.** That is, a rhetor who wishes to put forward a question or issue of policy must first deliberate about the need for it and then argue for its implementation.

Deliberative Policy Questions

Should some action be taken?

Given the rhetorical situation, what actions are possible? Desirable?

How will proposed actions change the current state of affairs? Or should the current state affairs remain unchanged?

How will the proposed changes make things better? Worse? How? In what ways? For whom?

Forensic Policy Questions

Should some states of affairs be regulated (or not) by some formalized policy?

Which policies can be implemented? Which cannot?

What are the merits of competing proposals? What are their defects?

How is my proposal better than others? Worse? When Lisa considers the questions of policy, she will ask herself some hard questions. She has already decided that some action should be taken. She needs now to ask herself whether her proposal to enact a dark-sky ordinance can be implemented (for instance: How much will it cost? What changes in technology or equipment will need to be made?) and whether it is a good thing for the community it will affect. She needs to consider changes that its implementation might bring about—loss of revenue to Springfield, possibly dangerous situations for citizens—and determine whether the seriousness of these changes outweighs the merits of her proposal. If anyone has made an alternative proposal, she needs to compare that to her plan and find arguments showing that her proposal is superior.

Lisa can find arguments for implementing her proposal by showing how it will improve the current state of things, by showing how alternative proposals are not as satisfactory as her own, and by showing that implementation of her proposal is entirely possible. For example, she should try to counter the opposing argument that lowered levels of light can endanger citizens' safety in other words, this argument requires **refutation.** If possible, she should point out in her proposal that current levels of light from streetlights do not pose a problem to astronomical observation.

Once she has considered all the questions raised by the policy questions, Lisa can draft a proposal of her dark-sky ordinance. The draft demonstrates the depth of her concern about the situation because she took the time to compose it. It also strengthens the possibility that her audience will use part or all of her draft when they actually write the ordinance, as busy people are likely to make use of work that has already been done.

So if you wish to recommend that a policy or procedure be implemented, you should first compose it. It will help if you can find out how similar policies are enacted in similar situations and compose a similar plan for implementing the one that you suggest. You should also determine how the policy that you recommend can be enforced. If you are recommending, on the other hand, that some public practice be changed, you must first compose your recommendation. Then find out who can make the changes you suggest, and find out what procedures must be followed to make the recommended change. You should also try to find out how your recommended change can be implemented and enforced, and offer suggestions for achieving this.

Using the Stases

The stases still prove surprisingly useful for beating a path through the thicket of issues that often surround a controversy. We suggest that rhetors begin by considering the issue under each the four stases: conjecture, definition, quality, and policy. Then compare the arguments generated under each head: Do any seem to capture the point at issue? Do any hold out the possibility of helping you with further investigation? Do any tell you something about issues that might be raised by a member of the audience, or by someone who disagrees with you? Do any help you to begin to develop an argument? Remember that this procedure is only intended to help you decide where to start. Its use does not guarantee that you will generate any useful proofs, much less that you can begin to draft a speech or paper at this stage of your preparation.

Works Cited

Breitenstein, Dave. "Amendments: 1, 4, 8 Fail; 2, 5, 6 Pass." <dbreitenstein@news-press.com>. November 2, 2010. Accessed 11/04/10.

Understanding Genres and Writing for Academic Audiences

7

The material that follows is taken from Amy Devitt, Mary Jo Reiff, and Anis Bawarshi's *Scenes of Writing*.

Imagine you are a clerk in a driver's license office—and there is no application form. Instead, each time someone needs a license, you say, "Please write down the necessary information." How many different sizes and shapes of paper would you receive, with how many different arrangements of information—and what would different people consider to be "the necessary information"? How messy would it be to try to work with all those pieces of paper?

Think then of how a driver's license application form saves time and energy for both applicants and clerks.

When frameworks for organizing texts get used repeatedly—as with application forms for a driver's license—then they become "genres."

Genres save us time and effort because they help both composers and audiences know what to do and what to expect. There are movie genres (Westerns, romantic comedies, horror movies), videogame genres (first person shooters, quests), and fiction genres (fantasy, science fiction, romance). There are genres for writing as well.

When you encounter a new rhetorical situation, you need to ask what genres your audience might expect in the situation and how tightly you need to stay within the confines of the genre if you are to achieve your purposes.

Genres as Social Scripts

As typical rhetorical ways of acting in different situations, genres function as social scripts. For instance, when you attend the first day of a typical college course, say this writing class, the first things you probably do are look around at the other students, check out the layout of the room, try to figure out what the teacher is like, and so on. In other words, you begin to read the scene in order to decide how best to act within it. But perhaps the best indication you will

Chapter 7, Understanding Genres and Writing for Academic Audiences, is taken from Anne Frances Wysocki and Dennis A. Lynch's *The DK Handbook*, pp. 196–199 (Part 5, Genres and Frameworks and Academic Genres); Amy Devitt, Mary Jo Reiff, and Anis Bawarshi's *Scenes of Writing*, pp. 18–63 and 92–97 (Chapter 2, "Using Genres to Read Scenes of Writing") and pp. 408–413 (Chapter 7, Writing Research-Based Genres); and Lester Faigley's *The Brief Penguin Handbook*, pp. 72–81 (Chapter 9, Write a Position Argument).

get about the nature of this scene is through the syllabus that the teacher distributes. As you know, the syllabus is a genre, one that teachers typically distribute on the first day of class. Beyond containing important information about the course goals, policies, and expectations, it helps *set the scene* of the course. By reading it carefully, you not only learn what you have to do in order to succeed in the course, when assignments are due, what the course policies are, and so on; you also learn something about how to behave in this scene; what kind of role your teacher will play and what kind of role she or he expects you to play; and what values, beliefs, and goals guide this course. The syllabus, in short, gives you early and important access to the "script" of the course. How well you read this script will impact how effectively you will act within the scene of the class and its various situations.

Writing Activity

Select a course other than this one for which you have received a syllabus. Before looking back at the syllabus, describe the "personality" of that course—the nature of the course that is conveyed through the class structure, activities, assignments, teacher-student interactions, student-student interactions, etc. Now look at the syllabus for that course: Does the syllabus share any "personality traits" with the course? Could you tell from the syllabus what kind of course it is turning out to be? If so, find some features of the syllabus that reveal that personality. If not, find some features of the syllabus that suggest a different personality.

Reading the Patient Medical History Form

For another example of how the language of genres reflects their situations, think about the scene of the doctor's office. Most of us can readily picture this scene, with its seating area, its coffee table piled with magazines, its reception desk, and its small examination rooms with health posters hanging on the walls. It is a familiar scene. What may be less familiar, however, is the role that genres play in scripting this scene.

The Patient Medical History Form (PMHF) is one such genre. You might recognize the form as the genre patients have to complete prior to meeting with the doctor on their initial visit to the doctor's office. The PMHF asks patients to provide critical information regarding their age, sex, weight, and height as well as their medical history, including prior and recurring physical conditions, past treatments, and, of course, a description of current physical symptoms. These questions are usually followed by a request for insurance information and then a consent-to-treat statement and a legal release statement that a patient signs. With these components, the PMHF is both a patient record and a legal document, helping the doctor treat the patient and at the same time protecting the doctor from potential lawsuits.

The PMHF does more than convey information from patient to doctor. In its content and visual design, it also tells us something about the scene that the patient is entering. Reading the genre, for instance, we notice that most if not all of its questions focus on a patient's physical symptoms. The genre is designed in such a way that there is very little space in which patients can describe their emotional state. The genre's focus on the physical reflects Western cultural views of medicine, which tend to separate the body and the mind. The medical assumption seems to be that doctors can isolate and then treat physical symptoms with little to no reference to the patient's state of mind and the effect that state of mind might have on these symptoms.

The attitude reflected in the language of this form resembles the description in Perri Klass's article earlier in this chapter of how doctors and nurses talk. As a genre, then, the PMHF reflects and preserves the habits of the medical community. It functions as one of the scripts by which the actors in this medical scene perform their roles and interact with one another. By completing the PMHF, an individual begins to assume the role of patient, one who has certain physical symptoms. And when the doctor meets the patient, the doctor will likely relate to the patient that way (it is not uncommon, for instance, for doctors and nurses to refer to patients by their physical symptoms, such as "I treated a knee injury today" or "the ear infection is in Room 3").

The Patient Medical History Form, thus, is one of the scripts that underwrites the scene of the doctor's office. Other genres within this scene (prescription notes, referral letters, patient files, letters to insurance companies, to name a few) set up other relations (between doctors and pharmacists, doctors and other doctors, etc.), other actions, and other social roles. Together, the genres provide a kind of rhetorical map that we can read in order to chart how people behave and communicate within this scene.

Collaborative Activity

Working with classmates, examine the visual elements of the sample PMHF we have included. Pay attention to the design of the document: The use of borders, boxes, headings and subheadings, font shape and size, color, etc. What else do these elements tell us about this genre and the scene in which it is used? In what ways do the visual elements support the claim we have been making about the PMHF?

Analyzing Genres

What we just did in reading the Patient Medical History Form to determine what it can tell us about how people behave and communicate in the doctor's office is called **genre analysis**. Genre analysis involves the close and critical reading of people's patterns of communication in different situations within scenes. As a process, it involves collecting samples of a genre, identifying patterns within it (recognizing, for example, that PMHFs focus almost exclusively on physical symptoms), and then drawing conclusions about what these patterns reveal about the situation or scene in which it is used. ***By doing this kind of genre analysis, you will gain access to the patterns of communication that will enable you to write more effectively within different situations and scenes.***

PATIENT HISTORY (Please Print)

THIS INFORMATION BECOMES PART OF YOUR CONFIDENTIAL MEDICAL RECORD

NAME _____ PRIOR PHYSICIAN _____

         LAST   FIRST   MIDDLE INITIAL

ADDRESS _____ TODAY'S DATE _____

         CITY   STATE   ZIP

TELEPHONE # (DAY)_____ (EVENING) _____ AGE _____ SEX M F

Chief Complaint and/or reason for visit _____

History of Present Illness - describe in detail _____

_____

_____

Medical Conditions (Give names and dates)

Condition	Personal	Date	Family	Date	Condition	Personal	Date	Family	Date
Hypertension	☐	___	☐	___	Anemia	☐	___	☐	___
Diabetes	☐	___	☐	___	Blood Disorders	☐	___	☐	___
Lung Disease	☐	___	☐	___	Obesity	☐	___	☐	___
Heart Disease	☐	___	☐	___	Ulcers	☐	___	☐	___
Cancer	☐	___	☐	___	Intestinal Disorders	☐	___	☐	___
Stroke	☐	___	☐	___	Jaundice	☐	___	☐	___
Chest Pain	☐	___	☐	___	Infertility	☐	___	☐	___
Abdominal Pain	☐	___	☐	___	Ear/Nose/Throat	☐	___	☐	___
Arthritis	☐	___	☐	___	High Cholesterol	☐	___	☐	___
Back Pain	☐	___	☐	___	Kidney Disease	☐	___	☐	___
Osteoporosis	☐	___	☐	___	Bladder Infections	☐	___	☐	___
Mental Disorders	☐	___	☐	___	TB Skin Tests	☐	___	☐	___
Phlebitis	☐	___	☐	___	Sleep Problems	☐	___	☐	___
Migraine	☐	___	☐	___	Alcoholism	☐	___	☐	___
Alcohol/Drug Abuse	☐	___	☐	___	Hepatitis C	☐	___	☐	___
Tobacco Abuse	☐	___	☐	___	Hepatitis B	☐	___	☐	___
Hereditary Disorders	☐	___	☐	___	Hepatitis Non A, Non B	☐	___	☐	___
Thyroid Disease	☐	___	☐	___					

Surgical Procedures (Give names and dates) _____

Blood Transfusions (Give dates) _____

Hospitalizations (Give dates) _____

Injuries/Trauma (Give type and dates) _____

Allergies _____

Immunization History

Influenza yearly ☐Y ☐N   Pneumonia ☐Y ☐N   Tetanus ☐Y ☐N   Hepatitis ☐Y ☐N

Social History

Marital Status _____ Occupation _____

Education _____ Housing/source of drinking water _____

Status of immediate and extended family _____ Number living in the household _____

Coffee/Tea intake?	☐Y	☐N	Amount? _____
Difficulty sleeping?	☐Y	☐N	
Wear seatbelts?	☐Y	☐N	
Do you have a Living Will?	☐Y	☐N	
Do you have a Durable Power?	☐Y	☐N	

Social History (continued)

Cigarette use?	❑ Y	❑ N	Amount? _____	Number of years? _____
Pipe? Cigars? Chew?	❑ Y	❑ N	Amount? _____	Number of years? _____
If you smoke, do you want to stop?	❑ Y	❑ N		
Alcohol use?	❑ Y	❑ N	Amount? _____	Number of years? _____

I.V. drug or intranasal cocaine use, even if only once, at present or in the past?   ❑ Y   ❑ N
Have tattoos or extensive body piercing?   ❑ Y   ❑ N
Multiple sex partners (now or in the past?)   ❑ Y   ❑ N

Have you ever:

Had blood transfusions or any blood products? .... ❑ Y   ❑ N
Been rejected for trying to donate blood? .... ❑ Y   ❑ N
Been told that your liver function tests were elevated? .... ❑ Y   ❑ N
Been stuck with a needle or had an exposure to blood? .... ❑ Y   ❑ N
Had any sexually transmitted diseases (i.e. syphilis, chlamydia, gonorrhea)? ... ❑ Y   ❑ N
Do you use condoms? .... ❑ Y   ❑ N

Family History

	AGE IF LIVING	AGE AT DEATH	PRESENT CONDITION/CAUSE OF DEATH
Father			
Mother			
Children			

DRUGS FREQUENTLY OR PRESENTLY USED (CHECK ALL THAT APPLY)

❑ Aspirin	❑ Decongestants	❑ Hormones	❑ Diet Pills
❑ Vitamins/Minerals/Herbals	❑ Antibiotics	❑ Diabetics	❑ Antidepressants
Over the Counter Meds	❑ Laxatives	❑ Insulin	❑ Sedatives
❑ Water Pill	❑ Antacids	❑ Birth Control Pills	❑ Sleeping Pills
❑ Blood Pressure	❑ Antihistamines	❑ Heart	❑ Cortisone
❑ Asthma	❑ Thyroid	❑ Nitroglycerin	❑ Anti-inflammatory Pills

Other _____

Symptom and System Review

❑ Headache	❑ Shortness of Breath	❑ Hemorrhoids	❑ Muscle Cramps
❑ Dizziness	❑ Coughed up Blood	❑ Abnormal EKG	❑ Varicose Veins
❑ Fainting	❑ Night Sweats	❑ Abnormal X-ray	❑ Phlebitis
❑ Seizures	❑ Cough	❑ High Blood Sugar	❑ Goiter
❑ Numbness	❑ Wheezing/Asthma	❑ Low Blood Sugar	❑ Hot Flashes
❑ Nervous	❑ Loss of Appetite	❑ Skin Rashes	❑ Fluid Retention
❑ Irritable	❑ Indigestion	❑ Dry Skin	❑ Tired
❑ Depressed	❑ Heartburn	❑ Heart Murmur	❑ Trouble Sleeping
❑ Ear Trouble	❑ Nervous Stomach	❑ Palpitations	❑ Kidney Trouble
❑ Sinus Trouble	❑ Abdominal Pain	❑ Irregular Heart Beat	❑ Difficulty Urinating
❑ Stuffy Nose	❑ Diarrhea	❑ Enlarged Heart	❑ Urinary Burning
❑ Nosebleeds	❑ Constipation	❑ Tire Easily	❑ Frequent Urination
❑ Vision Trouble	❑ Change in Bowel Habits	❑ Ankle Swelling	❑ Middle of Night Urination
❑ Nasal Allergies	❑ Gall Bladder Trouble	❑ Back Pain	
❑ Hoarseness of Voice	❑ Swallowing Trouble	❑ Neck Pain	MEN - ❑ Impotence
❑ Swallowing Trouble	❑ Yellow Jaundice	❑ Arm Pain	MEN - ❑ Loss of Libido
❑ Sore Throat	❑ Vomiting of Blood	❑ Bursitis	WOMEN - ❑ Loss of Libido
❑ Chest Pain/Pressure	❑ Passing Blood by Rectum	❑ Arthritis	WOMEN - ❑ PMS

Activity Level

❑ Sedentary life with little exercise   ❑ Mild exercise with job, house, or recreation (i.e. climb stairs)
❑ Occasional vigorous activity with work or recreation   ❑ Regular vigorous exercise program or heavy manual work

FOR WOMEN ONLY

Date last menstruated _____	Any menstrual problems?	❑ Y	❑ N
Period every _____ days	Heavy periods	❑ Y	❑ N
Number of pregnancies _____	Infrequent periods	❑ Y	❑ N
Number of miscarriages _____	Irregular periods	❑ Y	❑ N
Birth control method _____	Painful periods	❑ Y	❑ N
Date of last pap smear _____			

Check if you have had: ❑ D&C   ❑ Toxemia   ❑ Hysterectomy   ❑ Ovarian Failure
               ❑ Difficulty with pregnancy   ❑ with labor   ❑ with delivery

Genre analysis involves close reading and some observation by

1. Collecting samples of a genre
2. Finding out where, when, by whom, why, and how the genre is used
3. Identifying rhetorical and linguistic patterns in the genre
4. Determining what these patterns tell us about the people who use it and the scene in which it is used

BOX 7.1 GUIDELINES FOR ANALYZING GENRES

1. Collect Samples of the Genre

If you are studying a genre that is fairly public, such as wedding announcements, you can look at samples from various newspapers. You can also locate samples of a genre in textbooks and manuals about the genre, as we did with the complaint letters. If you are studying a less public genre, such as the Patient Medical History Form, you might have to visit several doctors' offices to collect samples. Try to gather samples from more than one place (for example, wedding announcements from different newspapers or medical history forms from different doctors' offices) so that you get a more accurate picture of the complexity of the genre. The more samples of the genre you collect, the more easily you will be able to notice patterns within the genre.

2. Identify the Scene and Describe the Situation in Which the Genre Is Used

Seek answers to questions about the genre's situation. Consider:

- **Setting:** Where does the genre appear? How and when is it transmitted and used? With what other genres does this genre interact?
- **Subject:** What topics, issues, ideas, questions, etc. does the genre address? When people use this genre, what is it that they are interacting about?
- **Participants:** Who uses the genre?
  Writers: Who writes the texts in this genre? Are multiple writers possible? What roles do they perform? What characteristics must writers of this genre possess? Under what circumstances do writers write the genre (e.g., in teams, on a computer, in a rush)?
  Readers: Who reads the texts in this genre? Is there more than one type of reader for this genre? What roles do they perform? What characteristics must readers of this genre possess? Under what circumstances do readers read the genre (e.g., at their leisure, on the run, in waiting rooms)?
- **Purposes:** Why do writers write this genre and why do readers read it? What purposes does the genre fulfill for the people who use it?

3. Identify and Describe Patterns in the Genre's Features

What recurrent features do the samples share? For example:

- What **content** is typically included? What excluded? How is the content treated? What sorts of examples are used? What counts as evidence (personal testimony, facts, etc.)?
- What **rhetorical appeals** are used? What appeals to logos, pathos, and ethos appear?
- How are texts in the genres **structured**? What are their parts, and how are they organized?
- In what **format** are texts of this genre presented? What layout or appearance is common? How long is a typical text in this genre?

- What types of **sentences** do texts in the genre typically use? How long are they? Are they simple or complex, passive or active? Are the sentences varied? Do they share a certain style?
- What **diction** (types of words) is most common? Is a type of jargon used? Is slang used? How would you describe the writer's voice?

4. Analyze What These Patterns Reveal about the Situation and Scene

What do these rhetorical patterns reveal about the genre, its situation, and the scene in which it is used? Why are these patterns significant? What can you learn about the actions being performed through the genre by observing its language patterns? What arguments can you make about these patterns? As you consider these questions, focus on the following:

- What do participants have to know or believe to understand or appreciate the genre?
- Who is invited into the genre, and who is excluded?
- What roles for writers and readers does it encourage or discourage?
- What values, beliefs, goals, and assumptions are revealed through the genre's patterns?
- How is the subject of the genre treated? What content is considered most important? What content (topics or details) is ignored?
- What actions does the genre help make possible? What actions does the genre make difficult?
- What attitude toward readers is implied in the genre? What attitude toward the world is implied in it?

Now that you have practiced doing genre analysis, how can you use what you know about genre to make more effective writing choices? Identifying a genre's patterns and analyzing what they mean does not give writers a ready-made syllabus or complaint letter. Just as readers bring their own knowledge and beliefs to their reading and can choose to resist the roles defined for them by genres, writers also do more than just copy these patterns. Unlike a script for a play, where actors have all their lines written and need to choose only how to perform those lines, a genre's pattern or "script" does not tell us, as writers, exactly what actions to take, what roles to perform, or what sentences and words to use. What it does give us is a general sense of the scene and situation and some *general* rhetorical patterns, and we can use this knowledge of the scene and people's rhetorical behaviors within it to make more effective and informed writing choices.

Rather than staring at a blank page or screen and guessing about how to begin writing or what to write about, you can turn to your knowledge of genres. Writing becomes choosing, not guessing. By analyzing any given genre, for example, you can make choices regarding major rhetorical elements:

Your purpose as writer   Knowing what genres are available in a given scene and how and why they are used will help you decide which one can best accomplish your purpose in writing. On the other hand, if you are *assigned* a genre to write and are not sure about your purpose for writing it, studying the genre can show you the purposes other writers have pursued with that genre. In either case, purpose and genre are inter-related: Your purpose for writing affects your choice of genre and your choice of genre affects your purpose.

Your role as a writer   Your role as a writer has to do with the kind of persona you choose to present in order to be persuasive as a speaker or writer. For example, should you be aggressive, soft-spoken, excited, subdued, or confident? The persona you choose will have a great deal to do with how effectively you write within a specific scene, as we saw in the example of the complaint letter. The patterns of behavior and communication within a genre will help you choose the role within that scene that will be the most appropriate in fulfilling your purpose.

Your readers   Certain genres are geared toward certain readers (the syllabus is geared toward students, the resumé toward an employer). By analyzing the genre, you learn something about your readers even though they may not be physically present. What do readers *expect* from the genre? For instance, do they expect to be treated with respect? Do they expect you to assume authority? Do they expect to laugh or cry or both? Do they expect you to be detailed, technical, and complicated, or do they expect simple and direct communication? Knowing something about your readers as revealed through the genre will help you "see" your audience, much like we began to "see" the audience during our analysis of the complaint letter. Such knowledge will help you decide what genre most suits your purpose.

Your subject matter   Any given subject can be treated in different ways depending on the genre used. A writer who analyzes the genres first is in a better position to decide which genre to write and then how to treat the subject matter. Using your knowledge of these genres, contemplate your subject matter: How should you introduce it? Should you treat it objectively or personally? Do you need to explain it in detail or is such explanation unnecessary? Should you present it logically or emotionally or sarcastically, etc.? Do you need to provide examples? Should you be descriptive, argumentative, or both? Should you present both sides of the subject? Do you need to quote experts on the subject or can you depend on your own authority? And so on. Knowledge of the genre will help you make some of these decisions about what and how to write.

Your format and organization   On a very obvious level, knowledge of a genre's patterns will help you decide how to format your writing. A resumé, for example, is formatted differently from a complaint letter. Knowing this, you begin to conceptualize the appearance of your text so that what may have begun as a blank page or screen suddenly has a shape. You can decide if you should present your content in the form of tables and charts, graphics, lists, prose, or poetry. The structural features of a genre will help you decide not only how to format the physical appearance of your writing; they will also help you decide how to present and organize your ideas. For example, by learning the patterns of a genre, you can decide what to mention first, second, third, and so on. You can learn whether the main ideas are stated at the beginning or at the end, whether to move from generalities to particularities or from particularities to generalities. You can also decide what kinds of transitions, if any, to use between different sections of the text. In short, not only will your genre knowledge help you approach your subject matter, but it will also help you present your subject matter in certain ways.

Your sentences and word choices   Having read samples of your genre should have given you a sense of the typical style used in that situation, a feel for what texts in that genre sound like. You can imitate that style, trying to make your text sound like the ones you studied. As you revise your draft and take a more explicit and conscious approach, knowing something about the genre's sentence and diction patterns will help you decide, for instance, whether to use active or passive sentences. It will also help you decide how long your sentences should be and what kind of complexity and variation is expected. In the resumé, for example, sentences often begin with a verb rather than a subject and need to be consistent ("Managed the sales department," "Served as liaison between employer and employees"). In other genres, of course, different sentence styles are preferred. The same applies to word choices. In scientific research articles, for example, the people being studied are often referred to as "subjects" while the pronoun "you" appears frequently in business letters. By looking at the patterns in word choice within a genre, you will be able to make more effective decisions about what words to use and why.

What we have just presented is meant only as a set of guidelines for using your knowledge of a genre to make more effective writing choices within that genre. There is no exact formula. The more you practice genre analysis, the more skillful you will become at reading genre scenes and situations. The better you are able to read and understand the patterns of a genre, the better you will become at knowing what purpose these patterns serve and how to make use of them in your writing. The next chapter will expand on this initial list and help you develop strategies for turning your reading of a genre into your writing of a genre.

Writing Activity

Review the genre you analyzed collaboratively in the last sets of activities, including the samples you collected, your notes, and your conclusions. Based on your analysis, describe what a writer needs to understand about the scene and situation in order to write that genre. Use our suggested guidelines in Box 7.1 and be as specific as you can. As a writer of this genre, what choices would you make regarding your role as writer, your readers, your subject matter, your format and structure, and your sentences and word choices? Record your responses and be prepared to share them with your teacher and classmates. Think of this activity as an exercise in prewriting, planning, and invention.

The material that follows is taken from Anne Frances Wysocki and Dennis A. Lunch's *The DK Handbook.*

A Comparison of Academic and Workplace Genres

	ACADEMIC GENRES	**WORKPLACE GENRES**
TEXTS	Academic papers, reports, articles in scholarly journals—also academic blogs	Memos, proposals, resumés, project plans, progress reports, white papers, executive summaries
AUDIENCES & PURPOSES	Academic genres help specialists build and share knowledge that is widely useful across the humanities, social sciences, sciences, engineering, and medicine.	Worksplace genres help people get work done quickly and efficiently—and so such genres address how people work together as well as the products, services, and processes they use and produce.
AUDIENCE EXPECTATIONS	Academic audiences expect academic texts to be: • serious • direct • explicit • objective and unbiased • supported with evidence • respectful of previous knowledge • cautious in their claims, only making claims that can be supported by evidence	Workplace audiences generally expect workplace texts to be: • short • focused • to-the-point • easy-to-read • full of immediately useful information supported by some degree of research

The Values of Academic Genres

As you will see in the following pages, different academic disciplines have different expectations about how writing within the discipline is organized, but all disciplines share these general expectations:

Academic Writing is about Building Knowledge

Academic audiences expect that you approach writing seriously because through writing you add to our understandings of the world and each other. This means that you have to take existing arguments seriously, research and gather evidence methodically and honestly, and make only the arguments that you can support with evidence.

Academic Writing uses Logical Development of Ideas and Tries to be Objective and Unbiased

Logic is about ideas that relate to each other because of their structure or form—as thesis statements do, and as papers that are organized around thesis statements do.

The point of view of academic writing is rarely personal, rarely focused on the writer. Instead, the emphasis is on the argument being made and on ideas that benefit as many people as possible.

Academic Writing Gets to and Stays on the Point

An introduction moves quickly to stating what the paper is about. The writer ought to be able to explain how each and every sentence helps move a reader to the conclusion. Any digression must fit well with purpose.

Academic Writing is Explicit

Academic writers say directly what their writing is about. In fiction and creative nonfiction, writers use figurative language frequently to pull readers in and suggest an overall point without ever stating the point; academic writing rarely does this.

Academic writers also give full definitions of the terms of their arguments because they understand that many readers have differing understandings of terms.

Academic Writing Always has an Element of Doubt

Academic writers accept that there are very few thoughts and ideas that apply to everyone, everywhere, at all times. Instead, academic writers consider a range of reasons and opinions.

To this end, academic writers often use phrases like *These facts suggest* … or *Given the available evidence, it would seem that* ….

Academic Writing is not Conversational

Academic writers strive for a thoughtful tone of voice, and rarely tell jokes or use emotional language or colloquialisms (such as *no-brainer* or *oh, snap!*). In some disciplines, writers will use **I** and will use their own experiences as evidence or examples; reading examples of writing in a discipline will help you learn the particulars of the discipline. (For help with writing assignments in classes in disciplines that are new to you, ask your teacher.)

Academic writing usually uses longer words and sentences, more vocabulary, and more complex grammar than spoken language.

Academic Writers are Responsible for Their Arguments and to Other Writers

Academic writers can't just say anything; instead, they must take responsiblity for any claims they make by giving supporting evidence and by helping readers check that evidence. In addition, they are responsible for showing when the evidence they offer comes from the work or words of others: Academic writers give careful and full acknowledgment of any use of the ideas of others.

The material that follows is taken from Lester Faigley's *The Brief Penguin Handbook*.

Writing an Academic Position Paper

When you imagine an argument, you might think of two people with different views, engaged in a heated debate—maybe even shouting slogans. In college courses, in public life, and in professional careers, written arguments are meant to persuade readers who refuse to accept a **claim** when it is expressed as a slogan.

Written arguments

- offer evidence and reasons,
- examine the assumptions on which the evidence and reasons are based,
- explore opposing arguments, and
- anticipate objections.

You may want to convince your readers to change their thinking about an issue or perhaps get them to consider the issue from your perspective. Or you may want your readers to take some course of action based on your argument. These two kinds of arguments can be characterized as **position** and **proposal arguments**.

Find an Arguable Topic and Make a Claim

In a position argument you make a claim about a controversial issue. You

- define or rebut the issue,
- take a clear position,
- make a convincing argument, and
- acknowledge opposing views.

Position arguments often take two forms—definition arguments and rebuttal arguments.

People argue about definitions (for example, is graffiti vandalism or is it art?) because of the consequences of something being defined in a certain way. If you can get your audience to accept your definition, then usually your argument will be successful.

Definition arguments take the form shown here.

Something is (or is not) _____ because it has (or does not have) Criteria A, Criteria B, and Criteria C (or more).

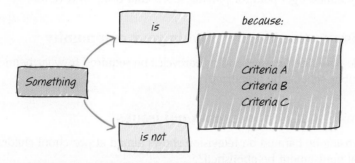

Graffiti is art because it is a means of self-expression, it shows an understanding of design principles, and it stimulates both the senses and the mind.

Rebuttal arguments take the opposite position. You can challenge the criteria a writer uses to make a definition or you can challenge the evidence that supports the claim. Often the evidence presented is incomplete or wrong. Sometimes you can find counterevidence.

Rebuttal arguments take this form.

The opposing argument has serious shortcomings that undermine the claim because
        flawed reason 1
        flawed reason 2

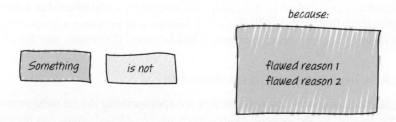

The great white shark gained a false reputation as a "man eater" from the 1975 movie *Jaws*, but in fact attacks on humans are rare and most bites have been "test bites," which is a common shark behavior with unfamiliar objects.

Finding an arguable topic

Probably you know people who will argue about almost anything. Some topics, however, are much better suited than others for writing an extended argument. One way to get started is to make a list of topics you care about. Below are examples of other starting points.

Think about issues that are debated on your campus

- Should admissions decisions be based solely on academic achievement?
- Should varsity athletes get paid for playing sports that bring in revenue?

Think about issues that are debated in your community

- Should people who ride bicycles and motorcycles be required to wear helmets?
- Should the public schools be privatized?

Think about national and international issues

- Should advertising be banned on television shows aimed at preschool children?
- Should capital punishment be abolished?

Read about your issue

- What are the major points of view on your issue?
- Who are the experts on this issue? What do they have to say?
- What major claims are being offered?
- What reasons are given to support the claims?
- What kinds of evidence are used to support the reasons?
- How can you add to what has been said about your subject?

Supporting claims with reasons

The difference between a slogan, such as *Oppose candidate X*, and an arguable claim, such as *Oppose candidate X because she will not lower taxes and not improve schools*, is the presence of a reason linked to the claim. A reason is typically offered in a ***because*** **clause**, a statement that begins with the word *because* and provides a supporting reason for the claim. The word *because* signals a link between the reason and the claim.

Claims must be specific and contestable

In addition to being supported by reasons that are appropriately linked to it, your claim must also be *specific*. Broad general claims, such as *The United States has become too crowded*, are nearly impossible to argue effectively. Often general claims contain more restricted claims that can be argued, such as *The United States should increase its efforts to reduce illegal immigration* or *The amount of land in national parks should be doubled to ensure adequate wild spaces for future generations.*

Your claim must also be contestable. Your claim that you like sour cream on a baked potato is specific, but not contestable. No matter how often you are told that a baked potato is less fattening without sour cream, the fact that you like sour cream won't change. You may stop eating the sour cream, but you won't stop wanting to eat it.

Organize and Write a Position Argument

Thinking of reasons to support a claim is not hard. What *is* hard is convincing your audience that your reasons are good ones. Imagine you will have critical readers. Whenever you put forward a reason, they will ask *So what?* You will have to have evidence, and you will have to link that evidence to your claim in ways they will accept if they are to agree that your reason is a good reason. Be open to new ideas while you are writing. Often you will go back and forth in developing a position argument.

---

1 | Before you write

Think about your readers
- What do your readers already know about the subject?
- What is their attitude toward the subject? If it is different from your position, how can you address the difference?
- What are the chances of changing the opinions and beliefs of your readers? If your readers are unlikely to be moved, can you get them to acknowledge that your position is reasonable?
- Are there any sensitive issues you should be aware of?

---

2 | Write an introduction

Engage your readers quickly
- Get your readers' attention with an example of what is at stake.
- Define the subject or issue.
- State your thesis to announce your position.

3 | Organize and write the body of your paper

Develop reasons
- Can you argue from a definition? Is _____ a _____?

Examples

Are cheerleaders athletes?
Are zoos guilty of cruelty to animals?
- Can you compare and contrast? Is _____ like or unlike _____?
- Can you argue that something is good (better, bad, worse)?
- Can you argue that something caused (or may cause) something else?
- Can you refute objections to your position?

Support reasons with evidence
- Can you support your reasons by going to a site and making observations?
- Can you find facts, statistics, or statements from authorities to support your reasons?

Consider opposing views
- Acknowledge other stakeholders for the issue, and consider their positions.
- Explain why your position is preferable.
- Make counterarguments if necessary.

4 | Write a conclusion

End with more than a summary
- Think of a strong way to end by offering more evidence in support of your thesis, reinforcing what is at stake, or giving an example that gets at the heart of the issue.

5 | Revise, revise, revise

Evaluate your draft
- Make sure your position argument meets the assignment requirements.
- Can you sharpen your thesis to make your position clearer?
- Can you add additional reasons to strengthen your argument?
- Can you supply additional evidence?
- Examine your language for bias and emotionally loaded words and reword if needed.
- When you have finished revising, edit and proofread carefully.

Two Sample Academic Position Papers
Sample Position Paper Using MLA

Mariela Martinez

Professor Barnes

English 102

13 April 2013

Should Students Have the Right of Freedom of Speech?

In January 2002, students at Juneau-Douglas High School in Juneau, Alaska, were dismissed from classes for a parade sponsored by a local business for the Winter Olympic Torch Relay, which passed in front of the school. Across the street and off of school grounds, high school senior Joseph Frederick, who had not attended school that day, and his friends waited until the torch and cameras approached. They then unfurled a banner that read "Bong Hits 4 Jesus." The outraged school principal, Deborah Morse, ran across the street and seized the banner. She then suspended Frederick for five days and later increased the penalty to ten days when Frederick quoted Thomas Jefferson on the right of freedom of speech (Sherman).

Frederick appealed to the Superintendent and the Juneau School Board, which denied his appeal. He then filed suit against Morse and the school board, claiming they had violated his First Amendment right to freedom of speech. The federal district court ruled in favor of Morse and the school board. The United States Court of Appeals for the Ninth Circuit, however, reversed the district court in a unanimous decision, ruling that

> The first and second paragraphs give the background of an issue that likely is unfamiliar to most readers.

Martinez 2

Frederick's right to freedom of speech had been violated (Hussain). The Juneau School Board then took the case to the United States Supreme Court, which heard oral arguments on March 19, 2007. Kenneth Starr, the Whitewater prosecutor during the Clinton administration, presented the case for the school board.

At first glance the incident seems blown enormously out of proportion, certainly unworthy of consuming many hours of a federal judge's time. Frederick's banner was a stupid prank done in poor taste by an adolescent. He is far from the ideal poster child for free speech. But the underlying issue is huge. I maintain that there is no reason to restrict the First Amendment rights of students when they are not disrupting the school. To give school authorities the right to control anything a student says anywhere far exceeds any reasonable interpretation of our Constitution.

In the third paragraph Martinez gives her interpretation that the event was not worthy of the attention it received. Then she states her thesis that students' rights to freedom of speech should be protected.

Attorney Kenneth Starr argued before the Supreme Court that Morse's censorship of Frederick was justified because of the precedent set in Bethel School District v. Fraser. In that 1986 case, the Supreme Court ruled that public schools could limit student speech at a school assembly. Vulgar or obscene speech could be censored. The court decided that

> [T]he undoubted freedom to advocate unpopular and controversial views in schools and classrooms must be balanced against the society's countervailing interest in teaching students the boundaries of socially appropriate behavior.

But that case involved a school assembly on school property. Starr argued that Frederick v. Morse is comparable because students had been collectively released from school to watch the Olympic torch pass by and were accompanied by their teachers.

Martinez examines the opposing position. She concludes that the evidence cited by the opposition does not apply to the Juneau case.

The case Morse v. Frederick is not, as Starr maintained, about protecting young people from "the scourge of drugs." The drug reference is a red herring. Frederick described the words as nonsense meant to get the attention of the television cameras (Biskupic). The banner was not pornographic or obscene. The banner did not incite violence. The only violent act was the principal's seizing the banner. Neither could it be interpreted as attacking Christianity. Organizations that litigate on behalf of the religious right including the Christian Legal Society and the American Center for Law and Justice, founded by the Rev. Pat Robertson, have sided with Frederick (Greenhouse).

Martinez argues that Frederick's banner neither broke any laws nor did it insult Christian organizations because the religious right sided with Frederick.

Instead the case is an effort by school administrators supported by their professional organizations to get the Supreme Court to allow them to censor anything they disagree with. This effort is chilling because they currently have the power to censor obscene, violent, and libelous speech. It is an attempt to use the public's fear about illegal drugs to justify heavy-handed authoritarian control of student expression, whether on or off campus. Morse and Starr may not like to admit it, but the First Amendment does apply in our nation's public schools. The U.S. Supreme Court decided in 1969, in the case of Tinker et al. v. Des Moines Independent Community School District, that students do have the right of political expression. The court ruled that as long as the student's expression does not disrupt

Martinez supplies evidence that students do have the right of political expression when they are not disruptive.

Martinez 4

the educational environment, officials cannot suppress it (Haynes). The Supreme Court has long maintained that speech that is unpleasant or uncomfortable is nonetheless protected.

Frederick's prank was stupid and boorish, but imagine that Frederick held up a banner protesting racial segregation in the South in 1961. We would now see his act as courageous. Indeed, students were at the forefront of the Civil Rights movement, and many school administrators opposed their actions. Principal Morse was not wrong to disagree with Frederick's message, but she was wrong to censor it. The Supreme Court declared in its Tinker ruling in 1969 that students do not "shed their constitutional rights to freedom of speech or expression at the 'schoolhouse gate.'" The First Amendment is fundamental to our sense of what the United States is about, and we should always be vigilant when those in power seek to limit freedom of speech.

In her conclusion, Martinez reiterates that she does not think Frederick's prank was a good idea, but the principal was wrong to deny his right to freedom of speech off of school property. She gives additional evidence that the Supreme Court has ruled in the past that students do have freedom of speech.

Martinez 5

Works Cited

Bethel School Dist. v. Fraser. 478 US 675. Supreme Court of the US. 1986. *Supreme Court Collection*. Legal Information Inst., Cornell U Law School, n.d. Web. 3 Apr. 2013.

Biskupic, Joan. "Justices Debate Student's Suspension for Banner." *USA Today*. 20 Mar. 2007: 3A. Print.

Greenhouse, Linda. "Free Speech Case Divides Bush and Religious Right." *New York Times*. 18 Mar. 2007, final ed.: A22. Print.

Haynes, Charles C. "T-shirt Rebellion in the Land of the Free." First Amendment Center. *First Amendment Center*, Vanderbilt U, 14 Mar. 2004. Web. 4 Apr. 2013.

Hussain, Murad. "The 'Bong' Show: Viewing Frederick's Publicity Stunt Through Kulmeier's Lens." *Yale Law Journal Pocket* Parts. Yale U Law School, 9 Mar. 2007. Web. 2 Apr. 2013.

Sherman, Mark. "'Bong Hits 4 Jesus' Banner Case Reaches Supreme Court." Lansing State Journal. *Lansing State Journal*, 16 Mar. 2007. Web. 2 Apr. 2013.

Tinker et al. v. Des Moines Independent Community School Dist. 393 US 503. Supreme Court of the US. 1969. *Supreme Court Collection*. Legal Information Inst., Cornell U Law School, n.d. Web. 3 Apr. 2013.

The material that follows is taken from Amy Devitt, Mary Jo Reiff, and Anis Bawarshi's *Scenes of Writing.*

Sample Position Paper Using APA Style

Elliott 1

Eugene Elliott

In Case of Emergency, Please Wait

The basic thought of having to wait is both unappealing and agitating to most people. However, when the concept of waiting is applied to emergency situations, the resulting behavior can be shocking. As Malign Akerstrom (1997) presented in her study of a Swedish emergency clinic, one of the most challenging aspects of a waiting room is "dealing with angry patients whose aggression mainly stemmed from their having to wait" (p. 504). As patients, waiting is a source of hostility primarily because we perceive waiting as a costly waste of our precious time (Akerstrom, 1997, p. 506). A key result of this hostility, from the perspective of both workers and waiters, is vented frustrations towards each other. In interviews with nursing staff, many "reported drastic physical events of aggression due to waiting" (Aker strom, 1997, p. 508). These events were reported to include staring, derogatory remarks "about their being ugly, fat, lazy," and also indirect comments referring to the staff's incompetence (Akerstrom, 1997, p. 508–509). The professionalism of the nurses usually seemed to override the urge to take revenge. Nevertheless, sometimes the irritation becomes so great that an inadvertent evil look or stare is directed towards the patient, and "sarcastic backstage talk" takes a "veiled" form of retaliation (Akerstrom, 1997, p. 517). Through observing the emergency waiting room at Pitt County Memorial Hospital, similar behavior can be assessed, as well as other responses to the anxiety of waiting.

In one corner of the waiting room, a mother sits with her children, anxiously awaiting news of her husband's condition (he had been brought in with severe chest pain). The kids, unaware of the importance of the situation, play loudly, running and shouting despite the quiet, tense atmosphere. Already upset by the events unfolding, she suddenly screams at the little boy while grabbing the girl's arm and orders them to "sit down and shut the hell up!" This outburst attracts the attention of everyone in the room. Some people glance quickly, while others look onward out of curiosity to see what would follow. One particular nurse, obviously used to this behavior, rolls her eyes, glances at her co-worker and continues working. The children sit quietly watching television carefully looking at their mother often.

For a while thereafter, the room is fairly calm. One gentleman sits reading Dubliners, by James Joyce, while the other nine people watch the six o' clock news on Channel 12. Gradually, some people go to the exam rooms while still more trickle in, and the conversations grow louder, until it becomes impossible to hear the television. A baby, about four or five months old begins crying hysterically, until her mother, apparently pregnant once again, lifts her from her carseat and breastfeeds her right

Elliott 2

there where they are sitting. Quite a response erupts. A rhythmic mumbling can be heard as women roll their eyes and stare, whereas the men seem to pretend not to notice, finding something else to look at. Oddly enough, although she had registered with the triage nurse only moments earlier, she is called back almost immediately. Representative of a society uncomfortable with the display of nursing young, this is an example of how changes in values through the years have effected responses to once ordinary daily events (Mead, 1930, p. 237).

As the waiting room gets more and more crowded, one elderly gentleman paces back and forth mumbling something unintelligible to anyone else. He maintains the same path until he is finally called. Apparently his wife is currently being treated. As he leaves, another lady sitting across from me quips, "He was getting on my nerves with that pacing," apparently unaware that for the last fifteen minutes she had been thumbing nervously through every magazine on the table. Within the next couple minutes, a seating situation becomes evident. As new patients check in, the difficult decision of choosing a seat is begun. A slight division in the seating arrangement becomes noticeable, with a majority of white patients against one wall, and another section where blacks and Hispanics are sitting. Similar to the observations of Margaret Mead (1930) where ". . . men who are of kin build their houses side by side . . .", so do people of the same race sit together (p. 236). This trend continues, as each new arrival carefully scans the room and chooses his or her seat likewise.

Eventually, the effects of waiting and being confined to the crowded quarters begins to take its toll, as several people approach the nurse's station and inquire on how much longer the wait should be. Phrases such as "I don't have all damn day" and "I'm glad I'm not dyin' as slow as this place is," can be heard in quiet whisper, mostly being said to oneself. Only when a man walks in with what appears to be a popsicle stick protruding from his arm, does the monotonous chatter break as everyone stares, some cringing at the sight but continuing to look out of curiosity. Following directly behind this man, there is a hospital security guard assisting as a Greenville police officer escorts a prisoner bearing handcuffs and foot chains. Yet again a unanimous stare ensues as he checks in, then is escorted outside to wait for his name to be called.

With an almost capacity crowd, conversations can be overheard from everywhere, ranging from the purpose of someone's emergency room visit, the news, and especially how long the wait is. One younger lady who had earlier stated her problem as having been nauseous for several days, jumps up and darts towards the bathroom, vomiting just by the payphones. Seeing that she is obviously sick, a nurse helps her on back, and within three minutes a janitor is cleaning up the accident. Moments later, a gentleman whom the nurse refers to as Mr. Curry walks up to the triage desk. He had been smoking about every ten minutes for the past hour, nervously awaiting his turn. On this approach however, he yells out "Never mind, f_ this s_t" and storms out. The nurse says that she was getting ready to call his name. From this moment,

Elliott 3

the complaining was minimal. The crowd dwindles down to about five people left waiting. The new waiters watching television or reading magazines make evident the endless cycle of emergency room visits.

Emergency room waiting can be a painstaking process that tests the patience of both the hospital staff and the waiting patients. The concept of being placed in a confined area with strangers of many different backgrounds and lifestyles can be tense, especially in a critical emergency situation. Even the sincerest person can become agitated and sometimes enraged to the point of saying or doing things that he or she wouldn't do normally. This dramatic effect on human behavior is worthy of further research. Other aspects of waiting room anxiety stem from the design, decor, climate control, etc., or the lack thereof, of the particular room (Akerstrom, 1997, p. 507). Possibly examining the influence of the environment as well as attention deterring activities such as movies, games, fish aquariums and other entertaining alternatives may lead to more adequate waiting rooms with less stress and irritation. Researching the combined effects of environment and intensity of waiting situations is essential to creating more hospitable, welcoming atmospheres. Nobody really likes to wait, but waiting is inevitable in a society with so many people and their individual needs. Through further experiments and research, waiting can be transformed from an agonizing dreaded experience, into an activity that can be done with minimal agitation and anxiety.

References

Akerstrom, M. (1997). Waiting—A source of hostile interaction in an emergency clinic. *Qualitative Health Research*, 7, 504–518.

Mead, M. (1930). Scenes from Manus life. In Comely, Hamilton, et al. *Fields of writing: Readings across the disciplines* (4th ed.) (pp. 235–241). New York: St. Martin's Press.

Planning Your Argument: Composing a Rhetorical Purpose

8

Working Toward a Statement of Purpose

In this chapter we show you how to analyze a composing situation—for a class, for work, for a nonprofit organization where you volunteer—so that you develop a rich and useful idea of what you need to accomplish, for whom, and when and where. We offer you an organized approach for thinking about your purposes, audiences, and contexts so that you can confidently approach producing the texts you need to produce.

The process of analyzing purposes, audiences, and contexts ends with **a statement of purpose**: This piece of writing helps you tie purposes, audiences, and contexts together, see how they interrelate, and suggest concrete choices for production.

How Does Developing a Statement of Purpose Fit into a Composing Process for Writing?

People who study writers and writing have learned that all effective writers have processes they follow to develop their writing. From writer to writer, these processes differ in their particulars, but generally involve:

- Figuring out the project: *What are the project's purpose, context, and audience?*
- Considering and planning different approaches to the project: *What choices does a writer need to make to shape writing for its audience, given its purpose and context?*
- Writing a draft.
- Getting feedback from the intended audience.
- Revising the draft in response to feedback.

(Note that it looks as though the steps are linear, but writers usually move back and forth among the steps as they figure out more about what they are doing and as, sometimes, they figure out that they have taken a wrong turn.)

Developing a statement of purpose aligns with the first step of the process: By developing a statement of purpose, you can figure out, in a structured and useful way, what it is you need to accomplish with a text you are composing.

Chapter 8, Planning Your Argument: Composing a Rhetorical Purpose Statement, is taken from Anne Frances Wysocki and Dennis A. Lynch's *Compose Design Advocate*, pp. 32–52 (Chapter 2, Composing a Statement Purpose).

What's the Difference Between a Statement of Purpose and a Thesis Statement?

A thesis statement summarizes the argument of writing:

> Modern language classes prepare students to live within the expanding global economy because modern language classes expose students to other cultures.

A thesis statement can suggest the points a writer needs to make in a piece of argumentative writing and so is highly useful. But a thesis statement does not help a writer think about tone of voice, how much emotion to fold into the writing, or what sorts of supporting examples (and in what order) will be most effective.

A statement of purpose, on the other hand, by helping a writer think deeply about purpose, context, and audience—and about their relations—sets a writer up to make those choices.

Looking Ahead: What Do You Do With a Statement of Purpose?

We've described how a statement of purpose ties together purpose, audience, and context, and so prepares a writer to make specific choices about writing or other composing projects.

Those choices start to happen when a writer develops a design plan out of the statement of purpose—as you will see in the next chapter. A design plan enables a writer to make direct connections between purpose, audience, and context and strategies, arrangement, and medium.

Purpose

WHAT ARE YOU TRYING TO DO?

To develop a sense of your purpose for any text you are composing, ask yourself the questions and follow the prompts below. Write down your answers: You need to be able to come back to your ideas to see how you can change or add to them after you think about your audience and context.

What is your motivation in this communication situation?

In other words, why are you communicating? What do you hope to achieve by building the piece of communication you are approaching?

It might be that you are thinking about this question because you have to write a paper for a class, which is an external motivation. You will do your best work if you are also motivated from within: If you have to put time into building communication, work to find reasons that matter to you. Your own curiosity about a topic is enough, but also think about building communication that helps you make connections with others or that helps you learn something new.

What do you hope your audience will do or feel or think after having experienced the communication you will produce?

Do you want more people to vote, or do you want your audience to know more about the situation in Iraq, or do you want others to understand how your relationship with your grandparents, aunts, and uncles was critical to who you are today? Do you want your teacher to be dazzled by the thoughtful, critical, hard work you have done? Do you want people to stop driving cars and ride bikes more, or do you want them be better at doing mathematical word puzzles?

Do you want to educate, entertain, or inform others—or to do some mix of these?

The more specific you can be here about how you want your audience to respond to the communication you are building, the more easily you will be able to shape your communication toward those ends.

If there is some event or situation that made you want to communicate with others, describe it in as much detail as possible.

Sometimes we are motivated to write by seeing something happen to others, or by reading something with which we agree—or disagree—strongly. Because this is motivation, it is important for you to recognize this, so that you can be sure to help your audience understand where you are coming from; the audience will be more likely then to understand your reasons for communicating what and how you do… and when the people who hear you understand your reasons, they are generally able to make better judgments about your communication.

What would be the best possible outcome of the communication?

If you can imagine exactly what you would like to happen, then you can use what you imagine to guide and encourage you as you work.

What would be the worst possible outcome?

Knowing what failure looks like can help you figure out strategies for avoiding it.

How will your communication change the situation in which you make the communication?

That is, is your purpose worthwhile? When you picture the best possible outcome for the communication you are building, are you imagining effects that are worth striving to achieve? If not, perhaps you should rethink what you are contemplating.

■ ■ ■ **PRACTICE WITH PURPOSE…**

The situations described below might seem obvious to you, but in working out a sense of purpose, you will clarify what it is you want to achieve—which will help you in thinking about audience and context in the next pages.

1. Imagine you've just found out your application to study abroad for a semester has been turned down by the committee that makes such decisions. You are thinking about appealing the decision. Use the questions above to write your sense of purpose in making the appeal.

2. A class you want to take is full, and you are planning to talk with the professor to try to get in. Use the questions above to write your sense of purpose in talking with the professor.

■ ■ ■

FURTHER DEVELOPING YOUR PURPOSE

The questions on the preceding two pages ask you to consider—regarding the text you are composing—where you are now and where you would like to be in the future. Thinking about purpose thus starts you toward "designing possible futures" for you and your audiences.

The future you envision needn't be a full-scale, fully worked out city, country, or universe. You can think about possible futures for your church, workplace, or neighborhood—changes like bike paths or recycling or fair access to resources or Sunday afternoon potluck dinners—and then work to compose communications to engage others with your imaginings.

developing your purpose for the present: complex motivations

Writing tasks often have "layers of motivation." Sometimes your motivation will seem simple—"I've been assigned a paper"—but it also can be more complex—"I want to build a webpage to teach others about neuropathic diseases because my father was just diagnosed and there's nothing available except in complex medical jargon and there's no way to communicate with others whose family members have this diagnosis."

It thus can be a good idea to try to separate the different parts of your motivation so you can be clear about your purposes.

For example, Martin Luther King Jr. wrote a now famous letter—"Letter from Birmingham Jail"—to eight clergymen explaining his participation in civil disobedience. As he composed, he realized that the letter would probably be published and read by more people. Dr. King thus had to make sure he spoke the language of the clergymen and connected his purpose to their beliefs and values, but he also had to keep in mind that arguments that might be effective with the clergymen might not be effective with others. In this case, Dr. King had to keep straight the different motivations for speaking to the two audiences, to make sure that his purposes in each case did not conflict.

Look at the motivation we described for the website about neuropathic diseases. There's strong and empathetic motivation in the desire to connect with and help others—but this also means the person building the website will need to be careful not to be too personal and not to make the website all about her experiences if she is to help others be comfortable.

developing your purpose for the present: when the motivation isn't yours

When you're asked to give a presentation or write a memo at work or for an organization at which you're volunteering, the motivation for communication comes from outside you; you will communicate not only for yourself but also for someone else. In such circumstances, you need to be clear about differences between your values and the institution's. If you cannot communicate the values of the institution without qualification, you must either find compromises acceptable to both you and the institution or you must back out.

developing your purpose for the future: how will you live up to your motivation?

Our actions have short- and long-term consequences, and it is easy to lose sight of one or the other—and to have our efforts then become tangled. Look at Dr. King's situation: In the short term he wanted the clergymen to understand how his civil resistance and desire to speak truth to power flowed from his religion, but he realized that in the long term his thoughts and actions needed to be answerable to a broader public, especially (in this case) to a white middle-class public that felt threatened by his actions. As you consider what you want to achieve with your communication, ask:

■ Are my short-and long-term aims in harmony?

■ Am I in a position to ask of my audience what I am asking of them? Do I have the proper authority, or have I built up the proper trust with them?

■ Do I want to draw attention to myself and my cause at this time?

developing your purpose for the future: when the motivation isn't yours

We talked above about outside motivation when you communicate for someone else. But motivation can come from outside in another way, as when you are assigned a class paper. Sometimes you'll want to write such papers, sometimes not. And when you don't, this is how the future enters: If you cannot find internal motivation for writing, you plan a lousy future for yourself. You're planning frustration, boredom, or time you hurry through. If you can find a larger motivation for communicating—learning about written structures, perhaps, or trying out a creative approach—you'll make a much better future for yourself

developing your purpose for the future: does it help to break your purpose into different parts?

When you plan communications, think incrementally about achieving the future you want. That is, you might break down what you want into steps and in each case ask: Is this step worthwhile? Can I achieve this?

This process may also help you discover strategies that get overlooked when you are focused on the big picture. You may need to think about making multiple or smaller communications rather than one big one.

YOUR RESPONSIBILITIES

■ As you work out your purpose in communicating, your responsibilities are to yourself, to the people with whom you'll be communicating, and to everyone around you:

1. *To yourself*, you are responsible for finding reasons to communicate that help you further your understandings of others and of communicating in general. There is no reason to do this work

(Continued)

if you are not learning, if you are not gaining in competence and confidence in moving through and improving the world.

2. *To those with whom you are communicating,* you are responsible for finding purposes that are worth their time and attentions and that show that you care about the matters that lie between you and them.

3. *To everyone else...* Because communication is what binds us together and helps build—for better or worse—our communities, you are responsible for finding communicative purposes that respond to what is needed around you, that contribute usefully to the networks in which we all live.

TO ANALYZE

■ **Write informally for a few minutes:** List five things that matter to you in the world or that you like to do. Take an assignment that's been given to you, one for which you have either a printed or an online description. Rewrite the assignment to give it a purpose that helps you engage with at least one of the things that matters to you.

■ **Write informally for a few minutes:** Imagine tuition at your school is being raised. You probably have a straightforward and personal motivation to argue against the raise. You might not have the money or it might be hard to find (and you're already working two jobs). But administrators who make the decision about tuition will probably be unmoved by such a narrow purpose because it is so personal. In what ways can you make your sense of purpose more complex—to include effects on others or on the school or your community—so that it is more likely to engage others?

Audience

WHOM ARE YOU ADDRESSING?

Audiences are not one-dimensional and they generally do not want to be treated that way. You probably do not like it when you are treated only as a student or as a young person who doesn't know anything or hasn't experienced anything in the world. You can probably remember times you were angered when someone spoke to you as though you were only a simple-minded stoner or metalhead or teenager or hair-club member. We are all more complex than any title or epithet can convey—and when we acknowledge that complexity in the ways we treat people, we shape better relations among us all.

Nor is any audience just three dimensional: We are all at least four dimensional, because we live in time. We all exist as bodies with histories, and we have particular identities, allegiances, roles, memberships, and commitments that have developed and shifted over time. All these qualities contribute to how we read, understand each other when we are talking, and look at all the paper and computer screens around us.

To develop a picture of your audience that can guide your other decisions in building communication, perform the following steps:

Generate a list of audience characteristics.

The idea here is to generate as full a list as you can of any and all characteristics shared by your intended audience. As you produce your communication, what may seem the oddest characteristics can sometimes suggest to you highly useful and persuasive strategies or arrangements.

There are many categories of characteristics you can think through to generate your list. Think of your audience's attitudes, beliefs, and habits. Think of audience members' backgrounds, how and where they grew up. Think of material qualities like age, race, gender, sexual orientation, and able-bodiedness. Think of their state of mind because of the time of day or place of communication.

Imagine your audience members at the moment they encounter the communication you make, no matter what you're making.

Try imagining using different media for your communication, to get the widest sense of the conditions under which your audience members can respond. What attitudes or moods are they likely to be in, and why? What might they be thinking? Why should they be interested in your communication? Why might they be disinterested, or hostile?

Add all your observations to the audience characteristic list you've made.

Filter your list.

Which characteristics are most relevant to the purpose you have so far developed? Cross out—tentatively—any characteristics that you can't see as shaping your audience one way or another toward what you hope to achieve.

If your purpose, as you've stated it so far, is to persuade women to join the "Fast Car" project, then you know that your audience is composed of women: But it will also be important that you recognize that the women might be curious but also a bit apprehensive because they are being addressed by men on a primarily male campus and about a project that had in the past included almost exclusively men. The women might also be tired, if your meeting with them is at night, or late in the semester.

The idea is not to shorten your lists as much as possible, but rather to develop as complex and rich an idea of your audience as you can. By thinking of your audience complexly, you will treat it as being composed of the complex people they are.

■ ■ ■ **PRACTICE WITH AUDIENCE…**

In the preceding section on purpose, we asked you to write your sense of purpose for two different situations, appealing a decision about studying abroad and trying to get into a closed class. For both situations, use the three steps on this page to write descriptions of the audiences for these situations. To write the most useful descriptions, ask others in your class what they know about these kinds of audiences on your campus; others may have experienced similar situations and have useful knowledge to share.   ■ ■ ■

FURTHER DEVELOPING YOUR SENSE OF AUDIENCE

To begin: Complex and Shifting Audience Characteristics

First, go through the list below and think about or discuss with others how these characteristics—when made concrete in a particular person of a particular age, and so on—impinge on communication. Also use the list to help you start thinking about the particular audience(s) you are addressing in any particular situation.

But the list is just a beginning . . .

been like leading up to the moment you see them. Notice how your thinking about someone changes when you look at the person while thinking perhaps he or she just came out of a difficult interview on which a career depends, or has been up all night helping a friend who's had a death in the family, or is just leaving on a well-deserved vacation.

When thinking about your audience, think of it not as an "audience" but as being composed of

---

consider an audience's . . .

- ❑ age
- ❑ gender
- ❑ ethnicity
- ❑ level of education
- ❑ able-bodiedness
- ❑ sexual orientation
- ❑ class
- ❑ upbringing
- ❑ place of living
- ❑ place of work
- ❑ emotional states (tired, angry, receptive . . .?)

- ❑ past experience with the topic/issue/matter
- ❑ learned habits (how audience members have learned to look at the topic/issue/matter)
- ❑ values/beliefs/commitments relative to the topic/issue/matter
- ❑ possible questions about the topic/issue/matter
- ❑ self-identity: the kinds of relations people see themselves as having with others (mother ± unemployed ± daughter ± Republican ± leftist ± rich ± boss ± worker ± student ± teacher ± friend ± poor ± ambitious ± ??)

The list complicates how we often judge people by age and gender. When we also think about the values audience members hold and their emotional states (because of a national crisis or a personal achievement) or the relationships that matter to them, we are more likely to think in ways that help us address them respectfully and so develop good relations with them.

Think about how . . .

the people in your audience have eventful lives

The next time you walk through a crowded space—a cafeteria or an airport, for example—look at the people around you and imagine what their days have

people who are free to move about the plane, who bite off more than they can chew, who get tangled up in blue . . . you get the idea. This makes them less formidable than when they seem like a faceless list of characteristics and helps you think about them generously and humanely.

(Some designers, in developing software or furniture or tools, make up imaginary people who might use what they are making. The designers give these imaginary people names, ages, occupations—all the characteristics in our list. Then the designers work as hard as they can to keep these imaginary people in mind as they design so that they think as concretely and complexly as possible about their audiences.)

Think about how . . .

you have preexisting institutional relationships with your audience

Imagine you are writing a paper for a teacher you hardly know (big stretch, eh?). If the teacher thinks of you as a *mere student* and so does not expect much from you but you want the teacher to see you as more, how can you design this relationship so that the teacher doesn't see you as *just another student*?

Look at this situation from the other angle. Being a teacher sets limits on how you can relate to students: You have a certain authority and students are (mostly) predisposed to acquiesce. What can you do if you do not want students just to fall in line but rather want them to be responsible for their own learning? You may shift your authority by giving students a range of choices and responsibilities, or by setting up small group discussions so that you are not always the center. Even so, when teachers do things like that, they can still undermine all their efforts by referring to students (for example) as "my" students. The possessive "my" can imply a certain paternalism that repositions students as children and thus undercuts a teacher's effort to get students to take more responsibility for the classroom and their educations. It is easy to fall back into old habits, especially around the roles we have in the institutions where we live, work, and play.

These examples show that our communications happen within already existing institutional relations. In addition to school, we go to church and we work in offices, fast-food outlets, chain stores, auto repair shops, and web design studios. We live in different kinds of families. Each of these institutions gives us titles—brother, *employee, head fry cook, niece, citizen, deputy chief*—and titles have meaning only relative to other people and their titles. You cannot be a father without a child, a head fry cook without an assistant (otherwise you are just "fry cook"), an employee without a boss, or a citizen without there being many other citizens.

Any time you communicate within such institutional frameworks, you need to keep the particularities of the relationships in mind. How do others see you because of who you are within the institution, and how do you see them? What expectations of behavior do people have about you—and you about them—because of your roles or titles or names? How might these expectations shape what you can say or write or show?

And do you need to step outside the relationships or call attention to them to achieve what you hope? Teachers can do this when they ask students to talk about the experiences of being students and when students then suggest how the teacher can change classroom structures or practices—such as grading policies or seating—so students feel more responsible in the class.

Put otherwise, the fact that you have a preexisting relationship with your audience does not need to hamstring your efforts to communicate. By thinking about your role and what your audience knows about you as part of the context of communication, your role becomes tied to your sense of purpose and thus becomes a part of what you need to strategize about.

Think about how . . .

you often have primary and secondary audiences

In a complicated world, what you want to accomplish can get complicated.

For example, the U.S. *Declaration of Independence* has layers of purposes addressed to multiple audiences. It was a declaration to the King of England that the authors—representing the people of the 13 original colonies—believed they had the right to break away from England and form a sovereign nation. But for the Declaration to do all the writers intended, they had to think about several other audiences as well: the people of England, not just the King; foreign governments with whom the colonies had been doing business and who would be worried about trading with "radical" people; and future generations of Americans who might look back and

(Continued)

wonder why the break with England was made. Neglecting any of these audiences would not only have made the *Declaration of Independence* less complex than it needed to be, but it would have excluded from consideration people who were being affected by the actions being declared.

Other texts can have multiple—primary and secondary—audiences. For example, you might be helping a domestic abuse shelter publicize its hotline, and, in working through this communication situation, you and the people at the shelter decide to put flyers about the hotline in restaurant and campus restrooms. But rather than just put the hotline's name and phone number on the flyer, you also describe all the different actions that count as domestic abuse, to help others understand whether they are in abusive relationships or perpetuating abuse. That is, your primary audience is those who have been abused and know it; your secondary audience is those who may not yet understand that they are in an abusive relationship.

Thinking long and hard about how your communication might have multiple audiences—sometimes hidden from view—is a good way to ensure that what you say is as complicated as it needs to be. It is also a good way to keep your eye on whom you are including and whom you are excluding (perhaps accidentally) by what you are saying or how you are saying it.

Think about how . . .
your audience is only ever your intended audience

You cannot compose communications that take into consideration every concern or feature of all audience members at the moment you communicate with them—even when you are speaking directly with them.

It is important, then, to keep in mind a distinction between your real audience and the audience you imagine as you prepare to communicate. As you plan and communicate you are living in the space between what you think, imagine, and believe about

your audience members and who they actually are and how they actually respond.

It can be humbling to remember that at the end of the day, after all the planning in the world, the moment the words leave your mouth (or the paper gets turned in), your communication is out of your hands.

Even though we can never be certain we have anticipated our audience's reactions correctly, we still must try. In the final analysis our audiences are both real and intended, both imagined and actual, and we have a hand in how our relationship to them plays out.

Think about how . . .
audiences step into the characteristics you imagine its members to have

Two pages ago we asked you to remember when you felt someone addressed you as though you were only a student or only a young person. We asked you to recall such memories because they are most often unpleasant.

But also recall when someone said something complimentary to you or introduced you as "the smartest person I know" or "my best friend." Remember how you probably felt a bit of a glow and more capable and at ease.

Now extend such memories into how you—and other communicators—address audiences.

This should remind us that we are responsible for how we imagine—or construct—our audiences, how we position their members, and whom we include and exclude in the process. When we address audiences, we are asking them to step into the characteristics we imagine they have. If we imagine those characteristics from a less than respectful view, audiences either must take on those characteristics or actively resist them. If we imagine the audience in positive ways, they will generally respond likewise.

As you consider your audience, then, do keep in mind how your decisions shape what you ask your audience to be and to do

YOUR RESPONSIBILITIES

- You are responsible for respecting your audiences as people who think and have good reasons for believing what they do.

- In order to make good on your responsibility to your audience, you need to listen carefully to what other people have to say about the piece of communication you are building. It is sometimes hard to hear critical feedback about what you produce, but it is important to acknowledge that others have good ideas about how you can strengthen what you make.

- You need to take seriously that any piece of communication you make—written, visual, oral, or any mix— affects other people. Take seriously that you can move other people for good or otherwise.

TO ANALYZE

- **Discuss with others:** David MacIntyre is a physics major. Here is his description of his audience and purpose as he was preparing to write a paper on space travel for a class:

  The audience for this paper is a person who has given little thought to the space program and probably sees no outstanding reason why he or she should be paying for it—in other words, nearly everyone. This is the type of person I hope to persuade to support the space program in general and in particular to support the idea of human spaceflight. This leads to two general ideas I have to keep in mind throughout my writing: First, I need to show that the space program as a whole is a benefit to society and, second, why sending humans into space is a valuable part of that project. At the end of my paper, my readers should not be asking themselves, 'Sure, that's great, but why not just send robots?'

  How does David's description connect his audience with his purpose? What more about his audience could David learn to help him achieve his purpose?

- **Write informally:** List the people with whom you have relationships shaped by the institutions within which you live and work. In your list, don't forget your religion, job, school, hospitals, civil institutions like the police and the Department of Motor Vehicles, your family, and the military. For each person you list, describe how your relationship shapes how you communicate.

- **Discuss with others:** Sometimes when you write papers you're told to consider your classmates as your audience—and yet you know you have to write to your teacher, too, since the teacher grades your writing. In such a situation, how do you think through these primary and secondary audiences? Who is primary to you—the teacher or the students? How do you address them?

  Similarly, you might in some classes produce communication for a client, with the communication aimed at still another group of people: For example, you might produce a poster—aimed at attracting young people to an after-school program—for a local nonprofit. The client has to approve the project—and it will be graded by the class teacher. What can you do to work with these primary and secondary audiences?

Context

WHERE AND WHEN IS YOUR COMMUNICATION?

As you work toward an effective piece of communication consider:

The time of the communication

Just when will the communication take place?

Is there a specific occasion that motivates the communication, such as a funeral where you've been asked to give the elegy or a presentation you must make at a conference about research you've been doing? Do you have to imagine the occasion because you won't be there, such as when someone comes to a website you've made, or when your teacher reads a paper you've written, or your father receives the birthday card you've sent him?

Can you picture the time of day or year? Does it matter to your audience the time at which they'll be receiving your communication? (For example, are you giving an oral presentation to your class as the last person of five speakers or at night, so that your listeners are likely to be tired and having a little trouble being attentive? Are you developing a fund-raising campaign for a nonprofit around Christmas time when people are likely to be a little more generous?)

The place of the communication

Where, exactly, will the communication take place? Will you be there?

Will your audience be in a temple, mosque, or church? And, if so, is it a large, formal, and imposing structure, or an informal, comfortable place? How will this shape the attitudes and expectations of your audience, as well as your comfort or level of nerves?

Will your audience be sitting in uncomfortable folding chairs, or in rows of desks? Will your audience be sitting at home, comfortable at their personal desks (or likely to doze in an armchair)?

Or will your audience see your posters up on a wall where all others are hanging their posters, too, so that you need yours to be a different color or size—or else taped to the sidewalk or some other place where your audience will be more likely to see them?

The broader context of the communication

How do time and place shape your audience's expectations? It's probably obvious that an audience at a funeral in a Gothic cathedral has different expectations than an audience for a business presentation—but nonetheless it's worth asking why.

In our time, Gothic cathedrals are not new—but the people who built them saw them as engineering marvels and signs of a community's willingness to commit years and tremendous resources to construct a representation of their belief in a God. Some of this sense has carried down to us, in part because of how our bodies feel in the large, light, airy spaces of cathedrals and in part because, whether or not we attend such cathedrals, we have seen and heard about them. Also, they are, simply, churches, built by their communities as holy spaces.

Most business meetings do not take place in holy spaces. Instead, business spaces are usually functional, and we have probably grown up associating business with getting things done, with moving quickly and getting to the point.

Asking about the spaces in which we communicate, and about the perceptions of time we attach to those spaces, gives us a better sense of audience expectations.

■ ■ ■ **PRACTICE WITH CONTEXT…**

In the sections on sense of purpose and audience, we asked you to consider two different situations, one in which you are appealing a decision about studying abroad, the other in which you are trying to get into a closed class. For both situations, describe the occasion of the communication you'll be making, its place, and its broader context of how and where decisions are made in schools. As with audience, if you find you need more information, describe what you need to learn and how you can learn it. You can ask others about their experiences in similar contexts on your campus. ■ ■ ■

FURTHER DEVELOPING YOUR SENSE OF AUDIENCE

On the preceding two pages, we asked you to consider the occasion of the communication, the place of the communication, and the broader context of the communication. Figuring out the specific event, time, and place is generally pretty easy. Determining other factors that might weigh on your communication can be difficult: It's hard to decide how broad your context is—but you can always benefit from thinking broadly.

You'll be most successful with context if you visualize the moment of communication. The more real you make this moment beforehand, the more you'll be able to develop strategies for approaching your audience and determine what media work best.

Notice also how context and audience overlap, as (for example) when you present a paper late on a panel or late in the day when your audience is tired and needs you to be more energetic and humorous than you might otherwise be. Because of this, revisit your description of your audience after you work through this section on context so that you can add any important characteristics you might have missed.

As you move on to consider a more complex understanding of your context you might:

ALSO Think about…

… how audiences perceive the time of communication

Arguing with a friend over which movie to see, you might understand the temporal context for the discussion to be just this one evening, but your friend may include past disagreements in which you always won. You might be giving a presentation about pollution's effects on frogs to a fourth-grade class: For you, this is a special 20 minutes; for the children, you are just part of every day's science hour.

These are examples of how you and your audience might perceive the time of communication differently. How each of you understands this aspect of context affects how your audience attends to the communication.

(Continued)

... how audiences perceive the place of communication

Have you ever gone to a religious service for a religion not yours? How did you feel the first day of college, in your first class? Being in a place we know well or in an unfamiliar place affects how at ease we are and hence how well we listen to others. Often, people in new circumstances are too distracted by just figuring out where they are to see posters on a wall or hear a speaker. Sometimes people are uncomfortable in places they know well (perhaps something bad happened there), and sometimes they are relaxed. If you can learn about an audience's general response to the place of communication, you can better shape your communication to fit.

... the contexts of bodies in space

We've asked you to visualize the contexts of your communications and how they might affect how people receive your productions. For instance, if you make an oral presentation, how do you ensure your audience sees and hears you comfortably? Such decisions depend on your purpose, of course: It could be the case that to achieve your purpose you want your audience to feel odd, cold, or uncomfortable so they will be slightly off balance. Sleazy people know that sleazy actions put other people at disadvantage: Imagine communication contexts like having an interviewee sit in a chair lower than the interviewer's, shaking someone's hand limply, or speaking a little too softly for someone to hear. Unethical communicators take these actions when they want audiences to feel weak or powerless. But you can also help

audiences feel comfortable and strong: You can ask them (even in a brochure) to sit if they are standing or take some deep breaths to relax. You can tell jokes. You can take care that a booklet you make has large enough type for their young or old eyes.

... institutional contexts

In addition to the physical dimensions of contexts, attend to the institutional dimensions. We talked in the section on audience about how audiences understand themselves through our institutions: families, religions, businesses and workplaces, and so on.

The contexts in which you communicate—classrooms, church halls, offices—might call to audience's minds some institutional relations more than others. When you give a speech in class, your audience sees you primarily as another student, an equal—but were you to present at a high school, students there would probably see you as a cool, older college person. If you are brought into a business or school to give a workshop about a topic you know well, your audience will see you as an authority, deserving respect for your knowledge.

The institutional relations audiences have with one another also affect how they respond. If you give a speech to family groups and talk only to the adults, they will notice that you ignore the children. Similarly, if someone in your class makes a comment during discussion and you ignore it and instead address only the teacher, other students can think of you as a snob or only out for a good grade.

Being alert to institutional contexts can help you think about whom to include as your audience and how to address it.

YOUR RESPONSIBILITIES

- If you have choices about where to communicate, be sure your audience will be comfortable, hear you, and, when possible, see and interact with you.
- The spaces within which we work with one another help or hinder our efforts to communicate effectively, so you will want to think about how you arrange such spaces. Is there room to move around? Is there plenty of elbow room? Are people isolated from one another? Lighting? Temperature?

- Context is more than just physical space, however. Contexts of communication also include what has led up to this point in time—peoples' histories as well as events that are happening around you (outside your building, or on the day before) and that may be relevant to you or members of your audience.

- Pay attention to the institutional context of your work as well. Do you have more authority than those you are speaking to, or less, and how will that affect what you can or cannot say and do? And how will your words—spoken with institutional force—affect those to whom you speak?

TO ANALYZE

- **Write informally:** Imagine you've been asked to give a speech to a group of 50 older people on the topic of what you learned about Indian art during your studies in Bombay. Sketch out—design—a space that would be the most conducive to their comfortable and attentive learning.

- **Write informally:** Consider an assignment on which you are now working for another class. Sketch out—design—the time and place in which you think that class's instructor would most generously respond to your work. How can you suggest that space and time through how you produce the assignment?

Statement of Purpose

With this step you will pull together what you have been writing and thinking about in the past three steps—purpose, audience, and context—into a **statement of purpose**.

A statement of purpose takes you beyond an initial sense of purpose because it asks you to tie purpose, audience, and context together. A statement of purpose should be detailed and specific enough to guide you through developing a design plan, for which you choose a medium or mix of media, decide on strategies, and then arrange, produce, and test what you compose. A final statement of purpose is usually about a half-page in length, depending on how concise you are.

To compose a statement of purpose

1. Look at what you have written about your sense of purpose, audience, and context and write one- to two-sentence summaries of each.
2. Write a one-sentence explanation of the relations among your purpose, audience, and context of communication. Use this as a draft of your statement of purpose.
3. Look at the one-sentence explanation you just wrote and ask these questions:
   - Does this explanation show how your purpose is tied to your audience's characteristics and the communication contexts you have identified?
   - Does this explanation make clear what the best possible outcome would be for your effort to communicate?

■ Does this explanation make clear the main things that could go wrong with your attempt to accomplish your purpose?

■ Does this explanation describe your responsibilities to other people as you move forward with this project?

4. Use your answers to these four questions to turn your one-sentence explanation into a paragraph—or more—that ties together your purpose, context, and audience.

AN EXAMPLE

Renee, from one of our classes, composed a statement of purpose to help her through a sticky but not unusual situation. Renee's sense of purpose, audience, and context are:

purpose	*I want to convince the Dean of Students that I should be allowed a late drop from the English class I'm failing. (It's my first semester, and Chemistry is harder than I thought, so I'm putting all my time into it—and not enough time into English. If I drop English then maybe I can get a better-than-passing grade in Chemistry.)*
audience	*My audience is the Dean of Students, who will demand strong reasons for my request—and will be reluctant to grant it—because the school has been tightening up on late drops.*
context	*The Dean will be in her office when she receives my request, and because there's only one month until the semester ends, everyone—including her—is probably pretty harried and rushed.*

■ This is Renee's one-sentence explanation (from step 2 on the previous page) of how her purpose, audience, and context of communication tie together:

I want to persuade a harried and reluctant Dean of Students that my circumstances warrant giving me a late drop in English.

■ After asking herself the questions on the bottom of the previous page, Renee realized she hadn't considered the possible negative outcomes of her request: She hadn't thought about what might make the Dean of Students turn down her request. By working that thought into her planning, Renee developed this statement of purpose:

I want to persuade a harried and reluctant Dean of Students that my circumstances warrant a late drop in English. I don't want her to think I'm only grade grubbing so that she turns down my request; instead, I want her to see I'm making the request because I'm serious about doing well and I learned a lot this semester about needing to manage my time.

By doing this revision, Renee sets herself up well to move into thinking about the next category of this rhetorical process—developing a design plan—and its steps of figuring out strategies, a medium, and arrangement. As we move through those steps in the next chapter, you'll see how Renee carried out her thinking, ending in a letter to the Dean.

FURTHER DEVELOPING STATEMENTS OF PURPOSE

As you continue working with the rhetorical process, and as your projects become more complex, your understandings of purpose, audience, and context will become more complex and your statement of purpose likewise will become more complex. For instance, since complex contexts sometimes mean that we have to juggle several purposes with respect to several different audiences, a corresponding statement of purpose will need to explain not only the relations among purpose, audience, and context but also the relations between different purposes and audiences.

composing a more complex statement of purpose

If you find yourself composing in complex situations, add the following questions to those listed under step 3 on page 125:

■ Does this statement of purpose explain the relations between my main purpose and any secondary or subpurposes I may have?

■ Does this statement of purpose reflect and respect the complexities of my audience?

Does it take into account primary and secondary audiences?

■ Is this a purpose everyone could share, or is it peculiar to my own interests or my social position?

■ Is this a purpose I would want others to have?

■ Is this purpose puerile, petulant, or petty? Am I base, brutish, or blind for having this purpose? Or is my purpose one that—when I achieve it—will help me feel proud and a useful member of the community I address?

recomposing a more complex statement of purpose

We hope you are seeing that even your statement of purpose is a strategy. How you state your purpose, how you represent your audience to yourself and to themselves, and how you envision your contexts are all strategic choices that shape how you think about and how you produce your communication—and will also shape how your audience responds.

(Continued)

YOUR RESPONSIBILITIES

■ Since your statement of purpose connects your sense of purpose to your specific audience and context, you are responsible for making sure that the connections leave room for your audience to respond, if they need to. Be careful not to subsume the audience to the context and treat people like rocks or the ground you walk on.

■ Try to use your statement of purpose to clarify for yourself how what matters to you connects with what matters to other people, given the contexts you share.

TO ANALYZE

■ **Discuss with others:** It is often useful to stop and tinker with a statement of purpose to see how—by changing parts of it—the overall picture of your task changes. Below is a statement of purpose for a research project being undertaken by Stephanie Hill (a sociology major). Read through the statement of purpose, and then with a partner discuss the questions that follow.

Men in their late teens and twenties are my audience. I want them to learn just how much body-image is a problem for women because of how men look at women. I know most men think this isn't really a problem and that eating disorders are just personal issues for individual women. But I want men to be thinking about their sisters and girlfriends (and even potential daughters), and about how they probably don't want these people they care about to be spending so much time thinking about their bodyshapes—even to the point of starving themselves. I want to try to put my readers into the position of women, who see thousands of magazine covers of skinny women on them (or think of all the women on TV!), and about how the repetition of all those skinny women makes women feel… and then I want my readers to think about what it's like to have a boyfriend or brother who constantly makes comments about how you look like you've just added a pound….

- Change the audience characteristics Stephanie describes. How does this change the overall statement of purpose?

- Stephanie doesn't say much about the context in which her audience will experience her communication. Imagine different contexts in which her audience could encounter her communication: How do the different contexts change your ideas about what media Stephanie could use? How do the different contexts suggest that the statement should be modified?

- Imagine Stephanie carrying out her purpose in several different media: How do different media change the context?

- What strategies does this statement of purpose suggest to you?

Thinking Through Production

■ In preceding sections you've described a purpose, audience, and context for two different situations: appealing a decision about studying abroad and trying to get into a closed class. Use the model of Renee's statement of purpose to write a short statement of purpose for each of the two situations.

■ Write a short, one-page paper in which you reflect on the following questions:

● How is the rhetorical process we've laid out here for developing a statement of purpose different from how you usually approach composing?

● What in the process do you think will be most useful to you given your strengths and weaknesses as a communicator?

● What in the process can you see giving you trouble?

● What in the process do you think will give you the most chances for being creative as you communicate with others?

■ Choose a project assignment you know is upcoming in a class or a communication task you've taken on for a church group, sorority or fraternity, or other organization to which you belong. Take 30 minutes to apply the rhetorical process of developing—and writing—a statement of purpose for the assignment or task. Afterward, write a bit in reflection: *How is your sense of the assignment or task different from your very first thoughts about how you were going to proceed?*

Convincing Your Audience: *Logos*

Classical argument is patterned after the persuasive speeches of ancient Greek and Roman orators. In traditional Latin terminology, the main parts of a persuasive speech are the *exordium,* in which the speaker gets the audience's attention; the *narratio,* which provides needed background; the *propositio,* which is the speaker's claim or thesis; the *partitio,* which forecasts the main parts of the speech; the *confirmatio,* which presents the speaker's arguments supporting the claim; the *confutatio,* which summarizes and rebuts opposing views; and the *peroratio,* which concludes the speech by summing up the argument, calling for action, and leaving a strong, lasting impression. (Of course, you don't need to remember these tongue-twisting Latin terms. We cite them only to assure you that in writing a classical argument, you are joining a time-honored tradition that links back to the origins of democracy.)

Let's go over the same territory again using more contemporary terms. We provide an organization plan showing the structure of a classical argument which shows these typical sections:

- **The introduction.** Writers of classical argument typically begin with an attention grabber such as a memorable scene, illustrative story, or startling statistic. They continue the introduction by focusing the issue—often by stating it directly as a question or by briefly summarizing opposing views—and providing needed background and context. They conclude the introduction by presenting their claim (thesis statement) and forecasting the argument's structure.

- **The presentation of the writer's position.** The presentation of the writer's own position is usually the longest part of a classical argument. Here writers present the reasons and evidence supporting their claims, typically choosing reasons that tie into their audience's values, beliefs, and assumptions. Usually each reason is developed in its own paragraph or sequence of paragraphs. When a paragraph introduces a new reason, writers state the reason directly and then support it with evidence or a chain of ideas. Along the way, writers guide their readers with appropriate transitions.

- **The summary and critique of alternative views.** When summarizing and responding to opposing views, writers have several options.

Chapter 9, Convincing Your Audience: *Logos*, is taken from John D. Ramage, John C. Bean, and June Johnson's *Writing Arguments*, pp. 55–71 (Chapter 3, The Core of an argument: A Claim with Reasons).

Organization Plan for an Argument with a Classical Structure

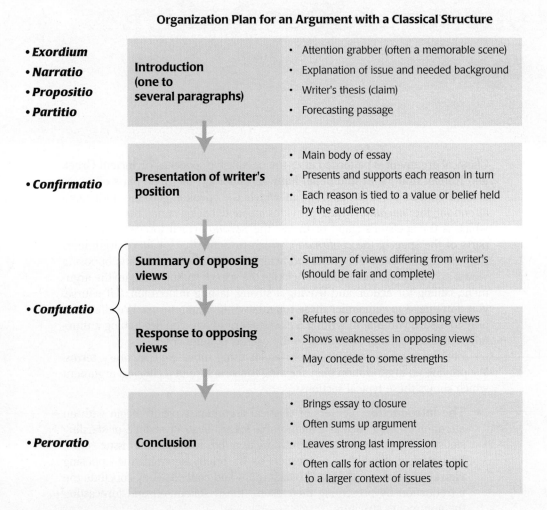

- *Exordium*
- *Narratio*
- *Propositio*
- *Partitio*

Introduction (one to several paragraphs)
- Attention grabber (often a memorable scene)
- Explanation of issue and needed background
- Writer's thesis (claim)
- Forecasting passage

- *Confirmatio*

Presentation of writer's position
- Main body of essay
- Presents and supports each reason in turn
- Each reason is tied to a value or belief held by the audience

- *Confutatio*

Summary of opposing views
- Summary of views differing from writer's (should be fair and complete)

Response to opposing views
- Refutes or concedes to opposing views
- Shows weaknesses in opposing views
- May concede to some strengths

- *Peroratio*

Conclusion
- Brings essay to closure
- Often sums up argument
- Leaves strong last impression
- Often calls for action or relates topic to a larger context of issues

If there are several opposing arguments, writers may summarize all of them together and then compose a single response, or they may summarize and respond to each argument in turn. As we will explain, writers may respond to opposing views either by refuting them or by conceding to their strengths and shifting to a different field of values.

■ **The conclusion.** Finally, in their conclusion, writers sum up their argument, often calling for some kind of action, thereby creating a sense of closure and leaving a strong final impression.

In this organization, the body of a classical argument has two major sections—the one presenting the writer's own position and the other summarizing and critiquing alternative views. The organization plan and our discussion have the writer's own position coming first, but it is possible to reverse that order.

For all its strengths, an argument with a classical structure may not always be your most persuasive strategy. In some cases, you may be more effective by delaying your thesis, by ignoring alternative views altogether, or by showing great sympathy for opposing views. Even in these cases, however, the classical structure is a useful planning tool. Its call for a thesis statement and a forecasting statement in the introduction helps you see the whole of your argument in miniature. And by requiring you to summarize and consider opposing views, the classical structure alerts you to the limits of your position and to the need for further reasons and evidence. As we will show, the classical structure is a particularly persuasive mode of argument when you address a neutral or undecided audience.

Classical Appeals and the Rhetorical Triangle

Besides developing a template or structure for an argument, classical rhetoricians analyzed the ways that effective speeches persuaded their audiences. They identified three kinds of persuasive appeals, which they called *logos, ethos,* and *pathos.* These appeals can be understood within a rhetorical context illustrated by a triangle with points labeled *message, writer or speaker,* and *audience* (see Figure 9.1). Effective arguments pay attention to all three points on this *rhetorical triangle.*

As Figure 9.1 shows, each point on the triangle corresponds to one of the three persuasive appeals:

- *Logos* (Greek for "word") focuses attention on the quality of the message—that is, on the internal consistency and clarity of the argument itself and on the logic of its reasons and support. The impact of *logos* on an audience is referred to as its *logical appeal.*
- *Ethos* (Greek for "character") focuses attention on the writer's (or speaker's) character as it is projected in the message. It refers to the credibility of the writer. *Ethos* is often conveyed through the writer's investment in his or her claim, through the fairness with which the writer considers alternative views, through the tone and style of the message, and even through the message's professional appearance on paper or screen, including correct grammar, flawless proofreading, and appropriate formats for citations and bibliography. In some cases, *ethos* is also a function of the writer's reputation for honesty and expertise independent of the message. The impact of *ethos* on an audience is referred to as the *ethical appeal* or *appeal from credibility.*
- *Pathos* (Greek for "suffering" or "experience") focuses attention on the values and beliefs of the intended audience. It is often associated with emotional appeal. But *pathos* appeals more specifically to an audience's imaginative sympathies—their capacity to feel and see what the writer feels and sees. Thus, when we turn the abstractions of logical discourse into a tangible and immediate story, we are making a pathetic appeal. Whereas appeals to *logos* and *ethos* can further an audience's intellectual assent to our claim, appeals to *pathos* engage the imagination and feelings, moving the audience to a deeper appreciation of the argument's significance.

A related rhetorical concept, connected to the appeals of *logos, ethos,* and *pathos,* is that of *kairos,* from the Greek word for "right time," "season," or "opportunity." This

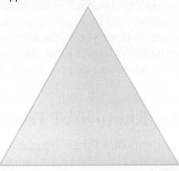

Message
LOGOS: *How can I make the argument
internally consistent and logical?
How can I find the best reasons and
support them with the best evidence?*

Audience
PATHOS: *How can I make the reader
open to my message? How can I best
appeal to my reader's values and
interests? How can I engage my
reader emotionally and imaginatively?*

Writer or Speaker
ETHOS: *How can I present myself
effectively? How can I enhance my
credibility and trustworthiness?*

FIGURE 9.1 The rhetorical triangle

concept suggests that for an argument to be persuasive, its timing must be effectively chosen and its tone and structure in right proportion or measure. You may have had the experience of composing an argumentative e-mail and then hesitating before clicking the "send" button. Is this the right moment to send this message? Is my audience ready to hear what I'm saying? Would my argument be more effective if I waited for a couple of days? If I send this message now, should I change its tone and content? This attentiveness to the unfolding of time is what is meant by *kairos.*

Given this background on the classical appeals, let's turn now to *logos*—the logic and structure of arguments.

Issue Questions as the Origins of Argument

At the heart of any argument is an issue, which we can define as a controversial topic area such as "the labeling of biotech foods" or "racial profiling," that gives rise to differing points of view and conflicting claims. A writer can usually focus an issue by asking an issue question that invites at least two alternative answers. Within any complex issue—for example, the issue of abortion—there are usually a number of separate issue questions: Should abortions be legal? Should the federal government authorize Medicaid payments for abortions? When does a fetus become a human being (at conception? at three months? at quickening? at birth?)? What are the effects of legalizing abortion? (One person might stress that legalized abortion leads to greater freedom for women. Another person might respond that it lessens a society's respect for human life.)

Difference between an Issue Question and an Information Question

Of course, not all questions are issue questions that can be answered reasonably in two or more differing ways; thus not all questions can lead to effective arguments. Rhetoricians have traditionally distinguished between *explication,* which is writing that sets out to inform or explain, and *argumentation,* which sets out to change a reader's mind. On the surface, at least, this seems like a useful distinction. If a reader is interested in a writer's question mainly to gain new knowledge about a subject, then the writer's essay could be considered explication rather than argument. According to this view, the following questions about teenage pregnancy might be called information questions rather than issue questions:

> How does the teenage pregnancy rate in the United States compare with the rate in Sweden? If the rates are different, why?

Although both questions seem to call for information rather than for argument, we believe that the second one would be an issue question if reasonable people disagreed on the answer. Thus, different writers might agree that the teenage pregnancy rate in the United States is seven times higher than the rate in Sweden. But they might disagree about why. One writer might emphasize Sweden's practical, secular sex-education courses, leading to more consistent use of contraceptives among Swedish teenagers. Another writer might point to the higher use of oral contraceptives among teenage girls in Sweden (partly a result of Sweden's generous national health program) and to less reliance on condoms for preventing pregnancy. Another might argue that moral decay in the United States or a breakdown of the traditional family is at fault. Thus, underneath the surface of what looks like a simple explication of the "truth" is really a controversy.

How to Identify an Issue Question

You can generally tell whether a question is an issue question or an information question by examining your purpose in relationship to your audience. If your relationship to your audience is that of teacher to learner, so that your audience hopes to gain new information, knowledge, or understanding that you possess, then your question is probably an information question. But if your relationship to your audience is that of advocate to decision maker or jury, so that your audience needs to make up its mind on something and is weighing different points of view, then the question you address is an issue question.

Often the same question can be an information question in one context and an issue question in another. Let's look at the following examples:

- **How does a diesel engine work?** (This is probably an information question, because reasonable people who know about diesel engines will probably agree on how they work. This question would be posed by an audience of new learners.)
- **Why is a diesel engine more fuel efficient than a gasoline engine?** (This also seems to be an information question, because all experts will probably agree on

the answer. Once again, the audience seems to be new learners, perhaps students in an automotive class.)

■ **What is the most cost-effective way to produce diesel fuel from crude oil?** (This could be an information question if experts agree and you are addressing new learners. But if you are addressing engineers and one engineer says process X is the most cost-effective and another argues for process Y, then the question is an issue question.)

■ **Should the present highway tax on diesel fuel be increased?** (This is certainly an issue question. One person says yes; another says no; another offers a compromise.)

■ ■ ■ **FOR CLASS DISCUSSION** Information Questions versus Issue Questions
Working as a class or in small groups, try to decide which of the following questions are information questions and which are issue questions. Many of them could be either, depending on the rhetorical context. For such questions, create hypothetical contexts to show your reasoning.

1. What percentage of public schools in the United States are failing?
2. Which is more addictive, marijuana or alcohal?
3. What is the effect on children of playing first-person-shooter games?
4. Is genetically modified corn safe for human consumption?
5. Should a woman with newly detected breast cancer opt for a radical mastectomy (complete removal of the breast and surrounding lymph tissue) or a lumpectomy (removal of the malignant lump without removal of the whole breast)?

Difference between a Genuine Argument and a Pseudo-Argument

Although every argument features an issue question with alternative answers, not every dispute over answers is a rational argument. Rational arguments require two additional factors: (1) reasonable participants who operate within the conventions of reasonable behavior and (2) potentially sharable assumptions that can serve as a starting place or foundation for the argument. Lacking one or both of these conditions, disagreements remain stalled at the level of pseudo-arguments.

Pseudo-Arguments: Committed Believers and Fanatical Skeptics

A reasonable argument assumes the possibility of growth and change; disputants may modify their views as they acknowledge strengths in an alternative view or weaknesses in their own. Such growth becomes impossible—and argument degenerates to pseudo-argument—when disputants are fanatically committed to their positions. Consider the case of the fanatical believer and the fanatical skeptic.

From one perspective, committed believers are admirable persons, guided by unwavering values and beliefs. Committed believers stand on solid rock, unwilling to compromise their principles or bend to the prevailing winds. But from another perspective, committed believers can seem rigidly fixed, incapable of growth or change. When committed believers from two clashing belief systems try to engage in dialogue with each other, a truth-seeking exchange of views becomes difficult. They talk past each other; dialogue is replaced by monologue from within isolated silos. Once committed believers push each other's buttons on global warming, guns, health care, taxes, religion, or some other issue, each disputant resorts to an endless replaying of the same prepackaged arguments. Disagreeing with a committed believer is like ordering the surf to quiet down. The only response is another crashing wave.

In contrast to the committed believer, the fanatical skeptic dismisses the possibility of ever believing anything. Skeptics often demand proof where no proof is possible. So what if the sun has risen every day of recorded history? That's no proof that it will rise tomorrow. Short of absolute proof, which never exists, fanatical skeptics accept nothing. In a world where the most we can hope for is increased audience adherence to our ideas, the skeptic demands an ironclad, logical demonstration of our claim's rightness.

A Closer Look at Pseudo-Arguments: The Lack of Shared Assumptions

As we have seen, rational argument degenerates to pseudo-argument when there is no possibility for listening, learning, growth, or change. In this section, we look more closely at a frequent cause of pseudo-arguments: lack of shared assumptions.

Shared Assumptions and the Problem of Ideology As our discussion of committed believers suggests, reasonable argument is difficult when the disputants have differing "ideologies," which is an academic word for belief systems or worldviews. We all have our own ideologies. We all look at the world through a lens shaped by our life's experiences. Our beliefs and values are shaped by our family background, our friends, our culture, our particular time in history, our race or ethnicity, our gender or sexual orientation, our social class, our religion, our education, and so forth. Because we tend to think that our particular lens for looking at the world is natural and universal rather than specific to ourselves, we must be aware that persons who disagree with us may not share our deepest assumptions and beliefs. To participate in rational argument, we and our audience must seek *shared assumptions*—certain principles or values or beliefs that can serve as common ground.

The failure to find shared assumptions often leads to pseudo-arguments, particularly if one disputant makes assumptions that the other disputant cannot accept. Such pseudo-arguments often occur in disputes arising from politics or religion. For example, consider differences within the Christian community over how to interpret the Bible. Some Christian groups choose a straightforward, literal interpretation of the Bible as God's inerrant word while other groups read some passages metaphorically or mythically and focus on the paradoxes, historical contexts, and interpretive complexities of the Bible; still other Christian groups read it as an ethical call for social justice. Members of these different Christian groups may not be able to argue rationally about, say, evolution or gay marriage because they have very different ways of reading Biblical passages and invoking the authority of the Bible. Similarly, within other religious traditions, believers may also differ about the meaning and applicability of their sacred texts to scientific issues and social problems.

Similar disagreements about assumptions occur in the political arena as well. Our point is that certain religious or political beliefs or texts cannot be evoked for evidence or authority when an audience does not assume the belief's truth or does not agree on the way that a given text should be read or interpreted.

Shared Assumptions and the Problem of Personal Opinions Lack of shared assumptions also dooms arguments about purely personal opinions—for example, someone's claim that opera is boring or that pizza is better than nachos. Of course, a pizza-versus-nachos argument might be possible if the disputants assume a shared criterion about nutrition. For example, a nutritionist could argue that pizza is better than nachos because pizza provides more balanced nutrients per calorie. But if one of the disputants responds, "Nah, nachos are better than pizza because nachos taste better," then he makes a different assumption—"My sense of taste is better than your sense of taste." This is a wholly personal standard, an assumption that others are unable to share.

■ ■ ■ **FOR CLASS DISCUSSION** Reasonable Arguments versus Pseudo-Arguments
The following questions can all be answered in alternative ways. However, not all of them will lead to reasonable arguments. Try to decide which questions will lead to reasonable arguments and which will lead only to pseudo-arguments.

1. Are the *Star Wars* films good science fiction?
2. Is it ethically justifiable to capture dolphins and train them for human entertainment?
3. Should cities subsidize professional sports venues?
4. Is this abstract oil painting created by a monkey smearing paint on a canvas a true work of art?
5. Are nose rings and tongue studs attractive?

Frame of an Argument: A Claim Supported by Reasons

We said earlier that an argument originates in an *issue question,* which by definition is any question that provokes disagreement about the best answer. When you write an argument, your task is to take a position on the issue and to support it with reasons and evidence. The *claim* of your essay is the position you want your audience to accept. To put it another way, your claim is your essay's *thesis statement,* a one-sentence summary answer to your issue question. Your task, then, is to make a claim and support it with reasons.

What Is a Reason?

A *reason* (also called a *premise*) is a claim used to support another claim. In speaking or writing, a reason is usually linked to the claim with connecting words such as *because, since, for, so, thus, consequently,* and *therefore,* indicating that the claim follows logically from the reason.

Let us take an example. In one of our recent classes, students heatedly debated the ethics of capturing wild dolphins and training them to perform in marine parks or "swim with dolphins" programs. One student had recently seen the 2009 documentary *The Cove*, about the gory dolphin hunts in Japan in which dolphins are killed en masse by fishermen and some are captured for display in shows around the world. Another student cited the 1960s family show *Flipper*, featuring a dolphin working harmoniously with—and often saving—his human friends. One student commented that his sister fell in love with marine biology on a family vacation in Hawaii when she swam with a dolphin, gave signals for the dolphin's jump, and touched its rubbery skin during a "swim with dolphins" program. In response, a few students remarked that the only ethical way to experience dolphins is with a pair of binoculars from a boat. Here are the frameworks the class developed for two alternative positions on this issue:

One View

CLAIM: The public should not support the commercial use of captured dolphins.

REASON 1: Aquariums, marine parks, and "swim with dolphins" programs separate dolphins from their natural habitat and social groups.

REASON 2: The unnatural environment of aquariums, marine parks, and dolphin programs places great stress on dolphins.

REASON 3: Aquariums, marine parks, and dolphin programs are mainly big businesses driven by profit.

REASON 4: What these aquariums, marine parks, and "swim with" programs call "education about dolphins" is just a series of artificial, exploitive tricks taught through behavior modification.

REASON 5: Marine parks and programs create a commercial market for dolphins, which directly or indirectly encourages dolphin hunts and captures.

REASON 6: Marine parks and programs promote an attitude of human dominance over animals.

Alternative View

CLAIM: The public should continue to support aquariums, marine parks, and "swim with dolphins" programs.

REASON 1: These parks and programs observe accreditation standards for animal welfare, health, and nutrition, and monitor the well-being of their dolphins.

REASON 2: These marine parks and "swim with" programs enable scientists and veterinarians to study dolphin behavior in ways not possible with field studies in the wild.

REASON 3: While creating memorable family entertainment, these parks and programs provide environmental education and teach appreciation for dolphins.

REASON 4: Accredited programs do not endorse dolphin hunts and have self-sustaining breeding programs to avoid the need for dolphin hunts.

REASON 5: In their training of dolphins, these programs emphasize animal husbandry and animal enrichment to exercise dolphins' intelligence and abilities.

REASON 6: Marine parks and "swim with dolphins" programs support research and conservation.

Formulating a list of reasons in this way breaks your argumentative task into a series of subtasks. It gives you a frame for building your argument in parts. In the previous example, the frame for the argument opposing commercial use of dolphins suggests five different lines of reasoning a writer might pursue. A writer might use all five reasons or select only two or three, depending on which reasons would most persuade the intended audience. Each line of reasoning would be developed in its own separate section of the argument. For example, you might begin one section of your argument with the following sentence: "The public should not support these dolphin programs because they teach dolphins clownish tricks and artificial behaviors, which they pass off as 'education about dolphins.'" You would then provide examples of the tricks and stunts that dolphins are taught, explain how these contrast with dolphins' natural behaviors, and offer examples of erroneous facts or information about dolphins supplied by these programs. You might also need to support the underlying assumption that it is good for the public to acquire *real knowledge* about dolphins in the wild. You would then proceed in the same way for each separate section of your argument.

To summarize our point in this section, the frame of an argument consists of the claim (the thesis statement of the essay), which is supported by one or more reasons, which are in turn supported by evidence or sequences of further reasons.

Expressing Reasons in Because Clauses

Chances are that when you were a child, the word *because* contained magical explanatory powers. Somehow *because* seemed decisive. It persuaded people to accept your view of the world; it changed people's minds. Later, as you got older, you discovered that *because* only introduced your arguments and that it was the reasons following *because* that made the difference. Still, *because* introduced you to the powers potentially residing in the adult world of logic.

Of course, there are many other ways to express the logical connection between a reason and a claim. Our language is rich in ways of stating *because* relationships:

- The public should not support marine parks and "swim with dolphins" programs because these programs place great stress on dolphins by separating them from their natural habitat and social groups.
- Marine parks and "swim with dolphin" programs place great stress on dolphins by separating them from their natural habitat and social groups. Therefore the public should not support the captivity of dolphins.
- Marine parks and "swim with dolphin" programs place great stress on dolphins by separating them from their natural habitat and social groups, so the public should not support these programs.

- One reason that the public should not support marine parks or "swim with dolphins" programs is that these programs place great stress on dolphins by separating them from their natural habitat and social groups.
- My argument that the public should not support marine parks and "swim with dolphins" programs is based mainly on the grounds that these programs place great stress on dolphins by separating them from their natural habitat and social groups.

Even though logical relationships can be stated in various ways, writing out one or more *because* clauses seems to be the most succinct and manageable way to clarify an argument for oneself. We therefore suggest that sometime in the writing process, you create a *working thesis statement* that summarizes your main reasons as because clauses attached to your claim.* Just when you compose your own working thesis statement depends largely on your writing process. Some writers like to plan out their whole argument from the start and often compose their working thesis statements with *because* clauses before they write their rough drafts. Others discover their arguments as they write. And sometimes it is a combination of both. For these writers, an extended working thesis statement is something they might write halfway through the composing process as a way of ordering their argument when various branches seem to be growing out of control. Or they might compose a working thesis statement at the very end as a way of checking the unity of the final product.

Whenever you write your extended thesis statement, the act of doing so can be simultaneously frustrating and thought provoking. Composing *because* clauses can be a powerful discovery tool, causing you to think of many different kinds of arguments to support your claim. But it is often difficult to wrestle your ideas into the *because* clause shape, which sometimes seems to be overly tidy for the complex network of ideas you are trying to work with. Nevertheless, trying to summarize your argument as a single claim with reasons should help you see more clearly what you have to do.

■ ■ ■   **FOR CLASS DISCUSSION**   Developing Claims and Reasons

Try this group exercise to help you see how writing *because* clauses can be a discovery procedure. Divide into small groups. Each group member should contribute an issue that he or she would like to explore. Discussing one person's issue at a time, help each member develop a claim supported by several reasons. Express each reason as a *because* clause. Then write out the working thesis statement for each person's argument by attaching the *because* clauses to the claim. Finally, try to create *because* clauses in support of an alternative claim for each issue. Recorders should select two or three working thesis statements from the group to present to the class as a whole.   ■ ■ ■

---

*A working thesis statement opposing the commercial use of captured dolphins might look like this: *The public should not support the commercial use of captured dolphins because marine parks and "swim with dolphins" programs place great stress on dolphins by separating them from their natural habitat and social groups; because these parks and programs are mainly big businesses driven by profit; because they create inaccurate and incomplete educational information about dolphins; because they create a commercial market for dolphins that directly or indirectly encourages dolphin hunts and captures; and because they promote an attitude of human dominance over animals.* You might not put a bulky thesis statement like this into your essay; rather, a working thesis statement is a behind-the-scenes way of summarizing your argument so that you can see it whole and clear.

Using Evidence Effectively 10

Consider a target audience of educated, reasonable, and careful readers who approach an issue with healthy skepticism, open-minded but cautious. What demands would such readers make on a writer's use of evidence? To begin to answer that question, let's look at some general principles for using evidence persuasively.

Apply the STAR Criteria to Evidence

Our open-minded but skeptical audience would first of all expect the evidence to meet what rhetorician Richard Fulkerson calls the STAR criteria:[1]

Sufficiency: Is there enough evidence?
Typicality: Is the chosen evidence representative and typical?
Accuracy: Is the evidence accurate and up-to-date?
Relevance: Is the evidence relevant to the claim?

Let's examine each in turn.

Sufficiency of Evidence How much evidence you need is a function of your rhetorical context. In a court trial, opposing attorneys often agree to waive evidence for points that aren't in doubt in order to concentrate on contested points. The more a claim is contested or the more your audience is skeptical, the more evidence you may need to present. If you provide too little evidence, you may be accused of *hasty generalization*, a reasoning fallacy in which a person makes a sweeping conclusion based on only one or two instances. On the other hand, if you provide too much evidence your argument may become overly long and tedious. You can guard against having too little or too much evidence by appropriately qualifying the claim your evidence supports.

> **Strong claim:** Working full time seriously harms a student's grade point average. (much data needed—probably a combination of examples and statistical studies)

---

[1]Richard Fulkerson, *Teaching the Argument in Writing* (Urbana, IL: National Council of Teachers of English, 1996), 44–53. In this section, we are indebted to Fulkerson's discussion.

Chapter 10, Using Evidence Effectively, is taken from John D. Ramage, John C. Bean, and June Johnson's *Writing Arguments*, pp. 89–108 (Chapter 5, Using Evidence Effectively).

Qualified claim: Working full time often harms a student's grade point average. (a few representative examples may be enough)

Typicality of Evidence Whenever you select evidence, readers need to believe the evidence is typical and representative rather than extreme instances. Suppose that you want to argue that students can combine full-time work with full-time college and cite the case of your friend Pam, who pulled a straight-A grade average while working forty hours per week as a night receptionist in a small hotel. Your audience might doubt the typicality of Pam's case since a night receptionist can often use work hours for studying. What about more typical jobs, they'll ask, where you can't study while you work?

Accuracy of Evidence Evidence can't be used ethically unless it is accurate and up-to-date, and it can't be persuasive unless the audience believes in the writer's credibility. As a writer, you must be scrupulous in using the most recent and accurate evidence you can find. Faith in the accuracy of a writer's data is one function of *ethos*—the audience's confidence in the writer's credibility and trustworthiness.

Relevance of Evidence Finally, evidence will be persuasive only if the reader considers it relevant to the contested issue. Consider the following student argument: "I deserve an A in this course because I worked exceptionally hard." The student then cites substantial evidence of how hard he worked—a log of study hours, copies of multiple drafts of papers, testimony from friends, and so forth. Such evidence is ample support for the claim "I worked exceptionally hard" but is irrelevant to the claim "I deserve an A." Although some instructors may give partial credit for effort, the criteria for grades usually focus on the quality of the student's performance, not the student's time spent studying.

Use Sources That Your Reader Trusts

Another way to enhance the persuasiveness of your evidence is, whenever possible, to choose data from sources you think your readers will trust. Because questions of fact are often at issue in arguments, readers may be skeptical of certain sources. When you research an issue, you soon get a sense of who the participants in the conversation are and what their reputations tend to be. Knowing the political biases of sources and the extent to which a source has financial or personal investment in the outcome of a controversy will also help you locate data sources that both you and your readers can trust. Citing evidence from a peer-reviewed scholarly journal is often more persuasive than citing evidence found on an advocacy Web site. Similarly, citing a conservative magazine such as the *National Review* may be unpersuasive to liberal audiences, just as citing a Sierra Club publication may be unpersuasive to conservatives.

Rhetorical Understanding of Evidence

In the previous section we presented some general principles for effective use of evidence. We now want to deepen your understanding of how evidence persuades by asking you to consider more closely the rhetorical context in which evidence operates.

We'll look first at the kinds of evidence used in arguments and then show you how writers select and frame evidence for persuasive effect.

Kinds of Evidence

Writers have numerous options for the kinds of evidence they can use in an argument, including personal-experience data, research findings, and hypothetical examples. To explain these options, we present a series of charts that categorize different kinds of evidence, illustrate how each kind might be worked into an argument, and comment on the strengths and limitations of each.

Data from Personal Experience   One powerful kind of evidence comes from personal experience:

Example	Strengths and Limitations
Despite recent criticism that Ritalin is overprescribed for hyperactivity and attention-deficit disorder, it can often seem like a miracle drug. My little brother is a perfect example. Before he was given Ritalin, he was a terror in school. . . . [Tell the "before" and "after" story of your little brother.]	▪ Personal-experience examples help readers identify with writer; they show writer's personal connection to the issue. ▪ Vivid stories capture the imagination and appeal to *Pathos*. ▪ Skeptics may sometimes argue that personal-experience examples are insufficient (writer is guilty of hasty generalization), not typical, or not adequately scientific or verifiable.

Data from Observation or Field Research   You can also develop evidence by personally observing a phenomenon or by doing your own field research:

Example	Strengths and Limitations
The intersection at Fifth and Montgomery is particularly dangerous because pedestrians almost never find a comfortable break in the heavy flow of cars. On April 29, I watched fifty-seven pedestrians cross the street. Not once did cars stop in both directions before the pedestrian stepped off the sidewalk onto the street. [Continue with observed data about danger.]	▪ Field research gives the feeling of scientific credibility. ▪ It increases typicality by expanding database beyond example of one person. ▪ It enhances *ethos* of the writer as personally invested and reasonable. ▪ Skeptics may point to flaws in how observations were conducted, showing how data are insufficient, inaccurate, or nontypical.

Data from Interviews, Questionnaires, Surveys   You can also gather data by interviewing stakeholders in a controversy, creating questionnaires, or doing surveys.

Example	Strengths and Limitations
Another reason to ban laptops from classrooms is the extent to which laptop users disturb other students. In a questionnaire that I distributed to fifty students in my residence hall, a surprising 60 percent said that they are annoyed by fellow students' sending e-mail, paying their bills, or surfing the Web while pretending to take notes in class. Additionally, I interviewed five students who gave me specific examples of how these distractions interfere with learning. [Report the examples.]	▪ Interviews, questionnaires, and surveys enhance the sufficiency and typicality of evidence by expanding the database beyond the experiences of one person. ▪ Quantitative data from questionnaires and surveys often increase the scientific feel of the argument. ▪ Surveys and questionnaires often uncover local or recent data not available in published research. ▪ Interviews can provide engaging personal stories, thus enhancing *pathos*. ▪ Skeptics can raise doubts about research methodology, questionnaire design, or typicality of interview subjects.

Data from Library or Internet Research For many arguments, evidence is derived from reading, particularly from library or Internet research.

Example	Strengths and Limitations
The belief that a high-carbohydrate–low-fat diet is the best way to lose weight has been challenged by research conducted by Walter Willett and his colleagues in the department of nutrition at the Harvard School of Public Health. Willett's research suggests that complex carbohydrates such as pasta and potatoes spike glucose levels, increasing the risk of diabetes. Additionally, some fats—especially monounsaturated and polyunsaturated fats found in nuts, fish, and most vegetable oils—help lower "bad" cholesterol levels (45).*	▪ Researched evidence is often powerful, especially when sources are respected by your audience; writers can spotlight source's credentials through attributive tags (see Chapter 16, pages 376–378). ▪ Researched data may take the form of facts, examples, quotations, summaries of research studies, and so forth (see Chapters 15 and 16). ▪ Skeptics might doubt the accuracy of facts, the credentials of a source, or the research design of a study. They might also cite studies with different results. ▪ Skeptics might raise doubts about sufficiency, typicality, or relevance of your research data.

Testimony Writers frequently use testimony when direct data are either unavailable or highly technical or complex. Testimonial evidence can come from research or from interviews:

Example	Strengths and Limitations
Although the Swedish economist Bjorn Lomborg claims that acid rain is not a significant problem, many environmentalists disagree. According to David Bellamany, president of the Conservation Foundation, "Acid rain does kill forests and people around the world, and it's still doing so in the most polluted places, such as Russia" (qtd. in *BBC News*).	▪ By itself, testimony is generally less persuasive than direct data. ▪ Persuasiveness can be increased if source has impressive credentials, which the writer can state through attributive tags introducing the testimony ▪ Skeptics might undermine testimonial evidence by questioning credentials of source, showing source's bias, or quoting a countersource.

Statistical Data Many contemporary arguments rely heavily on statistical data, often supplemented by graphics such as tables, pie charts, and graphs.

Example	Strengths and Limitations
Americans are delaying marriage at a surprising rate. In 1970, 85 percent of Americans between ages twenty-five and twenty-nine were married. In 2010, however, only 45 percent were married (U.S. Census Bureau).	▪ Statistics can give powerful snapshots of aggregate data from a wide database. ▪ They are often used in conjunction with graphics. ▪ They can be calculated and displayed in different ways to achieve different rhetorical effects, so the reader must be wary. ▪ Skeptics might question statistical methods, research design, and interpretation of data.

*Parenthetical citations in this example and the next follow the MLA documentation system.

Hypothetical Examples, Cases, and Scenarios Arguments occasionally use hypothetical examples, cases, or scenarios, particularly to illustrate conjectured consequences of an event or to test philosophical hypotheses:

Example	Strengths and Limitations
Consider what might happen if we continue to use biotech soybeans that are resistant to herbicides. The resistant gene, through cross-pollination, might be transferred to an ordinary weed, creating an out-of-control superweed that herbicides couldn't kill. Such a superweed could be an ecological disaster.	▪ Scenarios have strong imaginative appeal. ▪ They are persuasive only if they seem plausible. ▪ A scenario narrative often conveys a sense of "inevitability" even if the actual scenario is unlikely; hence rhetorical effect may be illogical. ▪ Skeptics might show the implausibility of the scenario or offer an alternative scenario.

Reasoned Sequence of Ideas Sometimes arguments are supported with a reasoned sequence of ideas rather than with concrete facts or other forms of empirical evidence. The writer's concern is to support a point through a logical progression of ideas. Such arguments are conceptual, supported by linked ideas, rather than evidential. This kind of support occurs frequently in arguments and is often intermingled with evidentiary support.

Example	Strengths and Limitations
Embryonic stem cell research, despite its promise in fighting diseases, may have negative social consequences. This research encourages us to place embryos in the category of mere cellular matter that can be manipulated at will. Currently we reduce animals to this category when we genetically alter them for human purposes, such as engineering pigs to grow more human-like heart valves for use in transplants. Using human embryos in the same way— as material that can be altered and destroyed at will—may benefit society materially, but this quest for greater knowledge and control involves a reclassifying of embryos that could potentially lead to a devaluing of human life.	■ These sequences are often used in causal arguments to show how causes are linked to effects or in definitional or values arguments to show links among ideas. ■ They have great power to clarify values and show the belief structure on which a claim is founded. ■ They can sketch out ideas and connections that would otherwise remain latent. ■ Their effectiveness depends on the audience's acceptance of each link in the sequence of ideas. ■ Skeptics might raise objections at any link in the sequence, often by pointing to different values or outlining different consequences.

Angle of Vision and the Selection and Framing of Evidence

You can increase your ability to use evidence effectively—and to analyze how other arguers use evidence—by becoming more aware of a writer's rhetorical choices when using evidence to support a claim. Where each of us stands on an issue is partly a function of our own critical thinking, inquiry, and research—our search for the best solution to a problem. But it is also partly a function of who we are as people—our values and beliefs as formed by the particulars of our existence such as our family history, education, gender and sexual orientation, age, class, and ethnicity. In other words, we don't enter the argumentative arena like disembodied computers arriving at our claims through a value-free calculus. We enter with our own ideologies, beliefs, values, and guiding assumptions.

These guiding assumptions, beliefs, and values work together to create a writer's "angle of vision." (Instead of "angle of vision," we could also use other words or metaphors such as *perspective, bias, lens,* or *filter*—all terms that suggest that our way of seeing the world is shaped by our values and beliefs.) A writer's angle of vision, like a lens or filter, helps determine what stands out for that writer in a field of data—that is, what data are important or trivial, significant or irrelevant, worth focusing on or worth ignoring.

EXAMINING VISUAL ARGUMENTS

Crowd surfing in a mosh pit

Angle of Vision

Because of nationally reported injuries and near-death experiences resulting from stage diving and crowd surfing at rock concerts, many cities have tried to ban mosh pits. Critics of mosh pits have pointed to the injuries caused by crowd surfing and to the ensuing lawsuits against concert venues. Meanwhile, supporters cite the almost ecstatic enjoyment of crowd-surfing rock fans who seek out concerts with "festival seating."

These photos display different angles of vision toward crowd surfing. Suppose you were writing a blog in support of crowd surfing. Which image would you include in your posting? Why? Suppose alternatively that you were blogging against mosh pits, perhaps urging local officials to outlaw them. Which image would you choose? Why?

Analyze the visual features of these photographs in order to explain how they are constructed to create alternative angles of vision on mosh pits.

An alternative view of a mosh pit

To illustrate the concept of selective seeing, we ask you to consider how two hypothetical speakers might select different data about homeless people when presenting speeches to their city council. The first speaker argues that the city should increase its services to the homeless. The second asks the city to promote tourism more aggressively. Their differing angles of vision will cause the two speakers to select different data about homeless people and to frame these data in different ways. (Our use of the word *frame* derives metaphorically from a window frame or the frame of a camera's viewfinder.

When you look through a frame, some part of your field of vision is blocked off, while the material appearing in the frame is emphasized. Through framing, a writer maximizes the reader's focus on some data, minimizes the reader's focus on other data, and otherwise guides the reader's vision and response.)

Because the first speaker wants to increase the council's sympathy for the homeless, she frames homeless people positively by telling the story of one homeless man's struggle to find shelter and nutritious food. Her speech focuses primarily on the low number of tax dollars devoted to helping the homeless. In contrast, the second speaker, using data about lost tourist income, might frame the homeless as "panhandlers" by telling the story of obnoxious, urine-soaked winos who pester shoppers for handouts. As arguers, both speakers want their audience to see the homeless from their own angles of vision. Consequently, lost tourist dollars don't show up at all in the first speaker's argument, whereas the story of a homeless man's night in the cold doesn't show up in the second speaker's argument. As this example shows, one goal writers have in selecting and framing evidence is to bring the reader's view of the subject into alignment with the writer's angle of vision. The writer selects and frames evidence to limit and control what the reader sees.

To help you better understand the concepts of selection and framing, we offer the following class discussion exercise to give you practice in a kind of controlled laboratory setting. As you do this exercise, we invite you to observe your own processes for selecting and framing evidence.

■ ■ ■ **FOR CLASS DISCUSSION** **Creating an Angle of Vision by Selecting Evidence**

Suppose that your city has scheduled a public hearing on a proposed ordinance to ban mosh pits at rock concerts. (See the Examining Visual Arguments feature, where we introduced this issue.) Among the possible data available to various speakers for evidence are the following:

- Some bands, such as Nine Inch Nails, specify festival seating that allows a mosh pit area.
- A female mosher writing on the Internet says: "I experience a shared energy that is like no other when I am in the pit with the crowd. It is like we are all a bunch of atoms bouncing off of each other. It's great. Hey, some people get that feeling from basketball games. I get mine from the mosh pit."
- A student conducted a survey of fifty students on her campus who had attended rock concerts in the last six months. Of the respondents, 80 percent thought that mosh pits should be allowed at concerts.
- Narrative comments on these questionnaires included the following:
  - Mosh pits are a passion for me. I get an amazing rush when crowd surfing.
  - I don't like to be in a mosh pit or do crowd surfing. But I love festival seating and like to watch the mosh pits. For me, mosh pits are part of the ambience of a concert.
  - I know a girl who was groped in a mosh pit, and she'll never do one again. But I have never had any problems.
  - Mosh pits are dangerous and stupid. I think they should be outlawed.

- If you are afraid of mosh pits, just stay away. Nobody forces you to go into a mosh pit! It is ridiculous to ban them because they are totally voluntary. They should just post big signs saying, "City assumes no responsibility for accidents occurring in mosh pit area."
- A teenage girl suffered brain damage and memory loss at a 1998 Pearl Jam concert in Rapid City, South Dakota. According to her attorney, she hadn't intended to body surf or enter the mosh pit but "got sucked in while she was standing at its fringe."
- Twenty-four concert deaths were recorded in 2001, most of them in the area closest to the stage where people are packed in.
- A twenty-one-year-old man suffered cardiac arrest at a Metallica concert in Indiana and is now in a permanent vegetative state. Because he was jammed into the mosh pit area, nobody noticed he was in distress.
- In 2005, a blogger reported breaking his nose on an elbow; another described having his lip ring pulled out. Another blogger on the same site described having his lip nearly sliced off by the neck of a bass guitar. The injury required seventy-eight stitches. In May 2008, fifty people were treated at emergency rooms for mosh pit injuries acquired at a Bamboozle concert in New Jersey.
- According to a 2008 ABC news special, a company specializing in crowd management at rock festivals estimated "that 10,000 people have been injured in and around mosh pits in the last decade." The company said further "that the most injuries incurred from mosh pits aren't actually by the moshers but by innocent bystanders."

Tasks: Working individually or in small groups, complete the following tasks:

1. Compose two short speeches, one supporting the proposed city ordinance to ban mosh pits and one opposing it. How you use these data is up to you, but be able to explain your reasoning in the way you select and frame them. Share your speeches with classmates.
2. After you have shared examples of different speeches, explain the approaches that different classmates employed. What principle of selection was used? If arguers included evidence contrary to their positions, how did they handle it, respond to it, minimize its importance, or otherwise channel its rhetorical effect?
3. In the first task, we assigned you two different angles of vision—one supporting the ordinance and one opposing it. If you had to create your own argument on a proposal to ban mosh pits and if you set for yourself a truth-seeking goal—that is, finding the best solution for the problem of mosh pit danger, one for which you would take ethical responsibility—what would you argue? How would your argument use the list of data we provided? What else might you add?

Rhetorical Strategies for Framing Evidence

What we hope you learned from the preceding exercise is that an arguer consciously selects evidence from a wide field of data and then frames these data through rhetorical strategies that emphasize some data, minimize others, and guide the reader's response.

Now that you have a basic idea of what we mean by framing of evidence, here are some strategies writers can use to guide what the reader sees and feels.

Strategies for Framing Evidence

- **Controlling the space given to supporting versus contrary evidence:** Depending on their audience and purpose, writers can devote most of their space to supporting evidence and minimal space to contrary evidence (or omit it entirely). Thus people arguing in favor of mosh pits may have used lots of evidence supporting mosh pits, including enthusiastic quotations from concertgoers, while omitting (or summarizing very rapidly) the data about the dangers of mosh pits.

- **Emphasizing a detailed story versus presenting lots of facts and statistics:** Often, writers can choose to support a point with a memorable individual case or with aggregate data such as statistics or lists of facts. A memorable story can have a strongly persuasive effect. For example, to create a negative view of mosh pits, a writer might tell the heartrending story of a teenager suffering permanent brain damage from being dropped on a mosh pit floor. In contrast, a supporter of mosh pits might tell the story of a happy music lover turned on to the concert scene by the rush of crowd surfing. A different strategy is to use facts and statistics rather than case narratives—for example, data about the frequency of mosh pit accidents, financial consequences of lawsuits, and so forth. The single-narrative case often has a more powerful rhetorical effect, but it is always open to the charge that it is an insufficient or nonrepresentative example. Vivid anecdotes make for interesting reading, but by themselves they may not be compelling logically. In contrast, aggregate data, often used in scholarly studies, can provide more compelling, logical evidence but sometimes make the prose wonkish and dense.

- **Providing contextual and interpretive comments when presenting data:** When citing data, writers can add brief contextual or interpretive comments that act as lenses over the readers' eyes to help them see the data from the writer's perspective. Suppose you want to support mosh pits, but also want to admit that mosh pits are dangerous. You could make that danger seem irrelevant or inconsequential by saying: "It is true that occasional mosh pit accidents happen, just as accidents happen in any kind of recreational activity such as swimming or weekend softball games." The concluding phrase frames the danger of mosh pits by comparing it to other recreational accidents that don't require special laws or regulations. The implied argument is this: banning mosh pits because of an occasional accident would be as silly as banning recreational swimming because of occasional accidents.

- **Putting contrary evidence in subordinate positions:** Just as a photographer can place a flower at the center of a photograph or in the background, a writer can place a piece of data in a subordinate or main clause of a sentence. Note how the structure of the following sentence minimizes emphasis on the rarity of mosh pit accidents: "Although mosh pit accidents are rare, the danger to the city of multimillion-dollar liability lawsuits means that the city should nevertheless ban them for reasons of fiscal prudence." The factual data that mosh pit accidents are rare is summarized briefly and tucked away in a subordinate *although* clause, while the writer's own position is elaborated in the main clause where it receives grammatical emphasis. A writer with a different angle of vision might say, "Although some cities may occasionally be threatened with a lawsuit, serious accidents resulting from mosh pits are so rare that cities shouldn't interfere with the desires of music fans to conduct concerts as they please."

■ **Choosing labels and names that guide the reader's response to data:** One of the most subtle ways to control your readers' response to data is to choose labels and names that prompt them to see the issue as you do. If you like mosh pits, you might refer to the seating arrangements in a concert venue as "festival seating, where concertgoers have the opportunity to create a free-flowing mosh pit." If you don't like mosh pits, you might refer to the seating arrangements as "an accident-inviting use of empty space where rowdies can crowd together, slam into each other, and occasionally punch and kick." The labels you choose, along with the connotations of the words you select, urge your reader to share your angle of vision.

■ **Revealing the value system that determines the writer's selection and framing of data:** Ultimately, how a writer selects and frames evidence is linked to the system of values that organize his or her argument. If you favor mosh pits, you probably favor maximizing the pleasure of concertgoers, promoting individual choice, and letting moshers assume the risk of their own behavior. If you want to forbid mosh pits, you probably favor minimizing risks, protecting the city from lawsuits, and protecting individuals from the danger of their own out-of-control actions. Sometimes you can foster connections with your audience by openly addressing the underlying values that you hope your audience shares with you. You can often frame your selected data by stating explicitly the values that guide your argument.

Special Strategies for Framing Statistical Evidence

Numbers and statistical data can be framed in so many ways that this category of evidence deserves its own separate treatment. By recognizing how writers frame numbers to support the story they want to tell, you will always be aware that other stories are also possible. Ethical use of numbers means that you use reputable sources for your basic data, that you don't invent or intentionally distort numbers for your own purposes, and that you don't ignore alternative points of view. Here are some of the choices writers make when framing statistical data:

■ **Raw numbers versus percentages.** You can alter the rhetorical effect of a statistic by choosing between raw numbers and percentages. In the summer of 2002, many American parents panicked over what seemed like an epidemic of child abductions. If you cited the raw number of these abductions reported in the national news, this number, although small, could seem scary. But if you computed the actual percentage of American children who were abducted, that percentage was so infinitesimally small as to seem insignificant. You can apply this framing option directly to the mosh pit case. To emphasize the danger of mosh pits, you can say that twenty-four deaths occurred at rock concerts in a given year. To minimize this statistic, you could compute the percentage of deaths by dividing this number by the total number of people who attended rock concerts during the year, certainly a number in the several millions. From the perspective of percentages, the death rate at concerts is extremely low.

■ **Median versus mean.** Another way to alter the rhetorical effect of numbers is to choose between the median and the mean. The mean is the average of all numbers on a list. The median is the middle number when all the numbers are arranged sequentially from high to low. In 2006 the mean annual income for retired families in the United States was $41,928—not a wealthy amount but enough to live on comfortably if you owned your own home. However, the median income was only $27,798, a figure that gives a much more striking picture of income distribution among older Americans. This median figure means that half of all retired families in the United States had annual incomes of $27,798 or less. The much higher mean income indicates that many retired Americans are quite wealthy. This wealth raises the average of all incomes (the mean) but doesn't affect the median.

■ **Unadjusted versus adjusted numbers.** Suppose your boss told you that you were getting a 5 percent raise. You might be happy—unless inflation rates were running at 6 percent. Economic data can be hard to interpret across time unless the dollar amounts are adjusted for inflation. This same problem occurs in other areas. For example, comparing grade point averages of college graduates in 1970 versus 2012 means little unless one can somehow compensate for grade inflation.

■ **Base point for statistical comparisons.** In 2008, the stock market was in precipitous decline if one compared 2008 prices with 2007 prices. However, the market still seemed vigorous and healthy if one compared 2008 with 2002. One's choice of the base point for a comparison often makes a significant rhetorical difference.

■ ■ ■ **FOR CLASS DISCUSSION** **Using Strategies to Frame Statistical Evidence**

A proposal to build a new ballpark in Seattle, Washington, yielded a wide range of statistical arguments. All of the following statements are reasonably faithful to the same facts:

■ The ballpark would be paid for by raising the sales tax from 8.2 percent to 8.3 percent during a twenty-year period.

■ The sales tax increase is one-tenth of 1 percent.

■ This increase represents an average of $7.50 per person per year—about the price of a movie ticket.

■ This increase represents $750 per five-person family over the twenty-year period of the tax.

■ For a family building a new home in the Seattle area, this tax will increase building costs by $200.

■ This is a $250 million tax increase for the residents of the Seattle area.

How would you describe the costs of the proposed ballpark if you opposed the proposal? How would you describe the costs if you supported the proposal?   ■ ■ ■

Gathering Evidence

We conclude this chapter with some brief advice on ways to gather evidence for your arguments. We begin with a list of brainstorming questions that may help you think of possible sources for evidence. We then provide suggestions for conducting interviews and creating surveys and questionnaires, since these powerful sources are often over-looked by students.

Creating a Plan for Gathering Evidence

As you begin contemplating an argument, you can use the following checklist to help you think of possible sources for evidence.

A Checklist for Brainstorming Sources of Evidence

- What personal experiences have you had with this issue? What details from your life or the lives of your friends, acquaintances, or relatives might serve as examples or other kinds of evidence?
- What observational studies would be relevant to this issue?
- What people could you interview to provide insights or expert knowledge on this issue?
- What questions about your issue could be addressed in a survey or question-naire?
- What useful information on this issue might encyclopedias, specialized reference books, or the regular book collection in your university library provide?
- What evidence might you seek on this issue using licensed database indexing sources for magazines, newspapers, and scholarly journals?
- How might an Internet search engine help you research this issue?
- What evidence might you find on this issue from reliable statistical resources such as U.S. Census Bureau data, the Centers for Disease Control, or *Statistical Abstract of the United States*?

WRITING ASSIGNMENT   A Microtheme or a Supporting-Reasons Argument

Option 1: A Microtheme   Write a one- or two-paragraph argument in which you support one of the following enthymemes, using evidence from personal experience, field observation, interviews, or data from a brief questionnaire or survey. Most of your microtheme should support the stated reason with evidence. However, also include a brief passage supporting the implied warrant. The opening sentence of your microtheme should be the enthymeme itself, which serves as the thesis statement for your argument. (Note: If you disagree with the enthymeme's argument, recast the claim or the reason to assert what you want to argue.)

1. Reading fashion magazines can be detrimental to teenage girls because such magazines can produce an unhealthy focus on beauty.

2. Surfing the Web might harm your studying because it causes you to waste time.

3. Service-learning courses are valuable because they allow you to test course concepts within real-world contexts.

4. Summer internships in your field of interest, even without pay, are the best use of your summer time because they speed up your education and training for a career.

5. Any enthymeme (a claim with a *because* clause) of your choice that can be supported without library or Internet research. (The goal of this microtheme is to give you practice using data from personal experience or from brief field research.) You may want to have your instructor approve your enthymeme in advance.

Option 2: A Supporting-Reasons Argument   Write an argument that uses at least two reasons to support your claim. Your argument should include all the features of a classical argument except the section on summarizing and responding to opposing views.

A *supporting-reasons argument* is our term for a classical argument without a section that summarizes and responds to opposing views. Even though alternative views aren't dealt with in detail, the writer usually summarizes an opposing view briefly in the introduction to provide background on the issue being addressed. Follow the explanations and organization chart for a classical argument as shown earlier in this chapter, but omit the section called "summary and critique of opposing views."

Like a complete classical argument, a supporting-reasons argument has a thesis-governed structure in which you state your claim at the end of the introduction, begin body paragraphs with clearly stated reasons, and use effective transitions throughout to keep your reader on track. In developing your own argument, place your most important, persuasive, or interesting reason last, where it will have the greatest impact on your readers. This kind of tightly organized structure is sometimes called a *self-announcing* or *closed-form* structure because the writer states his or her claim before beginning the body of the argument and forecasts the structure that is to follow. In contrast, an *unfolding* or *open-form* structure doesn't give away the writer's position until late in the essay.

In writing a self-announcing argument, students often ask how much of the argument to summarize in the thesis statement. Consider your options:

■ You might announce only your claim:

The public should not support the commercial use of captured dolphins.

■ You might forecast a series of parallel reasons:

There are several reasons why the public should not support the commercial use of captured dolphins.

■ You might forecast the actual number of reasons:

This paper presents four reasons why the public should not support the commercial use of captured dolphins.

■ Or you might forecast the whole argument by including your *because* clauses with your claim:

The public should not support the commercial use of captured dolphins because marine parks and "swim with dolphins" programs place direct stress on dolphins by separating them from their natural habitat and social groups; because they spread inaccurate and incomplete educational information about dolphins; because they create a commercial market for dolphins that directly or indirectly encourages dolphin hunts and captures; and because they promote an attitude of human dominance over animals.

This last thesis statement forecasts not only the claim, but also the supporting reasons that will serve as topic sentences for key paragraphs throughout the body of the paper.

No formula can tell you precisely how much of your argument to forecast in the introduction. However, these suggestions can guide you. In writing a self-announcing argument, forecast only what is needed for clarity. In short arguments, readers often need only your claim. In longer arguments, however, or in especially complex ones, readers appreciate your forecasting the complete structure of the argument (claim with reasons). ■

Sample Supporting-Reasons Argument

What follows is Carmen Tieu's supporting-reasons argument.

Why Violent Video Games Are Good for Girls
CARMEN TIEU (STUDENT)

It is ten o'clock P.M., game time. My entire family knows by now that when I am home on Saturday nights, ten P.M. is my gaming night when I play my favorite first-person-shooter games, usually *Halo 3,* on Xbox Live. Seated in my mobile chair in front of my family's 42-inch flat screen HDTV, I log onto Xbox Live. A small message in the bottom of the screen appears with the words "Kr1pL3r is online," alerting me that one of my male friends is online and already playing. As the game loads, I send Kr1pL3r a game invite, and he joins me in the pre-game room lobby.

In the game room lobby, all the players who will be participating in the match are chatting aggressively with each other: "Oh man, we're gonna own you guys so bad." When a member of the opposing team notices my gamer tag, "embracingapathy," he begins to insult me by calling me various degrading, gay-associated names: "Embracing apa-what? Man, it sounds so emo. Are you some fag? I bet you want me so bad. You're gonna get owned!" Players always assume from my gamer tag that I am a gay male, never a female. The possibility that I am a girl is the last thing on their minds. Of course, they are right that girls seldom play first-person-shooter games. Girls are socialized into activities that promote togetherness and talk, not high intensity competition involving fantasized shooting and killing. The violent nature of the games tends to repulse girls. Opponents of violent video games typically hold that these games are so graphically violent that they will influence players to become amoral and sadistic. Feminists also argue that violent video games often objectify women by portraying them as sexualized toys for men's gratification. Although I understand these objections, I argue that playing first-person-shooter games can actually be good for girls.

First, playing FPS games is surprisingly empowering because it gives girls the chance to beat guys at their own game. When I first began playing *Halo 2,* I was horrible. My male friends constantly put me down for my lack of skills, constantly telling me that I was awful, "but for a girl, you're good." But it didn't take much practice until I learned to operate the two joy sticks with precision and with quick instinctual reactions. While guys and girls can play many physical games together, such as basketball or touch football, guys will always have the advantage because on average they are taller, faster, and stronger than females. However, when it comes to video games, girls can compete equally because physical strength isn't required, just quick reaction time and manual dexterity—skills that women possess in abundance. The adrenaline rush that I receive from beating a bunch of testosterone-driven guys at something they supposedly excel at is exciting; I especially savor the look of horror on their faces when I completely destroy them.

Since female video gamers are so rare, playing shooter games allows girls to be freed from feminine stereotypes and increases their confidence. Culture generally portrays females as caring, nonviolent, and motherly beings who are not supposed to enjoy FPS games with their war themes and violent killings. I am in no way rejecting these traditional female values since I myself am a compassionate, tree-hugging vegan. But I also like to break these stereotypes. Playing video games offers a great way for females to break the social mold of only doing "girly" things and introduces them to something that males commonly enjoy. Playing video games with sexist males has also helped me become more outspoken. Psychologically, I can stand up to aggressive males because I know that I can beat them at their own game. The confidence I've gotten from excelling at shooter games may have even carried over into the academic arena because I am majoring in chemical engineering and have no fear whatsoever of intruding into the male-dominated territory of math and science. Knowing that I can beat all the guys in my engineering classes at *Halo* gives me that little extra confidence boost during exams and labs.

5   Another reason for girls to play FPS games is that it gives us a different way of bonding with guys. Once when I was discussing my latest *Halo 3* matches with one of my regular male friends, a guy whom I didn't know turned around and said, "You play *Halo*? Wow, you just earned my respect." Although I was annoyed that this guy apparently didn't respect women in general, it is apparent that guys will talk to me differently now that I can play video games. From a guy's perspective I can also appreciate why males find video games so addicting. You get joy from perfecting your skills so that your high-angle grenade kills become a thing of beauty. While all of these skills may seem trivial to some, the acknowledgment of my skills from other players leaves me with a perverse sense of pride in knowing that I played the game better than everyone else. Since I have started playing, I

have also noticed that it is much easier to talk to males about lots of different subjects. Talking video games with guys is a great ice-breaker that leads to different kinds of friendships outside the realm of romance and dating.

Finally, playing violent video games can be valuable for girls because it gives them insights into a disturbing part of male subculture. When the testosterone starts kicking in, guys become blatantly homophobic and misogynistic. Any player, regardless of gender, who cannot play well (as measured by having a high number of kills and a low number of deaths) is made fun of by being called gay, a girl, or worse. Even when some guys finally meet a female player, they will also insult her by calling her a lesbian or an ugly fat chick that has no life. Their insults towards the girl will dramatically increase if she beats them because they feel so humiliated. In their eyes, playing worse than a girl is embarrassing because girls are supposed to be inept at FPS games. Whenever I play *Halo* better than my male friends, they often comment on how "it makes no sense that we're getting owned by Carmen."

When males act like such sexist jerks it causes one to question if they are always like this. My answer is no because I know, first hand, that when guys like that are having one-on-one conversations with a female, they show a softer side, and the macho side goes away. They don't talk about how girls should stay in the kitchen and make them dinner, but rather how they think it is cool that they share a fun, common interest with a girl. But when they are in a group of males their fake, offensive macho side comes out. I find this phenomenon troubling because it shows a real problem in the way boys are socialized. To be a real "man" around other guys, they have to put down women and gays in activities involving aggressive behavior where men are supposed to excel. But they don't become macho and aggressive in activities like reading and writing, which they think of as feminine. I've always known that guys are more physically aggressive than women, but until playing violent video games I had never realized how this aggression is related to misogyny and homophobia. Perhaps these traits aren't deeply ingrained in men but come out primarily in a competitive male environment. Whatever the cause, it is an ugly phenomenon, and I'm glad that I learned more about it. Beating guys at FPS games has made me a more confident woman while being more aware of gender differences in the way men and women are socialized. I joined the guys in playing *Halo,* but I didn't join their subculture of ridiculing women and gays.

Moving Your Audience
Ethos, Pathos, and *Kairos*

11

At first, one may be tempted to think of *logos, ethos,* and *pathos* as "ingredients" in an essay, like spices you add to a casserole. But a more appropriate metaphor might be that of different lamps and filters used on theater spotlights to vary lighting effects on a stage. Thus if you switch on a *pathos* lamp (possibly through using more concrete language or vivid examples), the resulting image will engage the audience's sympathy and emotions more deeply. If you overlay an *ethos* filter (perhaps by adopting a different tone toward your audience), the projected image of the writer as a person will be subtly altered. If you switch on a *logos* lamp (by adding, say, more data for evidence), you will draw the reader's attention to the logical appeal of the argument. Depending on how you modulate the lamps and filters, you shape and color your readers' perception of you and your argument.

Our metaphor is imperfect, of course, but our point is that *logos, ethos,* and *pathos* work together to create an impact on the reader. Consider, for example, the different impacts of the following arguments, all having roughly the same logical appeal.

1. People should adopt a vegetarian diet because doing so will help prevent the cruelty to animals caused by factory farming.
2. If you are planning to eat chicken tonight, please consider how much that chicken suffered so that you could have a tender and juicy meal. Commercial growers cram the chickens so tightly together into cages that they never walk on their own legs, see sunshine, or flap their wings. In fact, their beaks must be cut off to keep them from pecking each other's eyes out. One way to prevent such suffering is for more and more people to become vegetarians.
3. People who eat meat are no better than sadists who torture other sentient creatures to enhance their own pleasure. Unless you enjoy sadistic tyranny over others, you have only one choice: become a vegetarian.
4. People committed to justice might consider the extent to which our love of eating meat requires the agony of animals. A visit to a modern chicken factory—where chickens live their entire lives in tiny, darkened coops without room to spread their wings—might raise doubts about our right to inflict such suffering on sentient creatures. Indeed, such a visit might persuade us that vegetarianism is a more just alternative.

Chapter 11, Moving Your Audience: *Ethos, Pathos, and Kairos*, is taken from John D. Ramage, John C. Bean, and June Johnson's *Writing Arguments*, pp. 109–123 (Chapter 6, Moving Your Audience: *Ethos, Pathos,* and *Kairos*).

Each argument has roughly the same logical core:

ENTHYMEME

CLAIM People should adopt a vegetarian diet

REASON because doing so will help prevent the cruelty to animals caused by factory farming.

GROUNDS

• Evidence of suffering in commercial chicken farms, where chickens are crammed together and lash out at one another

• Evidence that only widespread adoption of vegetarianism will end factory farming

WARRANT

If we have an alternative to making animals suffer, we should use it.

But the impact of each argument varies. The difference between arguments 1 and 2, most of our students report, is the greater emotional power of argument 2. Whereas argument 1 refers only to the abstraction "cruelty to animals," argument 2 paints a vivid picture of chickens with their beaks cut off to prevent their pecking each other blind. Argument 2 makes a stronger appeal to *pathos* (not necessarily a stronger argument), stirring feelings by appealing simultaneously to the heart and to the head.

The difference between arguments 1 and 3 concerns both *ethos* and *pathos.* Argument 3 appeals to the emotions through highly charged words such as *torture, sadists,* and *tyranny.* But argument 3 also draws attention to its writer, and most of our students report not liking that writer very much. His stance is self-righteous and insulting. In contrast, argument 4's author establishes a more positive *ethos.* He establishes rapport by assuming his audience is committed to justice and by qualifying his argument with the conditional term *might.* He also invites sympathy for the chickens' plight—an appeal to *pathos*—by offering a specific description of chickens crammed into tiny coops.

Which of these arguments is best? They all have appropriate uses. Arguments 1 and 4 seem aimed at receptive audiences reasonably open to exploration of the issue, whereas arguments 2 and 3 seem designed to shock complacent audiences or to rally a group of True Believers. Even argument 3, which is too abusive to be effective in most instances, might work as a rallying speech at a convention of animal liberation activists.

Our point thus far is that *logos, ethos,* and *pathos* are different aspects of the same whole, different lenses for intensifying or softening the light beam you project onto the screen. Every choice you make as a writer affects in some way each of the three appeals. The rest of this chapter examines these choices in more detail.

How to Create an Effective *Ethos:* The Appeal to Credibility

The ancient Greek and Roman rhetoricians recognized that an argument would be more persuasive if the audience trusted the speaker. Aristotle argued that such trust resides within the speech itself, not in the prior reputation of the speaker. In the speaker's manner and delivery, tone, word choice, and arrangement of reasons, in the sympathy with which he or she treats alternative views, the speaker creates a trustworthy persona. Aristotle called the impact of the speaker's credibility the appeal from *ethos.* How does a writer create credibility? We suggest four ways:

- **Be knowledgeable about your issue.** The first way to gain credibility is to *be* credible—that is, to argue from a strong base of knowledge, to have at hand the examples, personal experiences, statistics, and other empirical data needed to make a sound case. If you have done your homework, you will command the attention of most audiences.
- **Be fair.** Besides being knowledgeable about your issue, you need to demonstrate fairness and courtesy to alternative views. Because true argument can occur only where people may reasonably disagree with one another, your *ethos* will be strengthened if you demonstrate that you understand and empathize with other points of view. There are times, of course, when you may appropriately scorn an opposing view. But these times are rare, and they mostly occur when you address audiences predisposed to your view. Demonstrating empathy to alternative views is generally the best strategy.
- **Build a bridge to your audience.** A third means of establishing credibility—building a bridge to your audience—has been treated at length in our earlier discussions of audience-based reasons. By grounding your argument in shared values and assumptions, you demonstrate your goodwill and enhance your image as a trustworthy person respectful of your audience's views. We mention audience-based reasons here to show how this aspect of *logos*—finding the reasons that are most rooted in the audience's values—also affects your *ethos* as a person respectful of your readers' views.
- **Demonstrate professionalism.** Finally, you can enhance your *ethos* by the professionalism revealed in your manuscript itself: Appropriate style, careful editing and proofreading, accurate documentation, and adherence to the genre conventions expected by your audience all contribute to the image of the person behind the writing. If your manuscript is sloppy, marred by spelling or grammatical errors, or inattentive to the tone and style of the expected genre, your own credibility will be damaged.

How to Create *Pathos*: The Appeal to Beliefs and Emotions

Before the federal government outlawed unsolicited telephone marketing, newspapers published flurries of articles complaining about annoying telemarketers. Within this context, a United Parcel Service worker, Bobbi Buchanan, wanted to create sympathy for telemarketers. She wrote a *New York Times* op-ed piece entitled "Don't Hang Up, That's My Mom Calling," which begins as follows:

> The next time an annoying sales call interrupts your dinner, think of my 71-year-old mother, LaVerne, who works as a part-time telemarketer to supplement her social security income. To those Americans who have signed up for the new national do-not-call list, my mother is a pest, a nuisance, an invader of privacy. To others, she's just another anonymous voice on the other end of the line. But to those who know her, she's someone struggling to make a buck, to feed herself and pay her utilities—someone who personifies the great American way.

The editorial continues with a heartwarming description of LaVerne. Buchanan's rhetorical aim is to transform the reader's anonymous, depersonalized image of telemarketers into the concrete image of her mother: a "hardworking, first generation American; the daughter of a Pittsburgh steelworker; survivor of the Great Depression; the widow of a World War II veteran; a mother of seven, grandmother of eight, great-grandmother of three. . . ." The intended effect is to alter our view of telemarketers through the positive emotions triggered by our identification with LaVerne.

By urging readers to think of "my mother, LaVerne" instead of an anonymous telemarketer, Buchanan illustrates the power of *pathos,* an appeal to the reader's emotions. Arguers create pathetic appeals whenever they connect their claims to readers' values, thus triggering positive or negative emotions depending on whether these values are affirmed or transgressed. Pro-life proponents appeal to *pathos* when they graphically describe the dismemberment of a fetus during an abortion. Proponents of improved women's health and status in Africa do so when they describe the helplessness of wives forced to have unprotected sex with husbands likely infected with HIV. Opponents of oil exploration in the Arctic National Wildlife Refuge (ANWR) do so when they lovingly describe the calving grounds of caribou.

Are such appeals legitimate? Our answer is yes, if they intensify and deepen our response to an issue rather than divert our attention from it. Because understanding is a matter of feeling as well as perceiving, *pathos* can give access to nonlogical, but not necessarily nonrational, ways of knowing. *Pathos* helps us see what is deeply at stake in an issue, what matters to the whole person. Appeals to *pathos* help readers walk in the writer's shoes. That is why arguments are often improved through the use of stories that make issues come alive or sensory details that allow us to see, feel, and taste the reality of a problem.

Appeals to *pathos* become illegitimate, we believe, when they confuse an issue rather than clarify it. Consider the case of a student who argues that Professor Jones ought to raise his grade from a D to a C, lest he lose his scholarship and be forced to leave college, shattering the dreams of his dear old grandmother. To the extent that students' grades should be based on performance or effort, the student's image of the dear old grandmother is an illegitimate appeal to *pathos* because it diverts the reader from rational to irrational criteria. The weeping grandmother may provide a legitimate motive for the student to study harder but not for the professor to change a grade.

Although it is difficult to classify all the ways that writers can create appeals from *pathos,* we will focus on four strategies: concrete language; specific examples and illustrations; narratives; and connotations of words, metaphors, and analogies. Each of these strategies lends "presence" to an argument by creating immediacy and emotional impact.

Use Concrete Language

Concrete language—one of the chief ways that writers achieve voice—can increase the liveliness, interest level, and personality of a writer's prose. When used in argument, concrete language typically heightens *pathos*. For example, consider the differences between the first and second drafts of the following student argument:

First Draft

People who prefer driving a car to taking a bus think that taking the bus will increase the stress of the daily commute. Just the opposite is true. Not being able to find a parking spot when in a hurry to be at work or school can cause a person stress. Taking the bus gives a person time to read or sleep, etc. It could be used as a mental break.

Second Draft (Concrete Language Added)

Taking the bus can be more relaxing than driving a car. Having someone else behind the wheel gives people time to chat with friends or cram for an exam. They can balance their checkbooks, do homework, doze off, read the daily newspaper, or get lost in a novel rather than foam at the mouth looking for a parking space.

In this revision, specific details enliven the prose by creating images that trigger positive feelings. Who wouldn't want some free time to doze off or to get lost in a novel?

Use Specific Examples and Illustrations

Specific examples and illustrations serve two purposes in an argument. They provide evidence that supports your reasons; simultaneously, they give your argument presence and emotional resonance. Note the flatness of the following draft arguing for the value of multicultural studies in a university core curriculum:

First Draft

Another advantage of a multicultural education is that it will help us see our own culture in a broader perspective. If all we know is our own heritage, we might not be inclined to see anything bad about this heritage because we won't know anything else. But if we study other heritages, we can see the costs and benefits of our own heritage.

Now note the increase in "presence" when the writer adds a specific example:

Second Draft (Example Added)

Another advantage of multicultural education is that it raises questions about traditional Western values. For example, owning private property (such as buying your own home) is part of the American dream. However, in studying the beliefs of American Indians, students are confronted with a very different view of private property. When the U.S. government sought to buy land in the Pacific Northwest from Chief Sealth, he is alleged to have replied:

> The president in Washington sends words that he wishes to buy our land. But how can you buy or sell the sky? The land? The idea is strange to us. If we do not own the freshness of the air and the sparkle of the water, how can you buy them?[. . .] We are part

of the earth and it is part of us.[. . .] This we know: The earth does not belong to man, man belongs to the earth.

Our class was shocked by the contrast between traditional Western views of property and Chief Sealth's views. One of our best class discussions was initiated by this quotation from Chief Sealth. Had we not been exposed to a view from another culture, we would have never been led to question the "rightness" of Western values.

The writer begins his revision by evoking a traditional Western view of private property, which he then questions by shifting to Chief Sealth's vision of land as open, endless, and unobtainable as the sky. Through the use of a specific example, the writer brings to life his previously abstract point about the benefit of multicultural education.

Use Narratives

A particularly powerful way to evoke *pathos* is to tell a story that either leads into your claim or embodies it implicitly and that appeals to your readers' feelings and imagination. Brief narratives—whether true or hypothetical—are particularly effective as opening attention grabbers for an argument. To illustrate how an introductory narrative (either a story or a brief scene) can create pathetic appeals, consider the following first paragraph to an argument opposing jet skis:

I dove off the dock into the lake, and as I approached the surface I could see the sun shining through the water. As my head popped out, I located my cousin a few feet away in a row-boat waiting to escort me as I, a twelve-year-old girl, attempted to swim across the mile-wide, pristine lake and back to our dock. I made it, and that glorious summer day is one of my most precious memories. Today, however, no one would dare attempt that swim. Jet skis have taken over this small lake where I spent many summers with my grandparents. Dozens of whining jet skis crisscross the lake, ruining it for swimming, fishing, canoeing, rowboating, and even waterskiing. More stringent state laws are needed to control jet skiing because it interferes with other uses of lakes and is currently very dangerous.

This narrative makes a case for a particular point of view toward jet skis by winning our identification with the writer's experience. She invites us to relive that experience with her while she also taps into our own treasured memories of summer experiences that have been destroyed by change.

Opening narratives to evoke *pathos* can be powerfully effective, but they are also risky. If they are too private, too self-indulgent, too sentimental, or even too dramatic and forceful, they can backfire on you. If you have doubts about an opening narrative, read it to a sample audience before using it in your final draft.

Use Words, Metaphors, and Analogies with Appropriate Connotations

Another way of appealing to *pathos* is to select words, metaphors, or analogies with connotations that match your aim. We have already described this strategy in our discussion of the "framing" of evidence. By using words with particular connotations, a writer guides readers to see the issue through the writer's angle of vision. Thus if you want to create positive feelings about a recent city council decision, you can call it "bold and decisive"; if you want to create negative feelings, you can call it "haughty and autocratic." Similarly, writers can use favorable or unfavorable metaphors and analogies to evoke different imaginative or emotional responses. A tax bill might be viewed as a "potentially fatal poison pill" or as "unpleasant but necessary economic medicine." In each of these cases, the words create an emotional as well as intellectual response.

■ ■ ■ **FOR CLASS DISCUSSION** Incorporating Appeals to Pathos
Outside class, rewrite the introduction to one of your previous papers (or a current draft) to include more appeals to *pathos.* Use any of the strategies for giving your argument presence: concrete language, specific examples, narratives, metaphors, analogies, and connotative words. Bring both your original and your rewritten introductions to class. In pairs or in groups, discuss the comparative effectiveness of these introductions in trying to reach your intended audience.   ■ ■ ■

Using Images for Emotional Appeal

One of the most powerful ways to engage an audience emotionally is to use photos or other images. Although many written arguments do not lend themselves to visual illustrations, we suggest that when you construct arguments you consider the potential of visual support. Imagine that your argument were to appear in a newspaper, in a magazine, or on a Web site where space would be provided for one or two visuals. What photographs or drawings might help persuade your audience toward your perspective?

When images work well, they are analogous to the verbal strategies of concrete language, specific illustrations, narratives, and connotative words. The challenge in using visuals is to find material that is straightforward enough to be understood without elaborate explanations, that is timely and relevant, and that clearly adds impact to a specific part of your argument. As an example, suppose you are writing an argument supporting fund-raising efforts to help a third-world country that has recently experienced a natural catastrophe. To add a powerful appeal to *pathos,* you might consider incorporating into your argument the photograph shown in Figure 11.1 of the cleanup efforts in Port-au-Prince, Haiti, after the January 2010 earthquake. A photograph such as this one can evoke a strong emotional and imaginative response as well as make viewers think.

■ ■ ■ **FOR CLASS DISCUSSION** Analyzing Images as Appeals to Pathos
Working in small groups or as a whole class, share your responses to the following questions:

1. How would you describe the emotional/imaginative impact of Figure 11.1?
2. Many disaster-relief photos seek to convey the magnitude of the destruction and suffering, sometimes shockingly, by depicting destroyed buildings, mangled bodies, and images of human misery. How is your response to Figure 11.1 similar to

FIGURE 11.1 Cleanup in Port-au-Prince, Haiti, after the 2010 earthquake

or different from your response to commonly encountered close-up photographs of grief-stricken victims or to distance shots of widespread destruction? To what extent is Figure 11.1's story–with the woman carrying a basket juxtaposed against the enormous mechanical shovel–different from the more typical photographs of destroyed buildings or anguished faces?

Kairos: The Timeliness and Fitness of Arguments

To increase your argument's effectiveness, you need to consider not only its appeals to *logos, ethos,* and *pathos,* but also its *kairos*–that is, its timing, its appropriateness for the occasion. *Kairos* is one of those wonderful words adopted from another language (in this case, ancient Greek) that is impossible to define, yet powerful in what it represents. In Greek, *kairos* means "right time," "season," or "opportunity." It differs subtly from the ordinary Greek word for time, *chronos,* the root of our words "chronology" and "chronometer." You can measure *chronos* by looking at your watch, but you measure *kairos* by sensing the opportune time through psychological attentiveness to situation and meaning. To think *kairotically* is to be attuned to the total context of a situation in order to act in the right way at the right moment. By analogy, consider a skilled base runner who senses the right moment to steal second, a wise teacher who senses the right moment to praise or critique a student's performance, or a successful psychotherapist who senses the right moment to talk rather than listen in a counseling session. *Kairos* reminds us that a rhetorical situation is not stable and fixed, but evolves as events unfold or as audiences experience the psychological ebbs and flows of attention and care. Here are some examples that illustrate the range of insights contained by the term *kairos:*

- If you write a letter to the editor of a newspaper, you usually have a one- or two-day window before a current event becomes "old news" and is no longer interesting. An out-of-date letter will be rejected, not because it is poorly written or argued but because it misses its *kairotic* moment. (Similar instances of lost timeliness occur in class discussions: On how many occasions have you wanted to contribute an idea to class discussion, but the professor doesn't acknowledge your raised hand? When you finally are called on, the *kairotic* moment has passed.)

- Bobbi Buchanan's "Don't Hang Up, That's My Mom Calling," which we used to illustrate *pathos,* could have been written only during a brief historical period when telemarketing was being publicly debated. Moreover, it could have been written only late in that period, after numerous writers had attacked telemarketers. The piece was published in the *New York Times* because the editor received it at the right *kairotic* moment.

- A sociology major is writing a senior capstone paper for graduation. The due date for the paper is fixed, so the timing of the paper isn't at issue. But *kairos* is still relevant. It urges the student to consider what is appropriate for such a paper. What is the "right way" to produce a sociology paper at this moment in the history of the discipline? Currently, what are leading-edge versus trailing-edge questions in sociology? What theorists are now in vogue? What research methods would most impress a judging committee? How would a good capstone paper written in 2010 differ from one written a decade earlier?

As you can see from these examples, *kairos* concerns a whole range of questions connected to the timing, fitness, appropriateness, and proportions of a message within an evolving rhetorical context. There are no rules to help you determine the *kairotic* moment for your argument, but being attuned to *kairos* will help you "read" your audience and rhetorical situation in a dynamic way.

■ ■ ■   **FOR CLASS DISCUSSION** Analyzing an Argument from the Perspectives

of Kairos, Logos, Ethos, and Pathos

Your instructor will select an argument for analysis. Working in small groups or as a whole class, analyze the assigned argument first from the perspective of *kairos* and then from the perspectives of *logos, ethos,* and *pathos.*

1. As you analyze the argument from the perspective of *kairos,* consider the following questions:

   a. What is the motivating occasion for this argument? That is, what causes this writer to put pen to paper or fingers to keyboard?

   b. What conversation is the writer joining? Who are the other voices in this conversation? What are these voices saying that compels the writer to add his or her own voice? How was the stage set to create the *kairotic* moment for this argument?

   c. Who is the writer's intended audience and why?

    d. What is the writer's purpose? Toward what view or action is the writer trying to persuade his or her audience?

    e. To what extent can various features of the argument be explained by your understanding of its *kairotic* moment?

2. Now analyze the same argument for its appeals to *logos, ethos,* and *pathos.* How successful is this argument in achieving its writer's purpose?

How Audience-Based Reasons Enhance
Logos, Ethos, and *Pathos*

We conclude this chapter with the concept of audience-based reasons. Audience-based reasons enhance *logos* because they are built on underlying assumptions (warrants) that the audience is likely to accept. But they also enhance *ethos* and *pathos* by helping the writer identify with the audience, entering into their beliefs and values. To consider the needs of your audience, you can ask yourself the following questions:

Questions for Analyzing Your Audience

What to Ask	Why to Ask It
1. *Who is your audience?*	Your answer will help you think about audience-based reasons.
	■ Are you writing to a single person, a committee, or the general readership of a newspaper, magazine, blog site, and so forth?
	■ Are your readers academics, professionals, fellow students, general citizens, or people with specialized background and interests?
	■ Can you expect your audience to be politically and culturally liberal, middle of the road, conservative, or all over the map? What about their religious views?
	■ How do you picture your audience in terms of social class, ethnicity, gender, sexual orientation, age, and cultural identity?
	■ To what extent does your audience share your own interests and cultural position? Are you writing to insiders or outsiders with regard to your own values and beliefs?
2. *How much does your audience know or care about your issue?*	Your answer can especially affect your introduction and conclusion:
	■ Do your readers need background on your issue or are they already in the conversation?
	■ If you are writing to specific decision makers, are they currently aware of the problem you are addressing? If not, how can you get their attention?
	■ Does your audience care about your issue? If not, how can you get them to care?

What to Ask	Why to Ask It
3. *What is your audience's current attitude toward your issue?*	Your answer will help you decide the structure and tone of your argument.
	▪ Are your readers already supportive of your position? Undecided? Skeptical? Strongly opposed? ▪ What other points of view besides your own will your audience be weighing?
4. *What will be your audience's likely objections to your argument?*	Your answer will help determine the content of your argument and will alert you to extra research you may need.
	▪ What weaknesses will audience members find? ▪ What aspects of your position will be most threatening to them and why? ▪ How are your basic assumptions, values, or beliefs different from your audience's?
5. *What values, beliefs, or assumptions about the world do you and your audience share?*	Your answer will help you find common ground with your audience.
	▪ Despite different points of view on this issue, where can you find common links with your audience? ▪ How might you use these links to build bridges to your audience?

To see how a concern for audience-based reasons can enhance *ethos* and *pathos,* suppose that you support racial profiling (rather than random selection) for determining who receives intensive screening at airports. Suppose further that you are writing a guest op-ed column for a liberal campus newspaper and imagine readers repulsed by the notion of racial profiling (as indeed you are repulsed too in most cases). It's important from the start that you understand and acknowledge the interests of those opposed to your position. The persons most likely targeted by racial profiling would be Middle Eastern males as well as black males with African passports, particularly those from African nations with large Islamic populations. These persons will be directly offended by racial profiling at airports. From the perspective of social justice, they can rightfully object to the racial stereotyping that lumps all people of Arabic, Semitic, or African appearance into the category "potential terrorists." Similarly, African Americans and Hispanics, who frequently experience racial profiling by police in U.S. cities, may object to further extension of this hated practice. Also, most political liberals, as well as many moderates and conservatives, may object to the racism inherent in selecting people for airport screening on the basis of ethnicity or country of origin.

What shared values might you use to build bridges to those opposed to racial profiling at airports? You need to develop a strategy to reduce your audience's fears and to link your reasons to their values. Your thinking might go something like this:

Problem: How can I create an argument rooted in shared values? How can I reduce fear that racial profiling in this situation endorses racism or will lead to further erosion of civil liberties?

Bridge-building goals: I must try to show that my argument's goal is to increase airline safety by preventing terrorism like that of 9/11/01. My argument must show my respect for Islam and for Arabic and Semitic peoples. I must also show my rejection of racial profiling as normal police practice.

Possible strategies:

- Stress the shared value of protecting innocent people from terrorism.
- Show how racial profiling significantly increases the efficiency of secondary searches. (If searches are performed at random, then we waste time and resources searching people who are statistically unlikely to be terrorists.)
- Argue that airport screeners must also use indicators other than race to select people for searches (for example, traits that might indicate a domestic terrorist).
- Show my respect for Islam.
- Show sympathy for people selected for searching via racial profiling and acknowledge that this practice would normally be despicable except for the extreme importance of airline security, which overrides personal liberties in this case.
- Show my rejection of racial profiling in situations other than airport screening—for example, stopping African Americans for traffic violations more often than whites and then searching their cars for drugs or stolen goods.
- Perhaps show my support of affirmative action, which is a kind of racial profiling in reverse.

These thinking notes allow you to develop the following plan for your argument.

- Airport screeners should use racial profiling rather than random selection to determine which people undergo intensive screening
  - because doing so will make more efficient use of airport screeners' time, increase the odds of finding terrorists, and thus lead to greater airline safety (*WARRANT: Increased airline safety is good;* or, at a deeper level, *The positive consequences of increasing airline safety through racial profiling outweigh the negative consequences.*)
  - because racial profiling in this specific case does not mean allowing it in everyday police activities nor does it imply disrespect for Islam or for Middle Eastern or African males (WARRANT: *Racial profiling is unacceptable in everyday police practices. It is wrong to show disrespect for Islam or Middle Eastern or African males.*)

As this plan shows, your strategy is to seek reasons whose warrants your audience will accept. First, you will argue that racial profiling will lead to greater airline safety, allowing you to stress that safe airlines benefit all passengers. Your concern is the lives of hundreds of passengers as well as others who might be killed in a terrorist attack. Second, you plan to reduce adversaries' resistance to your proposal by showing that the consequences aren't as severe as they might fear. Using racial profiling in airports would not justify using it in urban police work (a practice you find despicable) and it would not imply disrespect for Islam or Middle Eastern or African males. As this example shows, your focus on audience—on the search for audience-based reasons— shapes the actual invention of your argument from the start.

■ ■ ■ **FOR CLASS DISCUSSION** Planning an Audience-Based Argumentative Strategy

1. How does the preceding plan for an argument supporting racial profiling make appeals to *ethos* and *pathos* as well as to *logos*?

2. Working individually or in small groups, plan an audience-based argumentative strategy for one or more of the following cases. Follow the thinking process used by the writer of the racial-profiling argument: (1) state several problems that the writer must solve to reach the audience, and (2) develop possible solutions to those problems.

   a. An argument for the right of software companies to continue making and selling violent video games: aim the argument at parents who oppose their children's playing these games.

   b. An argument to reverse grade inflation by limiting the number of As and Bs a professor can give in a course: aim the argument at students who fear getting lower grades.

   c. An argument supporting the legalization of cocaine: aim the argument at readers of *Reader's Digest,* a conservative magazine that supports the current war on drugs. ■ ■ ■

WRITING ASSIGNMENT Revising a Draft for *Ethos, Pathos,* and Audience-Based Reasons

Part 1: Choose an argument that you have previously written or that you are currently drafting. Revise the argument with explicit focus on increasing its appeals to *ethos, pathos,* and *logos* via audience-based reasons and other strategies. Consider especially how you might improve *ethos* by building bridges to the audience or improve *pathos* through concrete language, specific examples, metaphors, or connotations of words. Finally, consider the extent to which your reasons are audience-based.

Or

Multimodal option: Imagine an argument that you have previously written or are currently drafting that could be enhanced with effective photographs or images. Revise your argument to include these images, perhaps creating a desktop published document that wraps text around visuals chosen to enhance *pathos.* Other multimodal possibilities include transforming your argument into a speech supported by PowerPoint images, into a poster argument, or even into a podcast that includes music.

Part 2: Attach to your revision or transformed project a reflective letter explaining the choices you made in revising your original argument or in transforming it using a multimodal approach. Describe for your instructor the changes or transformations you made and explain how or why your new version enhances your argument's effectiveness at moving its audience. ■

Writing for Public Audiences

Perhaps no other scene so fully depends on its genres as does the **public scene.** Other scenes share locations (like schools and universities), share common objectives and values (like the belief in logic and reason), and may even share participants who see each other regularly as they go about their lives day to day, as is often true in workplaces. But where does the public scene exist? What values do all members of the public share? How many members of the public scene see each other in a week, a month, or even a year? For what we are calling public scenes, genres go far toward helping to identify their members, define their common situations, and shape their shared values. In many ways, genres serve as the sites in which members of the public communicate and interact with one another.

In this chapter, we will examine the nature of this public and explore a wide range of public genres, analyzing them for what they can tell us about how and why people communicate and behave in public scenes of writing. We will begin by describing how some public genres appeal to a specific public while others appeal to a more general public. Then we will focus on a segment of the public called the public sphere, in which people interested in political issues and issues of policy engage in rational debate. We will describe the genres, called civic genres (genres such as letters to the editor, editorials, pamphlets, and petitions), people use in order to shape public opinion and effect social change within the public sphere. As we will see, participating in civic genres can range from trying to influence a large, general public to having one's say within smaller groups with common interests. Having an impact on society, using writing to serve a public good, can even include contributing your writing talents to groups who need your services. This chapter, then, applies genre analysis and writing to scenes and situations in the world outside of work and school to see how people communicate information to broad audiences and to influence public actions. Such knowledge of how and why public genres work will serve you well as you use these genres to participate within public scenes of writing as a writer and a citizen.

Chapter 12, Understanding Genres and Writing for Public Audiences, is taken from Amy Devitt, Mary Jo Reiff, and Anis Bawarshi's *Scenes of Writing*, pp. 521–550 and 555–569 (Chapter 10, Reading and Writing within Public Scenes).

The Public and Its Genres

Grocery lists, letters to friends, diaries and journals, voice mail messages—these and many other genres help us go about our day-to-day lives and interact with important people in our lives. The genres we are interested in for this chapter are ones that work within broader scenes than work, school, or those that include only friends and family. The focus is on genres that address what some have called a **general public**—nameless people who need some information the writer has or whose opinion somehow matters to the writer or the scene.

Of course, various situations call for conveying information to as broad a public as possible. When a couple is married, many genres are used, including toasts, invitations, thank-you notes, and, of course, the ceremony. The traditional wedding scene is not just a private affair, however; it also includes situations that call for public broadcasting of the information, often through a wedding announcement in the newspaper. The significance of this public announcement is evident in the fact that gay couples are increasingly demanding, and gaining, the right to announce commitment ceremonies in the newspapers just as heterosexual couples do. Similarly, informing is a primary purpose of many articles in newspapers and magazines and many Web sites, genres designed to convey information to a broad public. Think about a news report on the most recent business scandal, a feature article on postpartum depression, or a Web site for the National Parks or Wildlife Service. Genres conveying specific information to a general public include dictionaries and other reference works, billboard advertisements, brochures from local services like health centers, bus schedules, and other written and electronic sources of information that a general public may need.

Unlike the academic genres we explored in previous chapters, the scenes that use these public genres are at most loosely defined. There is no well-defined group of dictionary-users as there is a group of molecular biologists, for example. The readers of news reports are a vague group compared to the readers of lab reports. It is in the very nature of public genres that the "public," the participants in the scene, constitutes a shadowy community.

How Public Genres Define Public Scenes and Situations

Perhaps even more so than in workplace and academic scenes, in public scenes genres help to constitute their own situations (settings of interactions involving certain participants, subjects, and purposes). *The nature of particular public genres helps to define who reads and writes them.* Although it is intended as a public broadcast of a marriage, for example, the wedding announcement in the newspaper is not read by everyone, not even by all newspaper readers. The newspaper article reporting last night's baseball game similarly is read only by a subset of the general public. Both genres define their publics by signaling the nature of their readership and defining the subject matter, purposes, and settings in which this readership interacts. They do so by such features as the kind of information included and the language used. Compare the two texts reprinted below, one a wedding announcement and one a game report. Pay special attention to what information is included and what is omitted, and note any special language used, including terms you might not know.

What differences in the kinds of information provided did you notice? Both genres include facts about what happened and names of participants, but the facts and the styles differ in obvious ways.

The wedding announcement includes information about who performed various roles, gives the family background of the bride and groom, and identifies the locations of the ceremony and reception. What information is not included? In the past (and still in some forums), wedding announcements also included descriptions of what the wedding party wore, how the locations were decorated, and what food was served. No wedding announcements, no matter how unconventional, describe what family tensions reared up in the seating arrangements, state how many times the bride had been married before, or quote the parents on whether or not they approve. In the wedding announcement genre, such information is not considered appropriate or relevant to the situation of announcing a marriage publicly.

Wedding Announcement

LEE-AUDUS

Jenny Lee, Eudora, and Ryan Audus, Lawrence, were married Aug. 11, 2001, at Trinity Episcopal Church in Lawrence with the Rev. Robert Lord officiating.

The bride is the daughter of Donna and Joseph Ketchum, Eudora, and Ronald Lee, Linwood. The groom is the son of Kenneth and Cheryl Audus, Lawrence.

Julie Avila was matron of honor. Aaron Kabler was best man.

Bridesmaids were Kristi Durkin, Maribeth Orr and Carly Audus. Groomsmen were Nathan Knust, Shawn Ferguson and Vicente Avila.

Alexis Avila and Jacqueline Black were flower girls. Dawson Kabler was ring bearer. Jafferty Costello was candlelighter.

A reception followed at Liberty Hall in Lawrence.

The bride is a graduate of Eudora High School and Kansas University, where she earned a bachelor's degree in business administration. She is an associate financial representative for Northwestern Mutual, Fairway.

The groom is a Lawrence High School graduate. He received a bachelor's degree in sports management from KU and is a product manager for TouchNet, Lenexa.

The couple live in Fairway.

Source: Lawrence Journal-World, Saturday, November 10, 2001, 2D.

Game Report
Arizona Denies New York Fourth Straight Crown

BY BEN WALKER
Associated Press Baseball Writer

Phoenix — The final World Series comeback belonged to the Arizona Diamondbacks, and it was the greatest of all.

Luis Gonzalez hit an RBI single to cap a two-run rally off Mariano Rivera in the bottom of the ninth inning, and Arizona stunned the New York Yankees, 3-2, in Game 7 on Sunday night.

"We went through sports' greatest dynasty to win our first World Series," said pitcher Curt Schilling, who shared the MVP award with fellow ace Randy Johnson.

The Yankees were only two outs from their fourth straight championship and fifth in six years when it suddenly fell apart.

Tony Womack tied it with an RBI double and, after Craig Counsell was hit by a pitch to load the bases with one out, Gonzalez blooped a soft single to center field.

Rivera, who had saved 23 straight postseason games, could do nothing but watch the ball fall in to end the Yankees' run.

"That's baseball," Rivera said. "There's nothing I can do about it."

The Yankees were trying to become the third team in history to win four titles in a row. The Bronx Bombers did it from 1936-39 and from 1949-53.

"We're obviously disappointed in the result, but not the effort," Yankees manager Joe Torre said.

Owner George Steinbrenner sounded the same tone.

"I'm proud of my team. We played our hearts out. It was a very tough loss. I will be a gracious loser," he said. "We'll be back. Mark that down. We'll be back. I'm not a good loser."

What began as a November duel between Schilling and Roger Clemens climaxed with the Diamondbacks winning the title in just their fourth year of existence.

It was the fastest rise in history, breaking the mark of five years set by the 1997 Marlins. That Florida team was the last to win when trailing in the ninth inning of a Game 7, doing it against Cleveland.

The Diamondbacks bounced back from two of the toughest losses in Series history. They dropped Games 4 and 5 at Yankee Stadium, blowing two-run leads in the bottom of the ninth both times.

Randy Johnson, 38, earned the victory in relief. He also won Game 6 on Saturday night, a 15-2 romp.

Johnson was 3-0, making him the first pitcher to win three times in a Series since Detroit's Mickey Lolich in 1968. The Big Unit won five times in this postseason.

Johnson, Schilling and several Arizona old-timers, including Gonzalez, Mark Grace, Matt Williams and Mike Morgan, won their first championship ring.

"They have a great ballclub over there, but this team was relentless," Gonzalez said. "This is probably going to go down as one of the best World Series ever."

Arizona's Bob Brenly became the first manager to win the championship in his first year since Ralph Houk did it with the Yankees in 1961.

"I felt that we outplayed them," Brenly said.

The Diamondbacks outscored New York 37-14 in a Series in which the home team won every game, just the third time that has ever happened.

The Yankees, the team that would not give up, nearly won it for the city that would not give in. A highly motivated bunch, they showed extra resolve after the Sept. 11 terrorist attacks in New York.

"That was the greatest Game 7 ever," said New York City Mayor Rudolph Giuliani, who went to the Diamondbacks locker room to offer his congratulations to them. "As a Yankees fan, I wish it turned out differently."

The Yankees were a home run swing away from elimination in the first round against Oakland, and lost the first two games at Bank One Ballpark.

But back in the desert, they looked lost.

Alfonso Soriano's solo homer off Schilling put New York ahead 2-1 in the eighth. Rivera, the most dominant reliever in postseason history, set down the Diamondbacks in the bottom half.

Then in the ninth, Arizona rallied.

Grace led off with a single and Rivera threw away Damian Miller's bunt for an error, putting runners at first and second.

Jay Bell bunted into a force play at third, but Womack lined a tying double to the right-field corner. Counsell, who scored the winning run in Game 7 with Florida in 1997, was hit by a pitch.

With the infield in, Gonzalez hit it hard enough for a game-winning single that set off fireworks, pounding music and deafening cheers.

Rivera had pitched six scoreless innings in the Series before Arizona won.

"That was the one guy we wanted to stay away from the whole World Series," Gonzalez said. "We got him the one time it counted."

The Yankees fell to 5-6 in deciding Game 7s of the Series.

Schilling was nearly untouchable at the start. The first pitcher to start three games in a Series since Minnesota's Jack Morris in 1991, he once again showed no ill effects from working on three days' rest.

Schilling allowed only one hitter to reach through six innings, and even that guy did not last long on the bases.

Paul O'Neill, playing his final game before retiring, was thrown out trying to stretch a double into a triple in the first.

But given a 1-0 lead in the sixth on Danny Bautista's RBI double, Schilling gave it back.

A strange wind started swirling through the ballpark to start the top of the seventh. Maybe it was a precursor of what was to come because moments later, Arizona had blown its edge.

Schilling retired 16 straight hitters before slumping. Derek Jeter led off with a single and O'Neill followed with a single in front of center fielder Steve Finley.

One out later, Tino Martinez tied it with an RBI single.

Clemens, pitching the biggest game of his great career, worked out of several early jams. The Diamondbacks caught up to him in the sixth after Finley led off with a single.

Bautista was next, and many people thought the man with five RBIs in Saturday's 15-2 romp would bunt. Brenly once again crossed up his critics and let Bautista swing away, and it worked.

Bautista hit a drive into the left-center gap, and Clemens simply stood on the mound with his right hand on hip, watching the play unfold.

Clemens was pulled after 6 1/3 innings with 10 strikeouts. He left without a Game 7 victory, the only thing missing on his Hall of Fame resume.

Notes: Yankees outfielder David Justice played in the previous two Game 7s and lost both times, with Atlanta in 1991 and Cleveland in 1997. He singled as a pinch-hitter in the eighth. ... All 50 players on the rosters appeared in at least one Series game.

Source: Lawrence Journal-World, Monday, November 5, 2001, 1C, 3C.

Compare the information included in the game report: scores at various points, including at the end, players who performed especially well or poorly, descriptions of key plays, comments by the coaches. Unlike wedding announcements, game reports do tend to refer to tensions between the teams, give past records of the participants, and quote the coaches on whether or not they approve of their players' performances. But game reports rarely report the family lineage of the players (unless the player is related to another known athlete). In turn, wedding announcements do not describe critical moments during the ceremony. Out of all the possible information one could include about a given event, whether a wedding or a game, each genre selects particular kinds of information as appropriate to the scene and situation of writing.

Defining Specific Publics

The kind of information included suggests the kind of audience, narrowing the readership from a completely unspecified general public to the particular public that reads the genre. Readers of wedding announcements may never see each other, but they share a common interest in local society as reflected in the genre they all read. Readers of game reports may well share the game experience as well, but, whether or not they attended the game, they share a common interest in that sport and that team and in the details of how a game played out. Those commonalities are partly *defined* by the genre they all read.

The narrowing of the public appears clearly in the language used. You probably noted the terminology used in the two examples you examined. The game report uses words known well by those who follow the sport: two-run rally, RBI, MVP, load the bases, blooped a soft single, for examples just in the first paragraphs. The wedding announcement uses its own technical terminology: matron of honor, groomsmen, ring bearer, candlelighter, for examples. To be a reader of each genre, a member of its public, you must be willing and able to learn and use that vocabulary. Of course, anyone may be an actual reader of a particular text. You may read your first wedding announcement when someone else shows you the announcement of the wedding of someone you know. You may read the report of a game that was your first experience in the sport, or you may read the report of Game 7 of the 2001 Arizona-New York World Series because you watched that particular game, even if you do not usually watch, much less read about, baseball. But such an occasional reader will not get the full implications of a genre meant for a special readership. Reflected in particular kinds of content and language, each public genre defines its audience from among the entire general public to create a particular public.

Collaborative Activity

Bring to class an example of a public genre other than wedding announcements and game reports. Make sure it is a genre written for an audience broader than family and friends and other than academic or workplace audiences. Compare the genres brought in by your group, using Box 7.1 (pp. 92–93) to help you describe the kinds of information they include, the way they present this information, and the kinds of language they use. In doing so, try to characterize the particular public each genre defines.

Defining More General Publics

While wedding announcements and game reports obviously appeal only to some readers within a general public, some other genres seem to define a broader public audience. Although readers must have general knowledge of the world, newspaper articles on the front page, for example, do not seem to require the technical knowledge that wedding and sports genres do. News reports tell *all* readers of the paper what has been happening in the world. Similarly, editorials comment on significant issues for general readers. Letters to the editor speak to all newspaper readers. Crossword puzzles offer a daily game, and comics offer daily amusement that any newspaper reader could understand. Advertisements announce sales. Ann Landers gives advice. Each of these genres is available to anyone who can pick up a copy of the newspaper and who can read—a truly general public. Along with newspapers, forums like magazines and Web sites commonly include such public genres.

Even though these genres seem more accessible than wedding and sports genres, these genres, too, define particular publics and reflect particular situations. First of all, not all newspaper readers read every genre, not even the front-page articles or the comics. Only those interested in the kind of news reported on the front page read those articles, and children may read only the comics. Some readers skim the first lines of news articles and read only a few articles in full. ***These facts of readership, parts of the genres' situations, influence how the genres are written.*** News articles report the most essential information in the first few sentences so that some readers can skip the rest and still have basic knowledge. Most comics use language easily understood by children as well as adult readers. Other such apparently general genres as editorials select subjects and presume background knowledge so as to define a narrower readership. Some editorial writers concentrate on international or political issues, for example, and feel no need to identify world leaders or explain long-standing or significant political debates. Other editorial writers focus on home or family issues, defining a readership with different knowledge and interests. Even the "general public" of the newspaper, then, divides into more specific publics based on common interests, and the genres help to define those more particular publics.

Not only do different genres within a newspaper appeal to different segments of the public, but also different newspapers reach different regional publics. The *Des Moines Register* does not reach the same national public as the *San Francisco Chronicle*, and neither reaches the same national public as the *New York Times* or *USA Today*. And some members of the general public do not read newspapers at all. Some might be members of a magazine-reading public, others might listen to television or radio talk shows, and still others might surf the Internet. In short, many "general publics" exist, just as we saw that many academic scenes exist. When we speak of the public, then, we need to acknowledge that no public includes everyone and that even the broadest-seeming genres reflect particular situations and create their particular publics.

Writing Activity

Make a list of all of the public genres you read (or watch or hear) that other people also follow. Which ones are accessible to a more generalized readership and appeal to a broader, more "general public"? What signals the genre's availability to a general public? Which ones define narrower publics with particular knowledge and interests? How are these particular publics defined by the genre and by its particular situations (subjects, settings, participants, and purposes)?

Civic Genres and Public Participation

One particular set of public genres works to define a public that is interested in political and policy issues and tries to influence public opinion in order to improve society. These kinds of public genres that try to shape public opinion and effect societal change are part of what are called **civic genres.** Before we examine some particular civic genres, we need to examine the shared objectives of their public scene and to consider some of the debates about its validity and importance.

Shared Objectives behind Civic Genres

Letters to the editor, editorials, guest columns, speeches, pamphlets, and petitions are all genres that address a large public in order to persuade people to agree with the writers. Some of these civic genres, like petitions and most pamphlets, also are meant to change behavior as well as minds. Petitions persuade people to sign but then are delivered to someone in authority who can effect change more directly. Writers of pamphlets typically want to persuade people to send money or change their lifestyles as well as to believe in the rightness of the pamphlet writer's cause. A letter to the editor might urge people to take action, or it might just urge people to believe differently (or to affirm their prior beliefs).

Often civic genres have no intention of changing people's behaviors *directly* or of making them do something immediately. Instead, writers of these texts want people to agree with the writers, perhaps to change their minds about an issue, perhaps to understand new arguments in favor of the writers' positions. Many of these writers mainly want to influence public opinion.

What good does it do just to influence public opinion instead of persuading people to take some action? Writers of civic genres believe that public opinion matters to the people who can make change happen. Built into the scene in which civic genres are used is the belief that government representatives and other people in positions of power care what "the public" thinks (and the dependence on public opinion polls reflects this), so influencing what the public thinks is influencing what people in power will do. This belief, of course, is built into representative governments and organizations that rest on democratic principles. If a public consensus can be developed, then the public's representatives in the state and organizations will need to follow that consensus. ***Writers of civic genres presume that a public consensus—and hence public policy—should be based in rational discussion of significant public issues.*** Editorials, letters to editors, speeches, and columns participate in the public, rational debate that should help us discover what is best for our common interest.

Writing Activity

Bring to class an example of a civic genre—a pamphlet, petition, flyer, letter to the editor, editorial, or any other genre that seeks to influence public opinion. Describe the public scene that is being targeted. What seem to be its common interests and shared objectives? Is the genre trying to change the minds of readers or their behavior or both?

Participating in the Public Sphere

Civic genres participate in what some scholars call the **public sphere.** In somewhat simplified terms, the public sphere is a forum for rational debate among all members of a group about issues of general concern. The public sphere is not a single location, like a town hall or an editorial page or an electronic discussion list. It includes all these locations and any others where people debate public issues in rational ways. The public sphere must also allow any person to voice any opinion about an issue, as long as the issue is generally relevant and the opinion is based in reason. And all people must have access to these forums, whether as speakers, writers, readers, or listeners. Through the use of civic genres that emerge from and shape these forums, individuals can participate in rational discussions of significant issues, thereby shaping the public opinion that represents the greatest good for the society at that time and place.

In some ways, this model of the public sphere is an idealized one, a model of what we wish would be in a perfect democratic world. It is also somewhat limited. In fact, the public debate about an issue often leaves out many people and many opinions. Public debate is not always rational, and the hallmarks of Western logic may dominate other ways of making significant arguments. Feminists in the 1960s and 1970s, for example, argued that the personal is political, an argument that leads among other things to basing rational argument in personal experience as well as public logic.

Also, everyone does not have equal access to the forums and genres of the public sphere. Vigorous public debate can silence less aggressive opinions, as you may have experienced in the classroom when heated debate leads to some participants dominating the conversation. In every society, too, some people have more power than others, and their opinions tend to be broadcast and listened to more than others'. Some entire groups may be underrepresented in the public sphere. Historically, members of minority groups have not received equal access to most public forums or public genres, and poorer members of society tend not to be those who are in a position to or can afford to write letters, circulate petitions, or offer guest columns.

Even if we somehow solved the problem of unequal access, some scholars would question whether there is such a thing as a general public or a "public sphere" that is common to everyone in a society. What forums exist in which *everyone* participates, so that public opinion can reflect a common general debate? Certainly the media—books, newspapers, magazines, radio, television—link us to others in society in ways that appear to create a space for general debate; however, even these forums may be limited in the public opinions represented. The word *media* is the plural form of *medium*, which comes from a Latin word meaning "middle," reminding us that media forums like television and radio are *mediated* experiences. In other words, what stories a newspaper decides to cover depends upon what stories the editorial board finds interesting or important. By functioning as gatekeepers and imposing their perceptions of significance on the audience, journalists and editorial boards can narrow and limit full public participation. In addition, not everyone reads a daily newspaper, much less contributes to one. Not everyone watches television, and not everyone is permitted to speak on the television stations that are widely watched. Some of the most widely shared genres—perhaps television shows, advertisements—are very restricted in who gets to produce them. While they may draw on and provide common cultural references, they do not allow the kind of access required for participating in shared public debate.

Collaborative Activity

In groups of three, assign each member of your group to bring to class a different newspaper published on the same date. You might choose to have one person bring a large national daily (like the *New York Times, Wall Street Journal,* or *Washington Post*), another your regional/local paper, and another either an independent or alternative paper from your city or a daily from another town/city (which you can find online or in the library). Analyze the similarities and differences in what the papers report. Do the papers reflect a shared public sphere, or do they define particular publics (or both)? What counts as news in each one? What different perspectives does each paper take on similar subjects? What opinions and points of view are left out? Examine any differences in coverage of politics, sports, entertainment, crime, etc. What do these forums indicate about their readerships or publics? What do the similarities or differences you noted tell you about the differing assumptions and expectations of these public forums?

What does this debate about the existence and accessibility of the public sphere mean? We believe that it makes it all the more important for us to speak up when the opportunity arises, to participate in the genres of civic discourse, to make our voices heard whenever and wherever we can, and to make a point of listening to as many different voices as possible. While access to the public sphere may be uneven, you can use the civic genres to which you *do* have access (like letters to your senator or congressional representative, letters to the editor, petitions, etc.) to influence public actions. Drawing on the rhetorical strategies of civic genres, you can carry out social actions and work to be heard and to hear others. For public debate and consensus to work in imperfect civic scenes, in which access and representation are unequal, everyone must participate in multiple public groups of differing memberships and participate in multiple public genres in order to obtain a more informed understanding of and to participate more fully in the issues. Read a daily newspaper or two, listen to multiple news shows on television and radio, seek out Web sites from a wide range of reputable sources, attend forums sponsored by groups you don't belong to and on subjects you don't usually consider. Read or listen to every source critically, knowing that the debate on each issue is larger than a single source. In a diverse and large society, the public sphere will be diverse and large and will require good citizens to work to be well-informed and to participate in public debate through public genres.

Writing Activity

List all the public forums you listen to or read, including newspapers and magazines but also Web sites, discussion lists, and radio and television shows. Note which of those sites use genres that allow the public to respond (for example, a Web site that includes a bulletin board, a newspaper that accepts letters to the editor, a radio show that has a call-in component). How do the genres in these public forums both enable and limit participation and response?

Collaborative Activity

Compare the list of public forums and genres that each member of your group has access to (listed in the preceding activity). Note how many forums many of you share and how many different forums appear among your lists. Discuss whether the particular publics of each forum overlap or are relatively distinct. Discuss also how you could broaden the range of publics you participate in, what different kinds of forums you could find, and how you could go about finding them.

Collaborative Activity

Compile for the class a list of public forums that your group believes include multiple public groups, use genres that allow the public to participate, and encourage rational debate. Annotate that list by describing for each forum its particular public and how someone could contribute to the forum's debate. What are the various genres that emerge from these forums and shape the goals of these forums? How might you change these genres to increase participation and debate?

Examples of Civic Genres

The genres through which people participate in the public sphere thus have significant objectives and can lead to significant change, even though they do not necessarily advocate that readers/listeners take a specific action and even though they might not reach everyone involved in an issue. A letter to the editor, guest column on an editorial page, or political Web site participates in a large, dynamic dialogue, with one text responding to others on the same issue so that people can see the issue more clearly in all its complexity. It is each citizen's responsibility not only to listen to this dialogue but also to join in. Democracy depends on citizens who speak up at public forums, contribute to discussion lists, write letters to the editor, offer columns to newspapers, magazines, and Web sites that are read by a public audience. If public consensus develops from public debate involving multiple voices, good citizens need to contribute their voices and opinions so that the common interest can be discovered.

In case you think your voice is too small or faint to be heard, consider the case of John, a student at one of our universities. Having researched the low pay of campus workers for an argument paper in his writing class, John discovered that campus workers were paid $5.65 per hour, well below the average wage for workers statewide ($9.50 per hour), and were not provided full benefits. To try to make a difference, John decided to join the Living Wage Campaign, an organized effort on the part of faculty, students, and staff to support campus workers. To assist in this effort, John turned his paper into a flyer that he posted on and off campus, attempting to inform and shape public opinion and to motivate individuals to lend their support to the campaign, including marching in campus protests. Unlike some other scenes in which genres might have immediate effect, like proposals in workplace scenes and syllabi in academic scenes, civic genres don't often have immediate, visible effects in their public scenes. Nonetheless, John's work may help to influence public opinion as others read his flyer. In any case, his rhetorical contributions enable people to become better informed through his participation in the public debate.

You may have opportunities to participate in many different public genres. Some groups publish newsletters, for example, that they distribute widely. Others develop Web sites containing essays or thought pieces. Some create pamphlets that broadcast the group's stances. Some organize town meetings or panels or run discussion lists. As you become more active in civic organizations, you will need to learn the particular genres used in their scenes of writing. Each offers a somewhat different response to somewhat different situations, of course, so you can use the genre analysis you have been learning in this book to understand and produce effective examples of the new civic genres you encounter. To help model how you can use genre analysis to understand and write civic genres more effectively, we will now guide you through detailed analyses of two civic genres: the letter to the editor and editorials, or guest columns.

Analyzing Letters to the Editor

One civic genre potentially available to all of us is letters to the editor. They are not really written for the editor at all. Rather, ***they are written to the particular public that reads that publication, to express someone's point of view and try to persuade others to see things the same way.*** Many kinds of publications accept letters, including magazines and newspapers as well as some online journals and regularly published newsletters. Let's begin with the examples of the genre. We will then help you analyze the situation and features of letters to the editor.

Below are all of the letters to the editor that appeared in one issue of one town's newspaper. We include *all* the letters so that you can see some range of what this genre encompasses without our selecting particular types of letters. As you read these letters, look for the underlying scenes and assumptions as well as the common situation and generic features.

Letters to the Editor

*(**LAWRENCE JOURNAL-WORLD**, NOVEMBER 8, 2001)*

1. Truck Traffic

To the editor:

Keep trucks out.

We voted to reduce traffic on 23rd Street. To do this all through traffic should be encouraged to use I-435. As for traffic on 31st street, we need traffic lights, turn lanes and limited zoning. We should not be pawns for politicians or the trucking industry, including the future Richards-Gabauer truck/rail exchange.

Steve King,
Lawrence

2. Driving Passion

To the editor:

I read several excellent letters in J-W recently that had comments about the traffic congestion in Lawrence and how KDOT's solutions would damage the wetlands.

To find sensible solutions, we need to look at history to see what caused this mess. The automobile, notwithstanding its shortcomings, is at the top of the list of what people want, whoever they are and wherever they live. High taxes designed to discourage car ownership have not had much effect, nor has the battle with urban traffic. People still drive under the most adverse conditions, or they move out when conditions become unbearable, then we have urban sprawl.

Federal, state and local governments in the U.S. subsidized the roads that accommodated the automotive revolution. However in Europe, public transit and the railways have received the subsidies, which public policy has been hostile or indifferent to the automobile. Perhaps that is because they don't have oil barons at the head of the government.

According to a recent study by Detroit Wayne State University, many suburban commuters now spend more than three hours in traffic each week day. Once home, they can't stop, except to switch hats, becoming taxi drivers, fetching children and running errands. According to author Tony Hiss, the average American family makes 14 car trips a day. More and more time in the car becomes almost intolerable when it occupies up to 30 hours and requires some 90 drives each week. People are no longer driving; they are driven.

Lawrence needs to maintain its unique character. Citizens need to join neighborhood groups to promote walking through neighborhoods to visit with neighbors.

Lester C. Marsh
Lawrence

3. Slap in the Face

To the editor:

The recent firing of two Allen Press employees for wearing Halloween paraphernalia is one of the most boneheaded and ridiculous moves I've ever seen a company make. As a business owner with over 100 employees on my payroll, I am saddened to realize that there are still bosses who behave and think in such intimidating and threatening ways.

At my company we have a laissez-faire attitude toward dress. I myself am guilty of wearing, dare I say, shorts, T-shirts and sandals in the summer, and I encourage my employees to do likewise. Halloween should be a time of fun for everyone. Unfortunately Allen management's only contribution to the mirth was a regressive, sick slap in the face directed at its employees.

Donald Phipps,
Lawrence

4. Trickle-Down Trick

To the editor:

We are gradually sliding into a recession, and lowering interest rates alone clearly hasn't helped much.

The cause of this recession seems evident. Obviously it is NOT a shortage of investments. Our factories, our retail stores, our transportation facilities, our service establishments, they all are laying off workers—over 415,000 in October alone—clear evidence that our economy is currently producing well below capacity. Why? Basically because consumers, economically insecure, have reduced their spending.

Now the president is proposing a "stimulus package" that, in professional lingo would be referred to as "supply side economics." What he proposes is a series of new tax cuts that would benefit primarily the wealthy (tens of thousands of dollars for the ones earning more than a million dollars a year), in the expectation that they will then invest it, which in turn will create jobs, and make the economy blossom again (I like to refer to it as feeding the horse so that the sparrows may eat). Now let me ask you: Honest, if you were in business and had an extra $50,000 or so, would you invest it in expanding your enterprise if you already can't sell the goods you have for sale? Does that make any sense to you?

Wouldn't it make more sense to place more purchasing power into the hands of those who do not have enough and would need and use this money for immediate consumer purchases? We could, for instance pay unemployment compensation for an additional three or six months to those who have lost their jobs without any fault of their own, or we could raise the minimum wage of workers that keeps them below the poverty level. Then, when these individuals spend their money and buy the goods that are for sale producers will have the incentive to produce more; and if they need to make more investments, they'll surely do so by using their own money or borrowing through bond sales from the public or, otherwise, from a bank.

Makes sense doesn't it? But try to sell that idea to those who believe that the way to go is to make the rich richer, and then some of it will surely trickle down to the poorer.

Harry G. Shaffer,
Lawrence

5. A Rigid Fiefdom

To the editor:

Regarding the recent flap about the firing of two employees at Allen Press, the company indeed has the right to fire employees because they don't adhere to the company's dress policy. Moreover, employees of the company have a right to seek employment elsewhere, and the company's customers have the right to seek another firm to do business with.

Allen Press' policy regarding dress reminds me of a recent excerpt I read in a book about the Taliban. A government official in Afghanistan issued an edict that women had to wear quiet shoes under their head-to-toe burqas. Failure to do so would result in serious penalties including beating or whipping. I am thankful that we are much more civilized here in the

U.S. Over here, one might lose one's livelihood for not adhering to some draconian policy, but at least we're not beaten or whipped.

U.S. and Afghan societies have something else in common. Both countries have at their hearts institutions whose beginnings are rooted in the Middle Ages. The fundamentalist interpretations of the Koran that the Taliban adhere to trace their beginning to the first millennium. Capitalism as we know it, owes much of its roots to Europe of the Middle Ages. We have been given some freedoms, but being employed by a large company has some parallels to serfdom. One need not think independently, nor express oneself. Just do the job and take the shekels paid. Companies preach empowerment, and send their employees to seminars about teamwork, then fire them because they wore a Halloween button.

I haven't had any dealings with Allen Press, and only know of them from the story I read. I hope that this incident represents an exception in the way they deal with employees. If it isn't, I hope at least some of their employees have the opportunity to find a less rigid fiefdom to serve.

Tim Bowles,
Olathe

6. A Sorry State

To the editor:

Terry Allen's dismissal only illuminates the sorry state of Kansas football. Rarely in collegiate athletics is a head coach fired while a season is in progress, regardless of how poorly a team is competing. College athletics, while driven by and dependent on revenue, should ultimately be about learning and it is hard to see how this late season dismissal helps the University of Kansas. Allen's firing will have little if any consequence on recruiting, and fans are not likely to flock to the remaining two home games to cheer on the Jayhawks because the message from the administration is that this season is officially a wash.

While that comes as no surprise to most, Allen's dismissal goes not only against the spirit of college athletics but against KU's institutional mission as well. This late-season move serves little more than a three-week headstart in the search process for a new coach. Regardless of the outcomes of the final games, the 2001 Jayhawks are Terry Allen's team and this move should have come at the end of the season.

I do not know Terry Allen, but by all accounts, he seems to be a decent, well-respected individual who was not met with success during his tenure at KU. And this does not distinguish him from any KU coaches in the recent past.

While a new era in KU football may loom on the horizon, the real shame lying beneath another losing season and another head football coach is that two varsity sports, men's swimming and tennis, were sacrificed last winter to pave way for increased spending for football. Dr. Bohl and the KU Athletic Department have a rare opportunity to correct a mistake and reinstate these programs that represented the best of the University of Kansas: scholarship, leadership, and athletic excellence.

Andrew Poggio,
Iowa City, Iowa

7. Credit is Due

To the editor:

What a slap in the face to all teaching librarians to find out in the Friday Journal-World that they are considered non-instructional personnel. I would dare to say that the people conducting this audit have not been in very many school libraries in Lawrence.

The librarian at my school spends most, if not all, of her day instructing groups of students. She is the central figure in all of our curricular studies, and is not just shelving books, as some people seem to think. I invite these people to visit Quail Run library any day of the week and see just what non-instruction really is!

Michele Trompeter,
Lawrence

Writing Activity

Choose one of the letters to the editor and try to reconstruct, as best you can, the writer's scene and situation. What shared objectives, values, beliefs, and assumptions are reflected in the editorial? What is the writer's purpose for writing? How does he or she transform a reported action into a significant public issue? What assumptions does the writer seem to make about audience?

Collaborative Activity

Using the samples provided and Box 7.1: Questions for Analyzing a Genre (pp. 92–93), work with your group to do an initial analysis of the genre of letters to the editor. Write a one-paragraph description of the scene of letters to the editor; then describe the situation of this genre—the readers, writers, purposes, subjects, and settings. Follow that paragraph with an initial list of generic features that these letters seem to have in common, despite their differences.

Some of the details of the letters you analyzed reflect the particular newspaper these letters were written for. Every forum has a policy on what letters they will accept. The *Lawrence Journal-World* states its "Letters Policy" as follows:

Letters Policy

The Journal-World welcomes letters to the Public Forum. Letters should be 350 words or less, be of public interest and should avoid name-calling and libelous language. The Journal-World reserves the right to edit letters, as long as viewpoints are not altered. Shorter letters are preferred and generally receive greater readership.

Letters must bear the name, address and telephone number of the writer. Letters may be submitted by e-mail to:

letters@ljworld.com

This letters policy appears in small print at the bottom of the editorial page in this newspaper. Other forums have similar statements that specify length, relevant subjects, and other details that make a letter more or less publishable in that forum. Note that the policy recognizes the place of letters to the editor in the public sphere, specifying that letters should be of public interest. The importance of rational debate may be suggested by the prohibition against name-calling and libelous language. This policy is not unusual, but each forum is different, so it is important to check the policy before writing a letter. Such policies are essential parts of the genre's situation.

By now, you have become so practiced at doing genre analysis that you probably handled the last group activity easily, recognizing the scene and situation in the genre and describing the genre's features. Rather than repeating the analysis you are capable of doing, then, let's concentrate on some of the more subtle features important to this particular genre, ones you probably noted but that deserve closer examination.

Public Issues

The letters reproduced here cover a range of subjects, including traffic congestion, the practices of a local business, the economy, college football, and the instructional value of librarians. These subjects did not simply occur to the writers as good subjects to write about. Each letter arose in response to someone else's action, usually an action reported in the newspaper. The newspaper story may have reported what happened, from its own perspective; the letters to the editor help turn those actions into debatable issues, ones that merit attention in the public sphere.

The general subjects become public issues in part through the actions of the letter writers. (We note, too, of course, that the newspaper's way of reporting the story initially may contribute to making an issue of what happened.) The last letter, "Credit is due," illustrates this move to public issue most obviously. The newspaper had referred to librarians as non-instructional personnel, and the letter writer "makes an issue of it" by writing a letter complaining and explaining the instructional role of librarians.

Other readers might not have noticed the wording or the implications, but one reader writes a letter to turn that wording into an issue of some public significance. Similarly, the newspaper had reported on the firing of employees for wearing Halloween-themed attire, and that act had become a private issue for the employees, who were considering filing suit. The act becomes a public issue, though, as people like the two letter writers here critique that action and what it represents of significance for the larger public. The fourth letter, "Trickle-down trick," responds to a less local action, the president's economic proposals, and "takes issue" with that plan. In writing a response to that plan, the letter writer creates a space for debating the president's proposals; the writer assumes that legislative actions need not simply be accepted but merit public review and discussion. He brings the action as an issue into the public sphere.

In the case of each letter, someone's reported actions have prompted the letter as a response, but ***it is the writing of the letter that has transformed the reported action***

into a significant public issue. This transformation of a reported action into a significant public issue is one of the rhetorical strategies a writer must make when writing a letter to the editor.

Civic discourse has as one of its major roles the enabling of public debate about actions affecting the public interest. Any subject that has potential significance for society can become a public issue. The public may not be in a position directly to enforce traffic laws, change a business's dress codes, implement economic policies, keep a football coach, or hire more librarians. However, through civic genres such as letters to

---

Writing Activity

Think of three subjects or actions that you might help "make an issue out of" by writing a letter to the editor. (You might think of issues for your campus newspaper as well as subjects of local and national significance.) List the actions your letters would respond to, and for each one state in a sentence the stance you would take to turn the action into an issue of public significance.

---

the editor, the public can call attention to the actions of those in power and to their beliefs and values (as well as the writer's own) and can sway public opinion to support or discourage their actions.

Openings and Closings

To sway public opinion, writers must not only call attention to an issue but must also get readers' attention. As you surely noted in your description of their situation, letters to the editor appear in a cluster on one or two pages, competing with each other and often with editorials for attention. Since newspaper readers are often in a hurry and selective (and newspapers prescribe a certain length for letters to the editor), letters have to grab their attention and have to try to make their point quickly and directly. Many readers will not read the entire letter. To be persuasive in such a situation, letters to the editor usually begin (after the obligatory "To the editor:") with a clear, direct assertion of the writer's position. Look at the openings of our sample letters, isolated below:

1. Keep trucks out.
2. I read several excellent letters in J-W recently that had comments about the traffic congestion in Lawrence and how KDOT's solutions would damage the wetlands.
3. The recent firing of two Allen Press employees for wearing Halloween paraphernalia is one of the most boneheaded and ridiculous moves I've ever seen a company make.

4. We are gradually sliding into a recession, and lowering interest rates alone clearly hasn't helped much.

5. Regarding the recent flap about the firing of two employees at Allen Press, the company indeed has the right to fire employees because they don't adhere to the company's dress policy.

6. Terry Allen's dismissal only illuminates the sorry state of Kansas football.

7. What a slap in the face to all teaching librarians to find out in the Friday *Journal-World* that they are considered non-instructional personnel.

You probably have no doubt of the writer's opinion, even if the issue is a local one you might not fully understand (like traffic on 23rd Street, for example). The one exception is letter 2, whose opening raises the subject but does not take a stand. Would you be likely to continue reading letter 2? Not only does the letter not make clear the writer's position, but also it does not grab the reader's attention. The other letters begin with a strong statement, sometimes the strongest statement of the entire letter. Imagine a newspaper reader scanning the letters quickly: The reader immediately knows what positions are being argued and can choose which to read further.

Letters to the editor usually end as they open, with a powerful statement of the writer's stance. Since readers typically scan the beginning and then the ending of a text, the closing statement gives the writer another shot at catching readers. Examine the last sentence of each letter to the editor below:

1. We should not be pawns for politicians or the trucking industry, including the future Richards-Gabauer truck/rail exchange.

2. Citizens need to join neighborhood groups to promote walking through neighborhoods to visit with neighbors.

3. Unfortunately Allen management's only contribution to the mirth was a regressive, sick slap in the face directed at its employees.

4. But we try to sell that idea to those who believe that the way to go is to make the rich richer, and then some of it will surely trickle down to the poorer.

5. If it isn't, I hope at least some of their employees have the opportunity to find a less rigid fiefdom to serve.

6. Dr. Bohl and the KU Athletic Department have a rare opportunity to correct a mistake and reinstate these programs that represented the best of the University of Kansas: scholarship, leadership, and athletic excellence.

7. I invite these people to visit Quail Run library any day of the week and see just what non-instruction really is!

Collaborative Activity

Analyze and describe the kinds of appeals (logical, emotional, ethical) used by the closing statements of each letter. Discuss why the writers might have chosen these appeals for the ending.

Notice that these final statements not only deliver a strong assertion of the main point but also do so more elaborately than the opening. The sentences are longer, the arguments more fully fleshed out. The closing comes at the end of the letter, after all, after the writer has had a chance to argue the point, offer details, and perhaps persuade the reader. The last sentence is the last chance to have an impact on the reader, to make a logical, emotional, or personal appeal that might sway readers to the writer's point of view.

Length and Detail

The *Journal-World*'s letters policy states a maximum length of 350 words and states that shorter letters gain more readers. So is shorter always better? No. If that were the case, the best letter would read simply, "No," or "Yes," or "Keep trucks out." While writers want their letters to be read, they also want to persuade those readers. Persuasion takes argument and detail.

The first letter on truck traffic, in fact, may be too undeveloped to persuade anyone. It states the writer's ideas (direct through traffic to an interstate and change 31st Street), and it offers a reason (reduce traffic and resist what politicians and trucking industry want). If you already agree with the problem, already are inclined to resist what politicians and industry want, and already want more restrictions on 31st Street, you are likely to agree with this letter. If you agree with the problem but had not thought of those proposed solutions, this letter may give you a new idea to consider. But if you agree with the problem but not with slowing down traffic on 31st Street, this letter offers little to persuade you otherwise. Such a short letter, in other words, works best for confirming readers' prior ideas or for raising new ideas. To persuade a wider public of the rightness of those ideas, a letter to the editor generally needs to offer more argument and evidence.

Compare the approach of the two longer letters, on the economy and on the firing of the football coach. Each offers reasons for the writer's stance and explains those reasons. The economy letter also offers some statistics as evidence of his point (and to enhance his ethos, his personal credibility). The drawback, of course, is that the letters require of readers more concentration and time. But neither letter is too long: Neither

Collaborative Activity

Compare the length and detail of the two letters on the employees fired for wearing Halloween paraphernalia. In what ways is each letter most effective? How well does each letter balance logos, pathos, and ethos? How might each letter be improved? Which letter do members of your group find most persuasive? Why? (Notice how your prior beliefs about dress codes and the roles of employees influence which letter you find persuasive.)

letter is so long that even those interested in the issue would not read the whole letter. Remember the scene and the readership of newspapers. The general public who reads this newspaper may scan the first sentences of the letters; the particular public of people interested in each issue is likely to read all of the letters on those issues. Good letters to the editor balance the need to reach as large a readership as possible with the need to persuade readers of the rightness of the writer's position.

Conciseness and Vividness

Within newspapers, the situation to which letters respond calls for brevity and engagement. Therefore, crafting concise sentences and using precise and vivid words is especially critical in letters to the editor. Each word of the 350 words maximum (or whatever the length your forum specifies) must count, both literally and figuratively. Letters must also grab readers' attention, and lively words can help do that.

Letters to the editor often use powerful words, ones packed with meaning and carrying an emotional punch. In our sample letters, the word *boneheaded* might have stood out because of its strong judgment, but this and other letters carry similarly powerful, though perhaps more subtle, words to make their points. Words that are both precise in meaning and lively in effect include *pawns, battle, oil barons, mirth, regressive, sick, flap, edict, draconian, serfdom, shekels,* and *sacrificed.* Phrases with impact include *athletic excellence, slap in the face, dare I say,* and *feeding the horse so that the sparrows may eat.* Statements including these less common, less everyday words and phrases hold the readers' attention more and carry emotional as well as logical weight. They also, of course, influence what readers think of the writer, the writer's ethos. Do you respect the thinking of someone who calls an action boneheaded? Do you admire his directness? Do you appreciate the knowledge of someone who compares the dress code to Taliban policies of burqas and shekels, or do you resent his trivializing of important international struggles? In short, writers must take care to make their letters lively and intriguing while conveying the most persuasive image of the writer and considering the effect on readers.

Collaborative Activity

Working through each letter, describe how the writer's choices of words and arguments affect how readers perceive the image of each writer. Based on these discussions, have each group member write a one-paragraph profile of one of the writers. What sort of persona do the writer's choices of words, phrases, and arguments help create? Who, that is, emerges from the language of the letter? And how does that constructed persona shape the way you as a reader might respond to the letter?

In such a situation requiring brief but persuasive statements, concise sentences help such vivid word choices stand out. Notice how the sentences in the letters consist of content-filled words, even those that are not especially vivid. "Keep trucks out" models the most concise sentences, ones with substantive words only. Of course, most English sentences require some emptier words like *the, have, of, in,* or *is,* but writing concisely pares sentences of as many of those emptier words as possible. Looking back at the first sentences of each letter, you can see how relatively few empty words appear. Compare "Terry Allen's dismissal only illuminates the sorry state of Kansas football" to a wordier version: "It seems to me as I consider the situation that the dismissal of one Terry Allen as the coach of the football team at the University of Kansas may be something that illuminates the state of football at the University of Kansas to be that of a sorry one." The livelier words are still present, but they are buried under a mass of verbiage.

Analyzing Editorials

Another genre that can contribute to public discussion is the editorial. Newspapers and magazines often use the title "guest column" for an editorial written by someone other than a member of the editorial staff. We will use the term *editorial* from now on to describe both guest columns and editorials.

The editorial shares many traits with academic analysis and argument papers as well as researched position papers, so it might at first seem hard to distinguish them. All of these genres present rational discussion of a significant issue, focus on a controlling idea, draw from reliable and credible sources, organize logically, and develop ideas with specific details. But consider the scene and situation of the editorial in contrast to that of the academic genres. Editorials speak to a public audience, not to a teacher or necessarily well-educated audience. The editorial writer has greater flexibility in defining a particular public, as we discussed earlier in this chapter, by his or her choice of subject, purposes, setting, and language; the academic writer usually has an assigned audience. The editorial writer can also often *choose* a public forum, whether a campus newspaper, an organization's newsletter, or an individual Web site, for example, further defining the editorial's audience.

Most significantly, perhaps, the *purpose* of the editorial differs from that of the academic genres that appear similar in form. Researched position papers and analysis papers aim to advance understanding of and knowledge about a significant subject in the academic scene; they need to demonstrate the reasonableness of their assertions and offer the writer's reasoned perspective. They need not persuade their readers to believe what they believe, even if they offer an argument. In addition, analysis papers and researched position papers take a more objective, critical stance rather than an invested persuasive stance. Editorials, on the other hand, like letters to the editor, participate in the ongoing discussion of the public sphere in order to help shape public consensus. To be effective, rather than critically examining and supporting an academic argument, editorials need to provide especially telling arguments or support, and they need to change some people's minds. This fundamentally persuasive purpose for editorials, along with the broader public nature of its audience and forum, leads to a fundamentally different genre.

Read the three editorials reprinted below and try to identify common features. Remember the kinds of generic traits we have analyzed throughout this book, including the type of content of the genre, its organization, choice and use of detail, style, and tone (for guiding questions to help you identify genre features, see Box 7.1, pp. 92–93). Note especially how the texts reveal their common scene, described in our preceding paragraph, and also how each defines its particular situations and particular publics.

Sample Editorials

1. Editorial By Robert Chamberlain, University Daily Kansan, October 10, 2001

Feminists Ignore Half the Problems

For some people, October means baseball. For others, it means Halloween. For me, it means an avalanche of sexism and questionable methodology. In fact, the first ominous pebbles began tumbling down Mt. Oread* in the form of a hysterical column by Shay O´Brien about the "domestic violence epidemic."

According to this piece, the age group with the highest rates of abuse, women ages 16 to 24, experienced "rates of domestic victimization at 19.6 per 1000." In the general population of women, the rate is about "240 women every day." Pretty scary, huh?

But let's look at them again. In the group most likely to be abused, less than two percent of women encounter domestic violence. Moreover, assuming what the column reports is true, in the general population only about one-tenth of one percent of women ever encounter domestic violence. Not exactly an epidemic.

But that's only the beginning. Given that abuse rates are 10 times higher for women age 16 to 24, it stands to reason that something is unique about the group. I would say it is their proximity to 16 to 24-year-old men. Given that young men are both disproportionately likely to commit violent crime and also more likely to hang around young women, I would say that the underlying cause of abuse isn't societal indifference. In fact, abuse is only symptomatic of a larger social problem: the plight of young men in our country.

Unfortunately, the women's movement is uninterested in helping young men. Thus, while you're sure to hear that women are far more likely to attempt suicide, you won't hear that men are far more likely to succeed. You won't hear that prostate cancer affects slightly more men than breast cancer does women. You won't hear that even though women aren't "natural" homemakers they are overwhelmingly given custody of the children in divorces.

You won´t hear about all this because so-called Third Wave Feminists still adhere to Second Wave ideologies and tactics. This October, feminist activists will undoubtedly trot out the same old tired (and inaccurate) numbers about 1 in 4 women being raped and a 27 percent wage gap between the genders. Personal experience will continue to trump careful analysis in academic gender debates. And silly references will still be made about an invisible, oppressive patriarchy that selectively subjugates women to advance the interests of men.

However, in order to really make a difference in solving the problems it identifies, feminism must move past gendered analysis. Disenfranchised young men, a phenomenal gap between the wages of workers and managers, and an underclass that goes without enough food, health care, and opportunity for advancement aren't gender-specific issues. Yet in our community there are those who select issues only on the basis of their effect on a single gender. In Women´s Studies 201, I learned a label for this sort of selection criteria: sexist.

Unfortunately, this sexism is insidious because it is well-meaning. The sexist activists are by and large good people who want to make our community better. But they fail to realize that unless the old models of single gender activism are rejected the only debate that can ensue will be the standard gender bickering that has occurred for the past 20 years.

* [nickname for the University of Kansas]

I fearlessly predict that for the vast majority of Third Wave Feminists at KU this article will be filed in the "Robert Chamberlain is sexist and we don't like him" archive. However, I sincerely hope that a select few will read it and take it seriously. It is only through the efforts of these motivated post-feminist scholars that a broader new movement for social justice will coalesce. And it is this movement that offers the best hope for our abused women, our forgotten men, and our nation as a whole.

2. Editorial by Amer G. Zahr (The Michigan Daily, November 26, 2001)

Fraternities and a Heightened Rape Culture

I must say I was quite disturbed. As I was walking through the Diag in the beginning of the school year, during the first waves of the fraternity rush period, I saw an interesting banner. It encouraged rushing for Chi Psi, a campus fraternity, using the attractive slogan, "Chi Psi, The Gentleman's Fraternity." Better yet, the black banner with white writing also included a white cutout of both the Playboy bunny and the Déjà Vu logo (a "gentleman's club" chain).

What we had here was the laying of a foundation for a fraternity culture that is, at best, passively encouraging male dominative roles or, at worst, outright misogynistic. Should we be surprised after seeing such a banner, embodying such an attitude, that campus women have reported being raped at the local Beta house a few weeks ago? Should we be surprised that Scot Boeringer, in a 1996 article titled "Influences of Fraternity Membership, Athletics, and Male Living Arrangements on Sexual Aggression," asserts that there exists more significant use of intoxicants and non-physical verbal coercion in obtaining sex by fraternity members? Should we be surprised that the journal *Gender and Society* published a study in which interviews with fraternity members found a tendency to give alcohol to women on the theory that women who were drinking would be less resistant to sexual advances? Should we be surprised that Peggy Reeves Sanday, in her book *Fraternity Gang Rape*, argues that alcohol is a tool that men in fraternities are taught to use to "work a yes out" of unwilling women? Should we be surprised that in their article, "Fraternity and Sorority Membership and Gender Dominance Attitudes," Linda Kalof and Timothy Cargill found a substantial difference in dominance attitudes among Greek and non-Greek students, concluding that affiliation with Greek organizations is associated with traditional male dominant-female submissive attitudes?

Colby Nordheimer, a woman who was raped at a fraternity party at the University of Arizona, gave an interview to the *Arizona Daily Wildcat* in 1996. When asked how much fraternity culture played into her being assaulted, Nordheimer replied, "I am a Greek … I don't think all fraternity men are rapists necessarily, but I do think that at times, there's a certain disrespect for women. It becomes a game, and sometimes they cross the line without necessarily knowing they've crossed it."

So what exists here is a number of studies and personal accounts showing that an overall American rape culture is highly and disproportionately prevalent in the campus fraternity environment. But this must concern us here in Ann Arbor to an even higher degree. Our university, unfortunately, holds the fraternities to no standards and to no accountability. Our university almost pretends like the frats don't exist, except for, of course, the Office of Greek Life. The office is located in the Michigan Union, and like other organizations, reapplies for office space every year. They are, however, unlike other groups, in no danger of ever losing their space. They employ a director, an assistant director and an administrative coordinator. They also house the four governing boards of the Greek community. It is a quite sophisticated operation. One would think that if such an organization were so prevalent in the Union's student organization office space, and such a visible presence on campus and in many students' lives, that our administration would hold them to the same types of standards as we hold other students and other organizations.

In my own view, the fraternities perhaps create as much benefit as other entities, while creating much more trouble. They are comparable to no student groups. A fraternity, to me, actually, is much more like a bar. They are cut from the same cloth. Frats encourage social interaction between members. Bars do the same (have you ever seen *Cheers*?). Frats cater to students. So do bars. In fact, I would suppose that many more students visit bars than ever visit frats. On the side of vice, frats are a hub for underage drinking. Bars house underage drinking, but much less, since they check identifications and use stringent standards since they are actually held accountable for allowing underage drinking. Back on the side of benefit, frats, like other students groups, carry out many community service activities, helping the local community. Bravo. Well, bars do the same thing. In fact, bars help the community not only by creating a social outlet, but also by creating a countless number of jobs for students as waiters and waitresses, line cooks, hostesses, bouncers, etc. That's community service if I ever heard of it.

In the end, frats=bars. The Union houses an Office of Greek Life. For fairness' sake, it should also house an Office of Bar Life. Greek Life representatives visit resident adviser training sessions to explain how they will relate to students' lives. Representatives from local bars should be afforded the same privilege. I don't see why not.

My proposal is that we treat the bars as we treat the frats. Now, another idea may be to treat the frats as we treat bars. In other words, we could treat the frats as if they don't exist. Sure, students can join them, and participate in all their virtues and vices, but not on the University's penny. Close down the Office of Greek Life. Let them seek private space to lease.

Or, finally, and probably most practically, our administration should create standards and regulations that the fraternities must live up to. And it must create real sanctions that make frats think twice before they create the kind of environment they are currently encouraging. Unfortunately, in the current context, it does not seem we are making any progress in stopping fraternities from egging on a dangerous misogynistic attitude, and viewing themselves as an untouchable "gentleman's club."

3. Editorial by Nick Woomer (The Michigan Daily, November 28, 2001)

Dancing on the Grave of the Protestant Work Ethic

It's Wednesday, a week after the start of Thanksgiving break, and (thankfully) politeness doesn't require you to ask everyone you have a conversation with "so how was your break?"

Every year, the responses are similar: "Pretty bad, I've got a bunch of work to do for this one class of mine and I'm still working on my personal statement for law school. . . . " "It was great, I saw a lot of my old high school friends at the bar and basically just chilled for a few days before things get real stressful again. . . ."

Generally, the lousy breaks aren't really "breaks" at all—just lulls in the school year that allow you to catch up on work. The good breaks tend to be the exact opposite—some quality time spent with friends and/or family, good conversation, good food, and reading material of one's choosing.

The lesson here is hardly a profound one: For most people, work = bad, and leisure = good. It's a simple, almost universally acknowledged truth and yet most Americans now regard the traditional 40-hour workweek as a luxury. The average American today works longer, harder and for less real income than ever before.

In the same way that the health care industry has convinced most Americans that any single-payer health care system will be a dystopian bureaucratic disaster ("Ever been to Canada? Talk about hell on earth. . . ."), Americans have somehow been convinced—although I suspect the so-called "Protestant Work Ethic" shares a big part of the blame—that work is some sort of end-in-itself.

Apparently it's harder to convince the French that obvious facts are, in fact, not true. Not only does everyone in France have access to health care (even those lazy poor people), but they also have a 35-hour workweek. And no, the country isn't on the verge of collapse; in fact, things over there are going just fine thank you.

By almost all accounts, the 35-hour workweek (or, rather, the 1,600-hour work year), which was adopted in 1998 by Lionel Jospin's government and now affects almost 50 percent of France's work force, is changing life there—dramatically. The legislation has caused affected employees to have between 11 and 16 extra days off per year. Now, more French people have more leisure time, and they're using it to go on more vacations (2000 saw an 18 percent jump in camper van purchases) and—this should please all you "family values" people—they're spending more time socializing with their friends and family. More people are working too; in June France's state planing commission estimated that the 35-hour workweek was responsible for creating one in six new jobs.

French employers have also seen the benefits of a reduced workweek—well-rested, happy workers are much more productive workers who make fewer mistakes and are less likely to mouth-off to customers. On the other hand, French employers (especially in capital-intensive industries) are trying to compensate for higher overhead costs—you lose money when you invest in machines that aren't being worked by someone—by cutting breaks and pushing employees to work at an uncomfortable pace. As a result, French labor ministry research indicates that only about 59 percent of those affected by the reduced workweek think it has made their lives better.

So, given its not-quite-overwhelming success, should we just give up on the reduced workweek? There's evidence that the problem isn't that 35 hours a week is too little, but that it's too much. An 8/8/01 column in the *Ottawa Citizen* cited an experiment in Finland where the traditional 8-hour workday is divided into two six-hour shifts. Even though they're required to pay workers for working eight hours a day, Finnish employers aren't losing money because the increased service hours, productivity and reduced overhead costs offset the cost of paying workers for two extra hours of work. Similar experiments are being conducted all over Europe.

According to Bruce O'Hara, the *Citizen* column's author, "the work-time issue has had so much attention in Europe that my guess is that some time in the next five years, at least one city or region will pilot-test a 28-hour workweek built around two community-wide shifts. I further predict that the model is so practical that it will quickly become the norm across Europe."

What the European and hypothetical experiments in shorter workweeks indicate (at the very least) is that it may be more than possible to significantly improve people's social lives at little or no economic cost. It's time to take a critical look at America's fabled "Protestant Work Ethic," do an economic cost-social benefit analysis, and start enjoying life.

Collaborative Activity

Analyze the editorials included in this chapter according to Box 7.1: Questions for Analyzing a Genre (pp. 92–93), and compile an initial list of the features of editorials you first notice—the patterns that they seem to share.

Because editorials appear in a wide range of settings and define many different publics, one editorial can appear quite different from another. Columnists like Ellen Goodman and Leonard Pitts, Jr., who often write about family issues or how issues affect women and minorities, may include their personal experiences with an issue or tell stories from other people's lives. The particular publics they define appreciate the human emphasis and find individual stories persuasive. Columnists like Molly Ivins or George Will, who often write about national political issues, tend to include statistics or quotations from experts or politicians to support their arguments, appealing to a different particular public. Yet all four write editorials, texts whose purpose is to persuade people to their way of thinking through rational argument about significant public issues.

Rhetorical Appeals

One of the markers of this persuasive genre, and one of the ways it differs from the academic genres we've described, is its use not only of logical but also of emotional and personal appeals (logos, pathos, and ethos). As you will recall, logos is appealing to an audience's rational mind, to the persuasiveness of logical and rational arguments; pathos is appealing to an audience's emotions, persuading readers by making them feel the writer's position, whether through sympathy, compassion, anger, or any other appropriate emotion; and ethos is appealing to an audience's belief in the personal qualities of the writer, persuading the readers that the writer should be believed or agreed with on this subject. In appeals from ethos, writers may try to convince readers that they are credible because of their expertise, sympathetic because of their experiences, or believable because they are in positions of power, for example. In the academic and workplace scenes, logical appeals are depended on heavily, but in the public sphere the most effective arguments draw on all three kinds of appeal.

Collaborative Activity

Reread the editorials above, and find places where each writer uses each of the three kinds of appeals. Make note of any areas where the appeals overlap (for instance, where an ethical appeal to the writer's credibility is based on identification with the audience or rational arguments/evidence).

Writing Activity

Describe which kinds of appeals you tend to find most effective, using these editorials for examples. If an editorial writer persuades you, do you tend to believe the writer because of who he or she is (ethical), because of how she or he makes you feel (emotional), or because of the rational arguments and evidence offered (logical)? (Of course, we all respond to all three kinds of appeals, but many of us gravitate toward one kind or another. Knowing which appeal you prefer can remind you not to depend too heavily on your own preference but to include other appeals that other readers might find persuasive as well.)

Subjects, Language, and Format

In addition to using all three appeals in their common situation, editorial writers share common types of subjects, ways of beginning and ending their texts, ways of integrating evidence and details, and even some aspects of style, tone, and voice. Effective editorialists who wish to persuade the widest range of readers do not denigrate their readers, for example, or ignore the arguments of people who disagree with them. Some use humor and some are stern, but they all choose words carefully, with attention to precision and vividness, necessary qualities for their persuasive purposes.

Writing Activity

Find at least three editorials from different forums. Analyze your editorials using Box 7.1: Questions for Analyzing a Genre (pp. 92–93). Write a 1-page description of the editorial genre for your classmates.

Collaborative Activity

Bring to class the editorials you gathered from different forums. Compare the descriptions you each wrote, and find points of similarity and difference among your analyses. Compile a list of generic features of the editorial that encompasses all the editorials your group gathered. Then discuss what the features of this genre reveal about the public scenes in which the editorial functions and about the individuals (writers/readers) who participate in that scene—their beliefs, assumptions, and expectations.

Collaborative Activity

Based on the analysis of editorials that you have done in the last several activities, write a list of writing tips for making effective choices when writing editorials. What do writers need to keep in mind? What content and organizational strategies might be useful? How should writers of editorials use the three kinds of rhetorical appeals? On the textual level, what kinds of sentence, word, and stylistic choices can and should writers make? Then, what writing process questions can you suggest for writers as they write their editorials?

Writing for Specific Publics

We have emphasized in this chapter writing in the public sphere at large, in forums that anyone can access like Web sites, magazines, or newspapers. We also noted that not everyone reads these forums and that each genre in fact defines a more particular public as its audience, a public of people interested in the same subjects or issues. Those people with common interests sometimes form smaller political groups, organizations of people banded together to try to influence public opinion and public policy toward the group's common interest. Organizations such as the National Organization for Women, the NAACP, the National Rifle Association, and Amnesty International are common ones with which you might be familiar. These smaller publics, too, try to influence public opinion in the public sphere. Some scholars in fact believe that most public policy results from negotiations and compromises among these groups, rather than from a broader public consensus in the public sphere. Another way to have some impact on society and its policies, then, is to become active in organizations that represent your interests. There, too, genres exist to help you have that kind of impact.

Many of the genres used in these more particular publics share situations and even names similar to those of the broader public sphere. Organizations' newsletters often include letters to the editor and guest columns, for example. Speeches and messages to electronic discussion lists serve both broad publics and special interest groups. The scenes of these special interest groups differ significantly to the extent that their participants represent a much narrower public and probably agree with the writer on some significant values and beliefs. The audience of such a specific public is much more homogenous, then, than the audience within most civic or public scenes. When you decide to join the conversation in a smaller political scene, then, you will need to adapt your understanding of the genres to these different audiences, whose beliefs will be more clearly defined.

Another significant way you can use writing to improve society is to contribute your writing talents and skills to a public organization. You can offer to write newsletter copy, a pamphlet or brochure, letters to potential donors or volunteers, advertising copy, news releases. Local organizations and local branches of national organizations, in particular, can often use help broadcasting their message to the larger public. Organizations even need to write letters to the editor or guest columns sometimes, especially to clarify misconceptions that might have appeared in a public forum or to ask for a community's support. One of our students volunteered for an organization that promotes education about the Bill of Rights and was asked to write a newspaper guest column to inform people. His column even gained him an invitation to serve on a televised panel about the Bill of Rights. When you write as a representative of an organization, of course, you are under some different strictures to represent *their* views and not just your own; this situation is similar in some ways to the situations common in workplace writing. To contribute your writing talents to an organization, you often need only to offer. If one organization does not need your help, another probably will. Seek out organizations whose purposes and values you support, of course, whether that is the local humane society, the campus recycling group, or your neighborhood association.

In short, your writing does matter in society. If you write to broadcast your wedding to the public, you are keeping others informed. If you write to persuade others that campus parking rules must change, you are contributing to public debate and helping to shape public opinion. If you write for smaller organizations, you advance a public cause and contribute their interests to the rational debate of the public sphere. If you choose not to write anything public, that choice, too, matters. Choosing not to participate in the debate about public issues leaves others to make decisions for you, permits the actions of authorities to go unchallenged, and undermines our democratic society and representative government. We earn our society by participating in it as good citizens.

WRITING PROJECTS

1. Write a letter to the editor, perhaps based in one of the issues you developed as you worked through this chapter. Be sure to specify the scene (which newspaper, magazine, or Web site). If an article or letter exists that shows the action your letter responds to, give your teacher a copy of that source, too. Seriously consider sending your letter to the forum for publication. After you write your letter to the editor, write a memo to your teacher explaining the writing choices you made and how these choices respond to the demands of your writing situation (the setting, the subject, the readers, and your purposes for writing) and to the demands of the scene (especially the objectives and constraints of the particular newspaper, magazine, or Web site).

1. Choose a newspaper, magazine, or Web site, and write an editorial in response to one of the following prompts. When you are finished drafting the editorial, write a memo explaining how the choices you made as a writer respond to the demands of the scene, situation, and genre of editorials.

Additional Guides to Writing for Public Audiences 13

Examining guidelines and models of the type of writing you are preparing to do enables you to think through your purpose, audience, and rhetorical strategies in light of the textual conventions for that genre. This chapter provides information about some common public writing genres that students often are asked to produce within their academic coursework.

The material that follows is taken from Lester Faigley's *The Brief Penguin Handbook*

How to Plan and Deliver Presentations

If you are assigned to give a presentation, look carefully at the assignment for guidance on finding a topic. The process for finding a topic is similar to that for a written assignment. If your assignment requires research, you will need to document the sources of information just as you do for a research paper.

Start with your goal in mind

What is the real purpose of your presentation? Are you informing, persuading, or motivating? Take the elevator test. Imagine you are in an elevator with the key people who can approve or reject your ideas. Their schedule is very tight. You have only thirty seconds to convince them. Can you make your case?

This scenario is not far-fetched. One executive demanded that every new idea had to be written in one sentence on the back of a business card. What's your sentence?

It's all about your audience

Who is your audience? In college your audience is often your instructor and fellow students—an audience you know well. Many times you will not have this advantage. Take a few minutes to answer these questions.

My audience

> Will they be interested in the topic?

> Why does it matter to them?

Chapter 13, Additional Guides to Writing for Public Audiences, is taken from Lester Faigley's *The Brief Penguin Handbook*, pp. 142–158 (Chapter 15, Design Presentations, and Chapter 16, Compose in Online Genres), and Amy Devitt, Mary Jo Reiff, and Anis Bawarshi's *Scenes of Writing*, pp. 425–438 (Chapter 7, Writing Research-Based Genres).

What are they likely to know and believe about the topic?

What are they likely to not know?

Where are they likely to disagree?

What do I want them to do?

How much time do I have?

If they remember only one thing, what should it be?

Get organized

Start with pen and paper before you begin creating slides. Post-it notes are another useful planning tool.

- **Make a list of key points.** Think about the best order for your major points.
- **Plan your introduction.** Your success depends on your introduction. You must gain the attention of your audience, introduce your topic, indicate why it's important, and give a sense of where you are headed. It's a tall order, but if you don't engage your audience in the first two minutes, you will lose them.
- **Plan your conclusion.** You want to end on a strong note. Stopping abruptly or rambling on only to tail off leaves your audience with a bad impression. Give your audience something to take away, a compelling example or an idea that captures the gist of your presentation.

Build content

Content alone does not make a presentation successful, but you cannot succeed without solid content. Support your major points with relevant evidence. Consider creating a handout so your audience can refer to important facts, statistics, and quotations.

- **Facts.** Speakers who know their facts build credibility.
- **Statistics.** Effective use of statistics can give the audience the impression that you have done your homework. Statistics can also indicate that a particular example is representative.
- **Statements by authorities.** Quotations from credible experts can support key points.
- **Narratives.** Narratives are brief stories that illustrate key points. Narratives can hold the attention of the audience—but keep them short or they will become a distraction.

Design Visuals for a Presentation

With slides, less is more. One text-filled slide after another is mind-numbingly dull. Presentations using slides can be better than a series of slides with bulleted points, one after the other seemingly forever.

Keep it simple

Compare the following examples.

Food Crisis in the United States

- The U.S. Department of Agriculture reported that over 50 million Americans lived with reduced-quality food or reduced food intake in 2011.

- The 2011 survey reports that over 20% of all households with children were food insecure.

- Over 8 million children lacked a healthy diet and at times did not have enough to eat.

■ Which slide makes the point most effectively?

Simple design rules!
>One point per slide
>Very few fonts
>Quality photos, not clip art
>Less text, more images
>Easy on the special effects

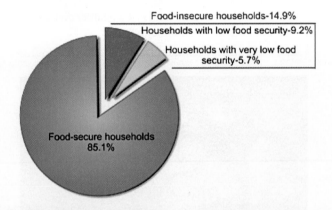

U.S. households by food security status, 2011

Food-insecure households-14.9%
Households with low food security-9.2%
Households with very low food security-5.7%

Food-secure households
85.1%

■ Charts and graphs make statistics easier to understand in a presentation.

Source: United States. Department of Agriculture. *Food Security in the U.S.* 4 Sept. 2012. Web. 6 Apr. 2013.

But what if you have a lot of data to show? Make a handout that the audience can study later. They can make notes on your handout, which gives them a personal investment. Keep your slides simple and emphasize the main points in the presentation.

Use effective charts

Again simpler is better. Limit your charts to only the details you need to make the point. If you have a complicated table or chart, distribute it as a handout.

Use audio and video clips strategically

Short audio and video clips can offer concrete examples and add some variety to your presentation. An audience appreciates hearing and even seeing the people you interview. *PowerPoint, Keynote, Prezi,* and other presentation software make it simple to embed the files within a presentation. Be careful, however, in using the built-in sound effects such as canned applause. Most sound effects are annoying and make you come off as inexperienced.

Deliver an effective presentation

If you are not passionate about your subject, you will never get your audience committed to your subject, no matter how professional looking your slides are. Believe in what you say; enthusiasm is contagious.

It's all about you

The audience didn't come to see the back of your head in front of slides. Move away from the podium and connect with them. Make strong eye contact with individuals. You will make everyone feel like you are having a conversation instead of giving a speech.

Prepare in advance

Practice your presentation, even if you have to speak to an empty chair. Check out the room and equipment in advance. If you are using your laptop with a projector installed in the room, make sure it connects. Begin promptly. Audiences become impatient if they have to wait several minutes for you to download your presentation.

Be professional

Pay attention to the little things.

- **Proofread carefully.** A glaring spelling error can destroy your credibility.
- **Be consistent.** If you randomly capitalize words or insert punctuation, your audience will be distracted.
- **Pay attention to the timing of your slides.** Stay in synch with your slides. Don't leave a slide up when you are talking about something else.
- **Use the "B" key.** If you get sidetracked, press the "B" key, which makes the screen go blank so the audience can focus on you. When you are ready to resume, press the "B" key again and the slide reappears.
- **Involve your audience.** Invite response during your presentation where appropriate, and leave time for questions at the end.
- **Add a bit of humor.** Humor can be tricky, especially if you don't know your audience well. But if you can get your audience to laugh, they will be on your side.
- **Slow down.** When you are nervous, you tend to go too fast. Stop and breathe. Let your audience take in what's on your slides.
- **Finish on time or earlier.** Your audience will be grateful.

STAYING ON TRACK

Avoid Death by PowerPoint

PowerPoint and similar slideware programs have become prevalent in businesses, organizations, and colleges alike, yet there are many critics of *PowerPoint* culture. And it's no mystery why. Think about all the bad presentations you have sat through. Write down what you don't like. Your list may look like the following:

What I don't like about PowerPoint presentations
    Data dump presentations—too much information
    Too much text on the slides, making it hard to
      read it all
    Text too small to read
    One bulleted point after another
    Cutesy clip art and distracting transitions
    Presenter reading word-for-word off the slides

The basic problem is that presenters don't acknowledge the difference between an oral presentation and a written document. *PowerPoint, Keynote, Prezi,* and other slideware were designed to support presentations with graphics, not to be the focus of the presentation. Why should an audience take the time to come to a presentation when they are asked to read the slides? Your audience expects to be informed and motivated by you.

How to Compose in Online Genres

Create a Blog Entry

Great bloggers who attract many readers share four qualities. They write with a lively, personal voice. They are well informed. They are honest about what they know and don't know. And they write their blog entries to initiate conversations, not to have the last word on a subject.

Blogs assigned for courses sometimes allow students a great deal of freedom to select their subject matter, and sometimes course blogs are on an assigned topic, such as responses to the readings.

Elements of a Successful Blog

Title	Include an informative title.
Content	Offer something new. If you don't have anything new, then point readers to the interesting writing of others.
Writing style	Engage readers with a conversational style.
Participation	Invite responses.

What you need to do

- Develop a personal voice that conveys your personality.
- Remember that your blog is a conversation. You want to get responses to what you write.
- Do your homework. Let your readers know the sources of your information.
- Keep it short. If you have a lot to say about different subjects, write more than one entry.
- Add images if they are needed.
- Provide relevant links.
- Remember that informal writing is not sloppy, error-filled writing.

Sample Reading Blog Entry

Blog

POSTED BY JILLIAN AKBAR AT 4:18 P.M. 3 COMMENTS OCTOBER 5, 2013

Sara Macdonald's *Holy Cow* (2002)

Sara Macdonald does not begin her voyage from Australia to India with the happiest of outlooks. Laden with memories of the terrible time she had there eleven years earlier, at first she finds her only consolation in being with her boyfriend Jonathan, a fellow journalist. Macdonald confesses that her motives are more than just companionship:

> Leaving my wonderful job was the hardest thing I've ever done but perhaps I didn't do it just for love. A part of me wanted to reclaim myself, to redefine my identity, to grow up professionally, to embrace anonymity and get rid of the stalker. (17)

Macdonald's account is engaging in her insightful depiction of India. Her observations of cultural norms, such as honoring one's family in marriage, are distant but detailed and nonjudgmental. The chapter titles suggest the irreverent tone and humor of the book including "Sex, Lies and Saving Face," "Three Weddings and a Funeral," "Insane in the Membrane," "Birds of a Feather Become Extinct Together," and "Hail Mary and Good-bye God."

Macdonald's attitude toward India lightens up in the second half of the book, and I finally could relate as she suffered an Indian summer with nothing but a television and power cuts—exactly like my boyfriend's apartment in August. She offers more on the exotic imagery of India: a lotus flower growing out of slimy water, a pink ten-foot high Mary in a sari, and the "candy-colored kingdom" of the Divine Mother in Kerala (199). She includes my favorite image of all when she returns to India and is submerged in "India's Kaleidoscope of Technicolor" to feel "like Dorothy in the land of Oz" (276).

Compose Wikis

Mention the word *wiki* and most people associate it with *Wikipedia*, the hugely popular people's encyclopedia. No doubt *Wikipedia* has had an enormous impact on our culture, but there are many other wikis besides *Wikipedia*, and many differ significantly from *Wikipedia*.

The underlying goal of wikis is to create a collective knowledge base. Unlike blogs and discussion posts, wikis are written and edited by a number of people. Individuals not only contribute their own ideas but edit the work of others. A wiki, in theory at least, is never finished.

Elements of a Wiki

Collaboration	Everyone can access the same information and can contribute.
Content	Wikis are "encyclopedic," meaning that they aim at creating comprehensive knowledge.
Revision	Wikis are by definition always works in progress. Everyone can add and revise.
Writing style	Writing in wikis should be factual and neutral.
Community building	No one takes individual ownership of a wiki.

What you need to do

- If you are selecting a subject for a wiki, ask is it worth your and your colleagues' effort? Who will be interested in reading it? Can you find enough information?
- If you are contributing to an article on a wiki, think about what you might add.
- Stay on the topic.
- Do your homework on the subject, and provide references for all facts.
- Avoid taking sides on an issue or interpretation.
- Respect others' views and convictions.
- Write clearly and in a neutral style.

Sample Educational Wiki

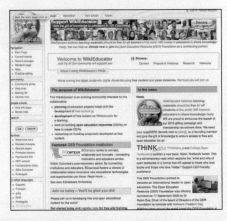

- The WikiEducator project invites experts from around the world to create free educational materials for both schools and informal learning settings.

WRITING SMART

Know How to Edit a Wiki

Wikis represent the collective effort of many people. You have a responsibility to respect their effort by being a helpful contributor.

1. **Understand your goal:** Wikis allow you to contribute your knowledge to a larger project. You may change or add to the content that others have contributed or you may post new articles on new subjects.

2. **Learn the tools:** Wikis have a different set of tools than those on a standard word processor. Find the markup tools before you start editing.

3. **Assume a neutral point of view:** Wikis are usually informative rather than persuasive. Attempt to represent all relevant viewpoints. If you include opinions, note them as opinions and attribute them if possible (e.g., Senator X maintains global warming is a hoax).

4. **Cite sources:** The sources of any information or facts that are not common knowledge should be cited.

5. **Copyright:** Don't cut and paste the work of others into a wiki. Paraphrase in your own words and cite the source.

6. **Courtesy:** Be open about disagreements, but don't resort to name calling.

Create a Web Page

Readers approach Web pages differently than they do older media like books and newspapers. Readers of Web pages expect to be able to move through your site according to their own interests, rather than starting on the first page and reading straight through to the last. Thus the information on a Web page needs to be clearly connected to other information on the site, but it must also, to a certain extent, stand on its own.

Elements of a Web page

Title and subheadings	The title of your Web page should appear in the page itself and at the top of the reader's browser window. Use subheadings to divide your information into readable sections.
Navigation menu	Navigation elements are the "table of contents" for a Web site. They should be clear and easy to find, but should not distract readers from the main content of the page.
Content	"Content" refers to the text, images, embedded videos, sound files, and all other material on your page.
Affiliation and credentials	Let your readers know who sponsors the Web site. If the site is for an organization or business, provide an "about" page and a link to the page in the main menu.

What you need to do

- If you do not have Web editing software such as *Dreamweaver* on your computer, find out where this software is available on your campus.
- Capture your readers' attention, and don't waste their time. Unlike readers of books, readers of Web pages can, with the click of their mouse, leave your page for thousands of other entertaining and informative sites. You must give them a reason to spend time on your site.
- Avoid large blocks of unbroken text. Divide your information into chunks, and if it runs longer than a page, consider dividing it between two or more Web pages.
- Build navigation into your content. Think about where people will need to go next after they read your page.
- Provide links to sources.
- Proofread carefully for mechanics, grammar, and spelling; they can make or break your credibility with readers.

Sample Web page for a Student Organization

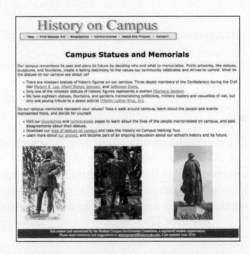

- Campus organizations, like nearly all organizations, create Web sites to publicize their mission and activities.

WRITING SMART

Evaluate the design of a Web site

You can learn a great deal about effective Web design by keeping these criteria in mind when you visit Web sites.

1. **Audience and purpose:** How does the site identify its intended audience? Why was the site created?
2. **Content:** How informative is the content? Has the site been updated recently? What do you want to know more about?

3. **Readability:** Is there sufficient contrast between the text and the background to make it legible? Are there paragraphs that go on too long and need to be divided? Are headings inserted in the right places, and if headings are used for more than one level, are the levels indicated consistently?
4. **Visual design:** Does the site have a consistent visual theme? Do the images contribute to the visual appeal or do they detract from it?
5. **Navigation:** Does the first page indicate what else is on the site? How easy or difficult is it to move from one page to another on the site? Are there any broken links?

Create a Podcast

Podcasts are easy to create using your own audio editor and your Web site or you can create them in a multimedia lab and post them on a third-party site. For a podcast with high audio quality, you'll need a headset with a noise-canceling microphone, a portable voice recorder, and podcasting software. All these may be available from your campus multimedia lab.

The Process for Creating a Podcast

Identify your purpose	What exactly do you want to accomplish?
Plan your content	Do you want to conduct interviews about a subject or an issue? Do a documentary of an event? Give practical advice or instructions? Give a history or an analysis? Make a persuasive argument?
Compose your audio	Arrange and record interviews. Write a script.
Know the law	If you use music created by someone else, you likely will have to pay for the right to broadcast that music. If someone agrees to be your guest, you have the right to broadcast that person's voice.
Record your podcast	Reserve a campus audio production lab or record on your computer. Create an audio file by combining the interviews with your narration.
Edit your podcast	Your multimedia lab may have instructions or consultants for using audio editing software. Allow ample time for editing.
Publish your podcast	Export the audio into a format such as WAV or MP3 that you can put on the Web or share as a downloadable file.

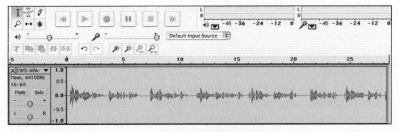

■ Free open-source editors are available for Windows, Mac, and Linux.

Create a Video

The cost and technical barriers for creating video have been significantly reduced. Phones and PDAs can now record video along with simple-to-use camcorders. Most new computers come with video editors installed including Apple's *iMovie* or Windows' *MovieMaker*. *YouTube* and other video-sharing Web sites make it easy to publish your video.

Nonetheless, making a high-quality video requires a great deal of effort. In addition to the technical demands, producing quality videos requires the hard work of planning and revising that extended writing tasks demand.

The Process for Creating a Video

Identify your subject and purpose	What exactly do you want to accomplish?
Decide on your approach	Do you want to conduct interviews? Do a documentary of an event? Make an announcement? Re-enact a past event?
Plan your content	Will all the video be original? Will you incorporate other video such as *YouTube* clips? Will you include still images? Maps or graphs? Music? Voiceover?
Draft a script and a storyboard	A storyboard is a shot-by-shot representation of your project that will help you organize your shooting schedule.
Make a schedule and plan your locations	Quality videos take many hours to shoot and edit. Visit all locations in advance to take into account issues such as lighting and noise.
Arrange for your equipment	At minimum you will need video and sound recording equipment and an editing suite. Find out what is available from your campus multimedia lab.
Compose your video	You can create more dynamic video by using techniques of still photographers. See pages 128–133. You can add movement by using the zoom feature on your camera.
Capture audio	The microphone installed in your camera is usually not the best option. Your multimedia lab may have external microphones that will give you better quality. Microphones record ambient noises—such as the wind noise, traffic, and computer fans—which you need to minimize.
Edit your video	Editing software allows you to combine video clips and edit audio. Your multimedia lab may have instructions or consultants for using video editing software. Allow ample time for editing.
Publish your video	Export the video into a format such as *QuickTime* that you can put on the Web or share as a downloadable file.

Create a Discussion Post

Productive writers often use discussion forums, e-mail, blogs, and instant messaging to communicate and discuss ideas. Your instructor will likely give specific instructions for how often you are required to participate in online discussion forums, and may also specify the number and kinds of posts you must make.

When you are posting the first entry in a discussion thread, give your post a clear, specific subject line that lets readers know what you are writing about before they open it. For new or response posts, offer the context (the assignment or reading name), the date and name of a previous post, or other background.

When you reply to other students' posts, use a respectful tone and keep your language clear and to the point. Think about the voice your writing creates and how classmates and your instructor will hear it. Follow commonsense rules of etiquette and avoid posting angry or personal attacks, taking special care to be respectful when you disagree. Finally, take time to re-read and edit your work before posting.

Discussion post assignment
DISCUSSION #2: VISUAL SIGNS

Think of some clothing or style that is popular among friends of yours: tattoos, baseball caps, piercings, jewelry, sneakers, and so on. Interview a friend who wears the item and photograph him or her, focusing on the item. Upload the photo to the discussion board. Write a post of 250–400 words about the significance of the item and what it says about the generation who values it.

Sample discussion post

Thread: Style or clothing? Magenta Chucks with Cartoon Laces

Author: Lindsey Rodriguez

Posted Date: Thursday, January 27, 2013 4:54:31 PM CST

Edited Date: Thursday, January 27, 2013 4:58:23 PM CST

Shoes are a versatile type of clothing because the wearer can consciously choose the size of the statement they make. People can pick a pair of subtle shoes that complement their outfit or wear a pair for their functionality. Alternatively, shoes may also serve as a statement—accessories that make a jarring contrast against the rest of the outfit or even serve as the focal point.

For example, a pair of well-worn, magenta Converse sneakers with mismatching laces can only be meant to generate intrigue as a clothing choice. While a magenta pair of Converses with Hello-Kitty and Spiderman laces would seem odd for the typical male, Rick Wang's closet is a sea of black, white, and shades of purple with the occasional ironic or vintage T-shirt lying on the floor. Rick is unlike any person I've ever met. For his senior yearbook portrait, he wore the same rented tux that was required for all guys with one exception: after much convincing of the photographer, on his shoulder sat the turtle beanie-baby he named Cornelius Alfonso Laramy Galileo III Esq. His eighteenth birthday party was held at Chuck E. Cheese's, where he gallivanted around with the cape and Chuck E. Cheese mask given to all birthday children. Like many of his generation, the shoes convey his embrace of the strange, fun, and colorful without any regard to dignity. The cartoon shoelaces are a display of his eccentricity and still lively inner-child.

As the technological revolution gave power and prestige to nerds, Converse's "Chucks" became popular among the generation that values socially awkward yet intelligent and quirky individuals. Crazy colored shoes have also grown in popularity because they express creativity and individualism for a generation that resists becoming boring.

The material that follows is taken from Amy Devitt, Jo Reiff, and Anis Bawarshi's *Scenes of Writing*.

Sample of a Newsletter

Volume 1, Issue 26

December 6, 2001

COLLEGE STUDENT'S SURVIVAL KIT

Plagiarism 101: How To Avoid It

Plagiarism 101

For the typical college student the words :mid-term" or "end-of-semester" are synonymous with unmitigated terror and panic as assignments pile up and tests are scheduled in every class. To a student overwhelmed with a 12 to 15 hour classload and multiple papers due in the same week, the only way out seems to be to just point, click and plagiarize. Don't even think about it! It's not worth failing a class or facing even worse consequences like being thrown out of school. Crunch times are a part of college life and also a part of the business world outside the walls of academe. It would be better to learn to deal with crunch times in college than in your first dream job.

Think about it. When your college hands you a degree at the end of four years, in essence the institution is saying that you possess the credentials and the knowledge necessary to be hired for a professional or managerial position. If you "earn" that degree by "cut and paste", then your degree has no real significance and you become your own victim of deceit.

What is Plagiarism?

Plain and simply, plagiarism is theft. When you use someone else's words, sentence structure, ideas, or any other part of **print** or **electronic** expression, you must put them in quotation marks and cite your source(s). You must give citations when using others' ideas, even if those ideas are paraphrased in your own words.

This issue will discuss and focus primarily on the issue of Internet Plagiarism which has become a huge problem nationwide on college campuses. This may come as a shock to some, but all the freely accessible information proliferating on the Internet is not free for the taking. There will be a price to pay if you don't cite what you find there. Please, read on...

Use the Internet — just don't abuse it.

Plagiarism and the World Wide Web

The World Wide Web is an awesome and powerful source of information, but with its accessibility has made another form of plagiarism a temptation: copy and paste and the use of Internet paper mills. The copy and paste mentality has become one of the biggest problems on college campuses today. According to a survey done by Plagiarism.org., "Almost 80% of college students admit to cheating at least once and that up to 30% of undergraduate students across the country may plagiarize on every assignment they turn in" (Harris).

Why you are here

You came to college to interact with scholars, to learn how to think critically, and to become a skilled professional in a discipline. Yes, the pressures on you are very real and they come from a myriad of directions. Students today are faced with fierce competition to maintain a high GPA for graduate schools, future job recruiters and pressure from their parents. Other causes range from poor time management, fear that your writing ability is inadequate, an overload of class hours, and uncertainty about what plagiarism includes (Harris). Buying or copying a paper may seem to be the easiest way out when you feel overwhelmed with assignments, but the risk is tremendous if you are caught. Your professors know about the paper mills and are trained to notice certain dead giveaways that shout, "I have copied and pasted this paper!" Don't take the risk and don't cheat yourself out of your education.

Internet Paper Mills

There are a number of sites on the Web advertising download-able student papers (for free or for sale). Some of these sites maintain that they do not provide these papers with the intention that students will claim them as their own; rather, the papers are for research or informational purposes. Others openly acknowledge that their sites were created in order to provide students with materials for plagiarism. Whatever the intent of the creators, these sites are being used as sources for plagiarized papers.

If you are thinking about buying or downloading your next research paper, be aware that many professors know about these sites and have visited them (familiarizing themselves with their contents). Remember too that your professor has become familiar with your writing style and can discern when text is a student's own and when it has been plagiarized (whether that text comes from the Web or not). Finally, that many of the papers available are poorly written; just because it's on the Web, or someone else wrote it, does not guarantee that it is accurate, grammatically correct or even spell-checked. In addition, the web paper could have been plagiarized in its entirety from yet another source.

Cut, Paste, Plagiarize

Cutting and pasting to create a paper from several sources is yet another plagiarism strategy. Don't believe for a minute that this is okay. These "assembly-kit" papers are often betrayed by wide variations in tone, diction, and citation style. The introduction and conclusion are often student-written and therefore noticeably different from the often glowing middle. The dead giveaways that pepper a copy and paste paper are immediately apparent to the trained eye. Don't take a chance. Do the research, write the paper, cite the sources and turn in your own honest work.

Citing Electronic Sources

If you are going to use source material from the Web (which is perfectly acceptable), you must cite your source in an acceptable format. Most English classes use the MLA style of formatting citations. Other disciplines may use the, such as psychology for example, may use the APA style of citation. Your professor will tell you which style is preferred for the class and the paper you are assigned.

Number One Rule: Buy a current edition of the MLA Handbook for Writers of Research Papers and the Harbrace College Handbook. These books will prove invaluable to you throughout your college career and may save you a lot of trouble, if you follow the guidelines in these books. In addition, barebones guidelines for the MLA documentation style can be found on the Web at: http://www.mla.org.

Reprinted here are some examples of on-line citation:

On-line Book

Wollstonecraft, Mary. <u>A Vindication of the Rights of Women</u>. New York: Everyman Library, 1929. [On-line] Available Telnet: gopher. wiretap.spies.com Directory:Library/Classics File:woman.txt.

On-Line Journal Article

Rosenberg, Martin E. "Dynamic and Thermodynamic Tropes of the Subject in Freud and in Deleuze and Guattari." <u>Postmodern Culture</u> 4.1 (1993): 32 paragraphs. [On-Line] Available Telnet: gopher. nebula.lib.vt.edu. Directory: Electronic Bookshelf/ejournals/ postmodern culture/PMCV4N1 File: rose0401.txt

On-Line Abstract

Natchez, Gladys. "Frida Khalo and Diego Rivera: The Transformation of Catasttrophe to Creativity." <u>Psychotherapy-Patient</u> 8 (1987):153-74. [On-Line] Abstract Available: DIALOG File: PsychINFO Item: 76-11344

CD-ROM Abstract

Natchez, Gladys. "Frida Khalo and Diego Rivera: The Transformation of Catastrophe to Creativity." <u>Psychotherapy-Patient</u> 8 (1987):153-74. [On-Line] Abstract Available: Silverplatter File: PsychLIT Item: 76-11344

All this information was taken from the fifth edition of the <u>MLA Handbook for Writers of Research Papers</u> which also features sections on computer research methods and other electronic resources.

Since professors may not distinguish between deliberate and accidental plagiarism, the heart of avoiding plagiarism is to make sure *you* give credit where it is due. This may be credit for something somebody said, wrote, emailed, drew, or implied. If you didn't write it—cite it!

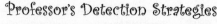

COLLEGE STUDENT'S
SURVIVAL KIT

1979 Downtown Blvd.
Center for Academic Excellence
Washington, D.C.

Phone: 555-555-5555
Fax: 555-555-5555
Email: center@gov.com

*The College Students
Resource Newsletter*

We're on the Web!
collegestudentsurvivalkit.com

Research it, write it, cite it!

Professor's Detection Strategies

Detection is becoming easier due to computer technology and is the latest strategy in an effort to deter the growing trend of Internet plagiarism. These detection sites utilize huge databases of online paper-mills in addition to searching millions of web pages for plagiarized material. Professors submit student's papers for analysis and if "if the service finds similarities, it notifies the teacher, who must then decide whether the similarities are coincidences, justified by proper footnotes or outright dishonesty" (Harris). These Internet services usually charge a fee by the number of students on a class, with discounts given for extra-large classes. Some detection sites include:

- Plagiarism.com at http://www.plagiarism.com. Educational materials and a software-screening program that creates a test of familiarity for a student to complete. The company says that no student has been falsely accused.

- Plagiarism.org at http://www.plagiarism.org. Online service that checks submitted student papers against a large database and provides reports of results. Also monitors term paper mills.

- Wordcheck at http://www.wordchecksystems.com. Keyword matching software. Requires local database of papers or texts to match.

- Integriguard at http://www.integriguard.com. Compares submissions against a database of other papers and Web sites.

- Eve at http://www.canexus.com/eve/index.shtml. Inexpensive software agent that searches the Web to compare a suspect paper with Internet content. Shows site and degree of match. (Virtual Salt)

Sources:

1. Gibaldi, Joseph. <u>MLA Handbook For Writers of Research Papers</u>. 5th ed. New York. The Modern Language Association of America. 1999. 1-293.

2. Harris, Robert. "Evaluating Internet Research." *VirtualSalt*. 17 Nov. 1997. 20 Nov. 2001. <http://www.virtualsalt.com/evalu8it.htm>.

Sample of a Letter to an Authority

February 16, 2001

Citizens of Clarksville,

As many of you already know, on January 1, 2001, five city council members were sworn into office for the first time. In an election where five of the six incumbents lost their positions, newcomers Gabriel Segovia, Marshall Ross, Phil Drew, Margie Clark, and Joe Couch won city council seats by promising lower property taxes. Now in office, these council members seek a drastic 82-cent reduction in our city's property tax rate. That the new council members won on the platform of lower property taxes speaks to the public's desire to lower these taxes. But, while the idea of paying fewer taxes on our property certainly appeals to us all, I feel that reducing our tax levels would be a terrible mistake.

As a concerned citizen of this city, I feel it is necessary to ask some questions about what our public officials are doing. I urge you, the citizens of Clarksville, to look at the answers to these questions before you make your decision; because it is only after answering these questions that we can decide whether a lower property tax rate is really what Clarksville needs.

How much is 82 cents per $100 worth to me? According to Clarksville tax code, residential property is taxed at 25% of its appraised value. The tax rate for this 25% of our property is $2.01 for every $100 of property owned. For example, if I own a house that, together with the land it was built on, is worth $50,000, I would pay $251 in property taxes. Commercial property is taxed at 40% of its value, so if my commercial property is worth $100,000, I would pay $804. So if I am lucky enough to be blessed with $150,000 worth of commercial and residential property, I would pay a little more than $1,000 in property taxes each year.

An 82-cent cut in property taxes would reduce the rate to $1.19 per $100 of property, saving the individual taxpayer a minimal amount of money. Using the hypothetical example above, I save $102 on my residential property and $328 on my commercial property for a total savings of $430. I am sure that $430 matters to anyone who pays taxes, no matter how much money they make. But is an extra $430 a year worth the sacrifices in public services that would occur after such a drastic tax cut?

How important is our tax money to the city? Our city functions on the taxes of its property owners. Our taxes pay for the police officers and firefighters who keep our homes and families safe. Our taxes pay for the upkeep of our public parks, pools, and other public recreation. Our taxes pay for the beautification of our city. In short, our city government needs our tax dollars to provide us with the public goods we want.

The city's budget for the coming fiscal year predicts revenue totaling about $53 million, 37% of which comes from the city's property tax. It seems to me that 37% of the city's budget is an important sum. It becomes more important when 22% of the city's projected budget comes from the local sales tax, beer and liquor tax, business tax, and hotel/motel tax, all of which are sensitive to the economy. If the local economy were to take a dip, the 37% of our budget provided by our property tax becomes vital to keeping the city's finances afloat.

Our property taxes become more important when we look at what they pay for. Two years ago, the city council elected to raise property taxes by eighty-two cents per $100 of property. With this increase, we have seen our city budget grow by about $14 million since 1999, and the city has done positive things with this money.

Since 1998, the number of city employees has increased dramatically. This increase has not been some bureaucratic expansion, however. The police force has increased by thirty-six, while the fire department gained twenty-five new employees. Parks and recreation will have fifteen new employees this year. These new employees who make us safe and give us valuable public goods were paid for with our property taxes.

This year alone, the police department will hire seventeen new employees, while the fire department will add eight. These new employees, along with the additional parks and recreation employees, will cost us $1.2 million, about $34,000 for each new employee. Since we will all enjoy the benefits of having the new city employees to provide us with public services, this is a price I will gladly pay.

Consider what we will get with a larger police force. Increased police presence will make our streets safer. With seventeen new officers, patrols could be expanded; and programs such as D.A.R.E., where police officers interact positively with the public, could be increased. If one of those seventeen new officers saves a life, prevents a home from being burglarized, or keeps a youth from trying drugs, then it is worth my extra $430.

Consider what the extra parks and recreation employees will do for us. Our city pools are just one place that parks and recreation employees work. Our public pools give us more than a fun summer activity for the youth of our city; they also serve as positive activity for the city's more at risk youth. With our tax money, the city can afford to hire more lifeguards, who will then be able to teach more swimming lessons to our youth. If one of those lifeguards becomes a positive role model to an at risk youth, then my extra $430 was well spent.

Another area where our tax money is well spent is capital projects. Clarksville's downtown area is in dire need of public money after the tornado of 1999. The capital projects budget, as well as the highway and streets budget will pay to rebuild the city streets of downtown Clarksville. Capital projects are also necessary if we want to revitalize our downtown area with more economic activity. If the capital projects budget is able to bring even a small amount of growth to downtown Clarksville, if my tax dollar fixes the damaged roads of downtown Clarksville, then I am more than happy to pay my $430.

After looking at the answers to my simple questions, I find it hard not to keep our property tax rate as it is. If you want a safer city, if you desire more public recreation, if you want our city to offer an exciting downtown area, then I urge you to contact the city council member from your ward and tell him or her that you are willing to pay the extra fee to make Clarksville great.

Can we afford to keep paying the current property taxes? I feel that we should all ask ourselves a more appropriate question: can we afford not to keep paying our current property taxes?

Sincerely,
James B. Weakley II

Sample of a Web Site

Help Save Memphis' Music Heritage

who we are

our goals

what you can do

history lesson

contact

who we are

Memphis has always been known as the home of the blues and the birthplace of rock n' roll. Now, that's even the city's catch phrase. After a decade and a half of rebuilding, downtown Memphis is trying to bring people back to the hotspot of old times, and they're undoubtedly succeeding. Despite the music heritage, developers are focusing on modernizing Beale Street and downtown Memphis. They are ignoring the music traditions that Memphis is home to, and they need to realize that history can be more important than making money on a new Beale. Developers need to bring Memphis back its glory as the groundbreaking spot for rock 'n' roll.

Truth?

The official Memphis Tourism logo

At Memphis Music, a large group of music–loving Memphians have joined forces in an effort to realign the focus of the investors in charge of Memphis' future. These investors need to focus on making Memphis what it appears to be – a haven for music fans. Is there any way for Memphis developers to return to the genuine blues, soul, and rock mecca it was for decades before now and still appeal to the typical consumer? We believe that the answer to that question just may be the key to making Memphis a hot commodity again.

Memphis has done a good job of representing itself in cultural and political history. There is the Civil Rights museum, dedicated to the memory of Martin Luther King, Jr. There is also the Peabody Hotel, an over 120-year-old hotel that chronicles the history of Memphis society. A. Schwab's on Beale Street refused to sell out to bulldozing developers after Beale's original clientele had dropped away, and continues to do well to this day, still reflecting its history as a general store in the early 20th century.

Cultural History:

The Peabody Hotel, the South's grandest.

Memphis has an extensive group of potential customers who could use a crash course in Memphis music history. Why won't the city take hold of this opportunity to show off the impressive history that it has waiting to be relived? We want to see the city become what it used to be, what it should be. It is our pleasure to do what we can in order to help Memphis' future blossom.

Help Save Memphis' Music Heritage

who we are

our goals

what you can do

history lesson

contact

our goals

Memphis has seen a lot of improvement in the downtown area. It is now an area that people will go to on the weekends, and has become a major hotspot for summer nights. Beale Street is as popular as ever. Developers have done a very good job of remodeling downtown to fit the new image of Memphis. They have forgotten, however, to remodel what we all know as an integral part of Memphis – the music. Memphis Music wants the city to realize that what they've accomplished is impressive, but we have some other ideas in mind.

- Bring real blues musicians back to Beale Street
- Honor the musicians of Beale Street past
- Build a museum representing the styles of music that have taken place in Memphis – the blues, the beginnings of rock and roll, and soul
- Ressurrect Mud Island's museum, chronicling cultural, historical, and musical happenings of the Mid–South
- Highlight the areas of the city that have been breeding grounds for music with plaques and/or more recognition in Memphis tourism guides
- Hold festivals in honor of Memphis music

Memphis has long been a highlight for music lovers on tour of the southeastern United States. The city boasts the 2nd largest tourist attraction in the United States – Graceland. Memphis is located in the center of at least 10 highly populated southern cities within a 400–mile radius. It attracts over 8 million tourists yearly, all willing to spend over $1.7 billion in retail. Downtown doesn't only attract those from outside Memphis. Memphis itself has 1.1 million residents, 200,000 of which live within 10 minutes of downtown, and many more within a 25–mile radius (City of Memphis Official Site).

Elvis Presley's Graceland:

The only reason to visit Memphis?

Dan Ball

Many tourists come while on a pilgrimage of all the important musical stops of the Mid–South, and also because Memphis is just a fun town to visit. Residents of Memphis should have enough pride in city history to bring them downtown so they can learn as much as possible. Memphis has the potential to educate so many people, and it is time to take the initiative. Memphis Music wants to do just that.

Memphis Music is also dedicated to supporting the new found success downtown. We also want to prove to the city that improving the coverage of its music history can also be a success, and bring money and prestige to what the city already has to offer. We are not builders, we are not lawyers, and we are not investors. However, we are the city of Memphis, and we will have a voice. Memphis Music is that voice, and our main goal is to use it to its very fullest.

Help Save Memphis' Music Heritage

who we are

our goals

what you can do

history lesson

contact

what you can do

Memphis Music can only do so many things. Since we are just a group of music lovers, we can't neccessarily be the movers and shakers in the fight to win back our music history. However, the little things can go a long way, so we shouldn't stand idly by as the suits behind the money make our decisions for us. After all, we are taxpaying citizens, and if we want the music back, we have to lend a hand in getting it.

So, in the spirit of joining in, here's a list of things that YOU can do to help:

- Write to city officials at this site
- Attend shows of Memphis musicians
- Write to the Commercial Appeal
  email: letters@gomemphis.com
- Write to the Memphis Flyer
  email: letters@memphisflyer.com
- Contribute to music education programs at your neighborhood schools
- Recommend musicians to play on Beale Street
- Purchase local musicians' music from local retailers
- Visit Sun Studios, Graceland, and Beale Street – explore the city for hidden treasures
- Educate yourself further through listening, watching, reading, and acting

The bottom line is that the future of our music history lies in the hands of everyone in the city. That includes you. To join us, all you have to do is contribute some of your time. It will reap rewards that we and our children will be able to enjoy for decades to come.

Help Save Memphis' Music Heritage

who we are

our goals

what you can do

history lesson

contact

history lesson

Back in the early 20th century, Beale Street was the haven for delta blues music. Incredibly talented black musicians brought their talent to downtown Memphis, what is known as the crossroads of music. For many decades, Beale Street was mainly this, a breeding ground for talent America had never experienced before.

Blues Greats:

Fred McDowell, Johnny Woods, Bukka White Nathan Beauregard, Furry Lewis, Sleepy John Estes

For a long time, America didn't know about the blues. To learn, people had to travel directly to the blues hotspots – Memphis, St. Louis, and Chicago. When recordings started becoming available, the blues left the streets of the black American and entered the living rooms of white America. During the 60's and 70's, Beale lost much of the fresh blues it used to offer. Instead, it gave Memphis a place to go on the weekends.

Take also, for example, Sun Studios on Union Avenue and Stax Records at College Street and McLemore Ave. These two record labels were major producers of soul, blues, and rockabilly hit records. Both labels were largely responsible for the immersion of American music into rock n' roll. Sun Studios boasted the bragging rights of Sam Phillips and Elvis Presley, not to mention later showcasing Jerry Lee Lewis. Elvis and Jerry Lee are widely known as two of the best rockers music has ever heard.

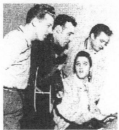

Sun Stars:

Jerry Lee Lewis, Carl Perkins, Elvis Presley, Johnny Cash

Stax was responsible for giving us the soul of the 60's and 70's. In 15 years, Stax had produced about 800 singles and 300 full albums. Plenty of well-known musicians either recorded at Stax, or really wanted to. Stax was even the fifth-largest black-owned business in America in 1974 (Soulsville, USA).

Sun Studios still stands at its original site, and offers tours and memorabilia. Stax, however, suffered a more severe sentence. The building was torn down in 1989, and a church was built in its place. Preservation of these two sites needs to be taken into better consideration.

These sites reflect the success of Memphis in the recording industry and further define the city as one that was able to start a music revolution that still exists today. The deterioration of historic music settings in the city is inexcusable and will certainly not be ignored.

Help Save Memphis' Music Heritage

who we are

our goals

what you can do

history lesson

contact

contact

You can reach us via e-mail, phone, or regular mail.

email: jherzog@utk.edu

phone: (901)754–0790

mailing address:

Memphis Music

1765 Crump Avenue

Memphis, TN 38107

Beale Street at night

Credits

Text

Page 12. Imagine you enter a parlor..., From "The Philosophy of Literary Form: Studies in Symbolic Action" by BURKE, KENNETH Reproduced with permission of UNIVERSITY OF CALIFORNIA PRESS in the format Republish in book via Copyright Clearance Center.

Page 13. Tony slowly got up from the mat..., Excerpt from Kathleen McCormick, The Culture of Reading and the Teaching of English, pages 20–21. Copyright (c) 1994 Reprinted by permission of Manchester University Press.

Page 16. We agree. We need viable alternatives. We're investing millions in geothermal, biofuel and solar technologies, http://www.chevron.com/weagree/?statement=renewables, Chevron Corporation.

Page 18. Illinois Plant Produces Alternate Fuel billboard, Scott Olson/Getty Images.

Page 18. Editorial cartoon by Robert Ariall. 4/22/08, Robert Ariail: © The State/Dist. By Newspaper Enterprise Association. Inc.

Page 26. Diagram of Inverted Pyramid Structure Recommended for Organizing Web Content, Used by permission, Kerry Radshaw (www.kerryr.net).

Page 27. In summary, the current study... (2 lines), Reprinted from Appetite, Vol. 57 No. 2, Serge V. Onyper, Timothy L. Carr, John S. Farrar, Brittney R. Ford, "Cognitive advantages of chewing gum. Now you see them, now you don't," p. 327, Copyright (c) 2012, with permission from Elsevier.

Page 28. Image of Page One of Research Report from the Scholarly Journal *Appetite*, Reprinted from Appetite, Vol. 57 No. 2, Serge V. Onyper, Timothy L. Carr, John S. Farrar, Brittney R. Ford, "Cognitive advantages of chewing gum. Now you see them, now you don't," p. 327, Copyright (c) 2012, with permission from Elsevier.

Page 29. Chew On This, Reprinted by permission from The University of California at Berkeley Wellness Letter, February, 2012. www.wellnessletter.com, Regents of the University of California.

Page 32. Preparing To Read: Sheri's Process, Gillespie, Paula; Lerner, Neal, Allyn & Bacon Guide To Peer Tutoring, The 1/e. (c) 2000. Reprinted and Electronically reproduced by permission of Pearson Education, Inc., Upper Saddle River, New Jersey.

Page 33. Physicists' Techniques For Efficient Reading, Academic literacy and the nature of expertise: reading, writing, and knowing in academic philosophy by GEISLER, CHERYL Copyright 1994 Reproduced with permission of TAYLOR & FRANCIS GROUP LLC BOOKS in the format Textbook via Copyright Clearance Center.

Page 34. Building a Context For Reading, Feldman, Ann Merle, Writing And Learning In The Disciplines, 1st Edition, (c) 1996. Reprinted and Electronically reproduced by permission of Pearson Education, Inc., Upper Saddle River, New Jersey.

Page 53. A Lifesaving Checklist, Atul Gawande, "A Lifesaving Checklist" New York Times, Op Ed, December 30, 2007. Copyright (c) 2007. Reprinted by permission of the author.

Page 65. How To Structure A Rhetorical Précis, Based on "The Rhetorical Précis," Rhetoric Review 7.

Page 67. Excerpt from Chap. 6, Monument Wars: Washington, D.C. the National Mall, and the Transformation of the Memorial Landscape by Kirk Savage, (c) 2009 by the Regents of the University of California. Published by the University of California Press. Editorial art drawing by Randy Mack Bishop, by permission of Randy Mack Bishop.

Page 67. Vietnam Veterans Memorial, GOL/Fotolia.

Page 79. From News-Press.com, November 2, 2010. © 2010 News-Press.com. All rights reserved. Used by permission and protected by the Copyright Laws of the United States. The printing, copying, redistribution, or retransmission of this Content without express written permission is prohibited.

Page 177. Lee-Audus, "Wedding Announcement," www.ljworld.com, *Lawrence Journal-World*. Reprinted by permission.

Images